Social Work, Social Welfare, and Social Development in Nigeria

This groundbreaking book provides a comprehensive account of social work, social welfare, and social development in Nigeria from a postcolonial perspective. It examines the historical development of social work and social welfare and the colonial legacies affecting contemporary social welfare provision, development planning, social work practice, and social work education.

Against this historical backdrop, it seeks to understand the position of social work within Nigeria's minimalist structure of welfare provision and the reasons for the profession's struggle for legitimacy and recognition today. It covers contexts of social work practice, including child welfare, juvenile justice, disabilities, mental health, and ageing, as well as areas of development-related problems and humanitarian assistance as new areas of practice for social workers, including internally displaced and trafficked people, and their impact on women and children. It seeks to understand Nigeria's ethnoreligious diversity and indigenous cultural heritage to inform culturally appropriate social work practice.

This book offers a global audience insight into Nigeria's developmental issues and problems and a local audience – social science and human service researchers, educators, practitioners, students, and policymakers – a glimpse of what's possible when people work together toward a common goal. It will be of interest to all scholars and students of social work, development studies, and social policy.

Mel Gray (PhD) is Professor Emeritus (Social Work) at the University of Newcastle, New South Wales, Australia. She has a longstanding interest in social work in Africa, having published widely on indigenisation and issues relating to cultural relevance, as well as social welfare and social development. This study of social work in Nigeria follows the first *Routledge Handbook of Social Work and Social Development in Africa* (2017), which she edited.

Solomon Amadasun is a graduate of the University of Benin in Nigeria and a PhD student at Deakin University, Victoria, Australia. He has published widely on Nigerian social work education and practice, and related issues, including human trafficking, disabilities, and the COVID-19 pandemic. He previously published *Social Work for Social Development in Africa* (September Publishing House, 2020).

Routledge Advances in Social Work

Revitalising Critical Reflection in Contemporary Social Work Research, Practice and Education
Edited by Christian Franklin Svensson and Pia Ringø

Revolutionary Social Work
Promoting Systemic Changes
Edited by Masoud Kamali

Social Work and Human Services Responsibilities in a Time of Climate Change
Country, Community and Complexity
Amanda Howard, Margot Rawsthorne, Pam Joseph, Mareese Terare, Dara Sampson and Meaghan Katrak Harris

Social Work and Climate Justice
International Perspectives
Edited by Devendraraj Madhanagopal and Bala Raju Nikku

Boys' Stories of Their Time in a Residential School
'The Best Years of Our Lives'
Mark Smith

Social Work, Young Migrants and the Act of Listening
Becoming an Unaccompanied Child
Marcus Herz and Philip Lalander

Rights-Based Community Practice and Academic Activism in a Turbulent World
Putting Theory into Practice in Israel, Palestine and Jordan
Jim Torczyner

Reforming Child Welfare in the Post-Soviet Space
Institutional Change in Russia
Meri Kulmala, Maija Jäppinen, Anna Tarasenko and Anna Pivovarova

For more information about this series, https://www.routledge.com/Routledge-Advances-in-Social-Work/book-series/RASW

Social Work, Social Welfare, and Social Development in Nigeria

A Postcolonial Perspective

Mel Gray and Solomon Amadasun

Routledge
Taylor & Francis Group

LONDON AND NEW YORK

First published 2023
by Routledge
4 Park Square, Milton Park, Abingdon, Oxon OX14 4RN

and by Routledge
605 Third Avenue, New York, NY 10158

Routledge is an imprint of the Taylor & Francis Group, an informa business

© 2023 Mel Gray and Solomon Amadasun

British Library Cataloguing-in-Publication Data
A catalogue record for this book is available from the British Library

Library of Congress Cataloguing-in-Publication Data
Names: Gray, Mel, 1951- author. | Amadasun, Solomon, author.
Title: Social work, social welfare and social development in Nigeria : a postcolonial perspective / Mel Gray, Solomon Amadasun.
Description: 1 Edition. | New York, NY : Routledge, 2023. |
Series: Routledge advances in social work | Includes bibliographical references and index.
Identifiers: LCCN 2022056689 (print) | LCCN 2022056690 (ebook) |
Subjects: LCSH: Social service--Nigeria. | Nigeria--Social policy–21st century. | Nigeria--History--21 century.
Classification: LCC HV465.5 .G73 2023 (print) | LCC HV465.5 (ebook) |
DDC 36109669--dc23/eng/20230202
LC record available at https://lccn.loc.gov/2022056689
LC ebook record available at https://lccn.loc.gov/2022056690

ISBN: 978-1-032-46528-9 (hbk)
ISBN: 978-1-032-46529-6 (pbk)
ISBN: 978-1-003-38212-6 (ebk)

DOI: 10.4324/9781003382126

Typeset in Goudy
by MPS Limited, Dehradun

Contents

List of tables   vii
Abbreviations   viii
Key dates   x
Main ethnic groups index   xi
States by poverty rate   xiii
States by geopolitical zone   xvi
States (alphabetical list)   xviii
Preface by Solomon Amadasun   xix

1 Introduction   1

2 Revisiting the development of social welfare and social
   work in Nigeria   9

3 Nigeria's social development record   37

4 Child welfare – a system in need of care   51

5 Social exclusion, gender, and disability in Nigeria and the
   social work response   66

6 Mental health and ageing   79

7 '5Ps' approach to human trafficking and the social work
   response   92

8 Nigerian social work and its quest for professional
   recognition   107

9 Enhancing the relevance of social work education   124

10 Conclusion   140

References   143
Index   178

Tables

2.1 Chronology of social policy, social welfare, and social work
      development   32
6.1 Mental health policy   80
9.1 Institutions offering social work education and related
      programs   128
9.2 BMAS guidelines for undergraduate courses   130

Abbreviations

AMSWON	Association of Medical Social Workers of Nigeria
ASWEN	Association of Social Work Educators in Nigeria
ATR	African Traditional Religion
AU	African Union has 55 member states; launched in 2002 as a successor to the Organisation of African Unity (OAU)
BMAS	Benchmark Minimum Academic Standards
C-ISOWN	Chartered Institute of Social Work Practitioners of Nigeria
CBR	Community-based rehabilitation
DPO	Disabled people's organisation
ECOWAS	Economic Community of West African States; established 1975, 15 member states
FCPTSWN	Forum of Concerned Professional and Trained Social Workers in Nigeria
FRN	Federal Republic of Nigeria
GDP	Gross domestic product
IDS	Institute for Development Studies (UK)
ISWON	Institute of Social Work of Nigeria
JONAPWD	Joint National Association of Persons with Disabilities
LGA	Local government area
NASoW	Nigerian Association of Social Workers
NBS	National Bureau of Statistics
NDP	National Development Plan
NGO	Non-government organisation
NUC	National Universities Commission
OAU	Organisation of African Unity (1963–1999)
SSA	Sub-Saharan Africa
UN	United Nations
UNDP	United Nations Development Program
UNIBEN	University of Benin

UNN	University of Nigeria, Nsukka
US	United States (of America)
USA	United States of America
USD	United States Dollar (currency)
WHO	World Health Organisation

Key dates

1472–1850	Precolonial Nigeria
1850s–1960	(British) colonial Nigeria
1914	Amalgamation of north and south Nigeria
1941	The first social welfare officer in Lagos, Donald Faulkner, pioneered official social work in Nigeria
1942	First social welfare department established under the Ministry of Labour
1960	Independence from Britain
1962–1968	NDP1
1963–1966	First republic
1966	Military coups
1967–1970	Civil war (one of many attempts to repeal the 1914 amalgamation)
1970–1974	NDP2
1975–1980	NDP3
1981–1985	NDP4
1993	Annulment of the presidential election
1996	National Human Rights Commission established
1999	Constitution of Republic of Nigeria
2010–2020	Vision 20:2020
2017–2020	Economic Recovery and Growth Plan (ERGP)
2021–2025	NDP5
2021–2030	Vision 20:2030

Main ethnic groups index

Ethnic group	Region	Description
Annang (also spelt Annaang)	Southern Nigeria with land in primarily 8 of 31 LGAs in Akwa Ibom State and 3 of the 17 LGAs in Abia State	
Edo (also called Bini) (1.7%)	Southern Nigeria west of the Niger River – from hilly country in the north to swamps in the Niger Delta	Most follow ATR, with strong reverence for culture symbolised by the *oba* or king
Fulani (Fula) (6%)	Northern Nigeria and further east, into the Benue River valley systems of northeastern Nigeria. Rural Fulani are pastoralists. (Hausa–Fulani have adopted Hausa language)	Fulani are predominantly Muslim. The President of Nigeria, Muhammadu Buhari is of Fulani descent
Gbari (Gwari)	Central Nigeria – the Niger, the FCT-Abuja, and Kaduna State Gbari are the largest ethnic group in the south of Kaduna State in northern Nigeria	Adherents of Islam, Christianity, and ATR
Hausa (30%)	30% of Hausa live in the north and northwest regions of Nigeria, in an area known as Hausaland.	Largest ethnic group in West Africa. Most follow Islam.

(Continued)

Ethnic group	Region	Description
Ibibo (Ibibio) (1.8%)	Coast of southern Nigeria, mainly Akwa Ibom and Cross River States	Related to the Annang and Efik peoples. During the colonial period, the Ibibio Union asked the British to recognise them as a sovereign nation.
Idoma	Lower western areas of Benue State and some in Cross Rivers State, Enugu State, Kogi State, and Nasarawa State	Most follow ATR
Igbo (Ibo) (15.2%)	Nigerians of southern origin	Predominant adherence to Christianity
Ijaw (Izon) (1.8%)	People of the forests of the Niger Delta in southern Nigeria	Largely inhabiting the coastal areas of the Niger Delta with fishing a predominant means of subsistence
Jukun	Taraba, Benue, Nasarawa, Plateau, Adamawa, and Gombe States	Also in parts of northwestern Cameroon
Kanuri (Beriberi) (2.4%)	Bornu state in northeastern Nigeria and southeastern Niger	
Nupe (1.2%)	Middle Belt	The dominant ethnicity in Niger State and important minority in Kwara State
Tiv (2.4%)	Central-eastern state of Taraba in the valley of the Benue River	Prosperous subsistence farmers and traders growing yams, millet, and sorghum and raising small livestock and cattle
Yoruba (15.5%)	Southwestern Nigeria	One of the more religiously diverse ethnic groups, practising Islam, Christianity, and ATR

States by poverty rate

	State	Region	Poverty %	Aspects mentioned in text/literature
1	Sokoto	North West	87.73	Poorest state
2	Taraba	North East	87.72	Second highest poverty rate; insecurity affecting children's education
3	Jigawa	North West	87.02	Borders the Republic of Niger; third highest poverty rate and highest birth rate
4	Ebonyi	South East	79.76	Fourth highest poverty rate; biggest rice producer
5	Adamawa	North East	75.41	Fifth highest poverty rate; insecurity affecting children's education
6	Zamfara	North West	73.98	Sixth highest poverty rate; has not adopted the Child Rights Act and insecurity affecting children's education
7	Yobe	North East	73.20	Insecurity leaving children in need of emergency-education support
8	Niger	North Central	66.11	High adult illiteracy, lack of access to food, shelter, water, health, sanitation, and electricity. Over 80% agriculturists
9	Gombe	North East	62.32	Has not adopted the Child Rights Act; insecurity affecting children's education
10	Bauchi	North East	61.53	Has not adopted the Child Rights Act; insecurity affecting children's education; has benefitted from overseas aid
11	Enugu	South East	58.13	Anti-trafficking taskforce
12	Nasawara	North Central	57.30	
13	Katsina	North West	56.42	Insecurity affecting children's education
14	Kano	North West	55.10	Second highest birth rate; has not adopted the Child Rights Act; insecurity affecting children's education; has benefitted from overseas aid

(Continued)

	State	Region	Poverty %	Aspects mentioned in text/literature
15	Plateau	North Central	55.10	High concentration of minority ethnic groups; occurrence of inter-ethnic conflict
16	Kebbi	North West	50.20	Third highest birth rate; has not adopted the Child Rights Act; insecurity affecting children's education
17	Kaduna	North West	43.50	High rate of insecurity, kidnapping, banditry, and crime. Almost all the Hausa and Fulani inhabitants in the north of Kaduna State are Muslims. There are about 30 other ethnic groups in the south of the state. Not all are Muslim. The Gbari (Gwari) is the largest ethnic group in the southern part of the State. The assassination in Kaduna (the old northern region capital city from 1954 to 1967) of Sir Ahmadu Bello, sultan of Sokoto and Northern premier, in an Igbo military coup in January 1966, led to the Nigerian Civil War (1967–1970).
18	FCT – Abuja*	North Central	38.70	Has adopted the Child Rights Act; insecurity affecting children's education; has benefitted from overseas aid
19	Cross River	South South	36.30	Anti-trafficking task force; has benefitted from overseas aid
20	Benue	North Central	32.90	Major source of food production and bastion of recent herders-farmers conflicts. Though one of the top 10 most populous states, Benue is not among the richest, with 49% of the population in the two lowest quintiles of Nigeria's wealth index. Most people engage in agriculture and live in rural areas. Exacerbating poverty are sporadic episodes of community violence and flooding that have displaced populations in some areas; thousands of refugees from neighbouring Cameroon crossing the border into Benue State; and one of the highest prevalence rates of AIDS and HIV in the country. Most people in Benue State are Tiv, Idoma, or Igede speakers (Ryan et al., 2020)

(Continued)

	State	Region	Poverty %	Aspects mentioned in text/literature
21	Abia	South East	30.70	Study of IDPs (Enwereji, 2008)
22	Imo	South East	28.90	Ohachenu's (2016) study on child adoption found positive attitudes
23	Kogi	North Central	28.50	Part of the multi-ethnic Middle Belt
24	Ekiti	South West	28.00	Passed the Mental Health Service Bill into law in October 2021
25	Akwa Ibom	South South	26.80	Anti-trafficking task force
26	Rivers	South South	23.90	Anti-trafficking task force
27	Bayelsa	South South	22.60	
28	Kwara	North Central	20.40	
29	Anambra	South East	14.80	
30	Ondo	South West	12.50	
31	Edo	South South	12.00	Source of over 94% of people trafficked internationally and 90% of women and children trafficked to Europe
32	Oyo	South West	09.83	Capital is Ibadan; anti-trafficking task force
33	Ogun	South West	09.32	
34	Osun	South West	08.52	
35	Delta	South South	06.00	Pervasive use of cultural preventive childrearing measures to ward off evil spirits, protect babies from witchcraft or sorcery, and prevent untimely death, misfortune, and bad luck, all of which could have harmful health implications (John et al., 2015)
36	Lagos	South West	04.50	Commercial hub; Lagos is one of the world's largest cities
37	Borno	North East	NO STATS	Displacement epicentre, home to Boko Haram. Capital Maiduguri where IDP camp is situated

*Territory Source: Statista (2022) based on NBS (2019).

States by geopolitical zone

North Central
Benue, Kogi, Kwara, Nasarawa, Niger, and Plateau States, as well as the Federal Capital Territory.

Conflict arising from territorial disputes between nomadic farmers and local communities, and ethnoreligious issues (Adesina et al., 2020).

North East
Adamawa, Bauchi, Borno, Gombe, Taraba, and Yobe States.

Highest number of recorded conflict, due to Boko Haram insurgencies and military operations affecting nearly 15 million people between 2009 and 2017 (Adesina et al., 2020).

North West
Jigawa, Kaduna, Kano, Katsina, Kebbi, Sokoto, and Zamfara States.

Homeland of Hausa people with the second largest ethnic group the Fulani.

South East
Abia, Anambra, Ebonyi, Enugu, and Imo States.

One of the most populous, largely rural regions, homeland of the Igbo with traditional attachments to land. Most engaged in crop farming, forestry, and oil industry (Okali et al., 2001).

South South (also known as Niger Delta region)
Akwa Ibom, Bayelsa, Cross River, Delta, Edo, and Rivers States.

Major source of oil; ecological degradation due to oil spillage; high unemployment; political tensions; high rates of criminal activity, including banditry, oil pipeline explosions, abductions, and robberies (Adesina et al.,

2020). Relatively sparsely populated, due to harsh environmental conditions (Okali et al., 2001).

South West
Ekiti, Lagos, Ogun, Ondo, Osun, and Oyo States.

Mostly Yoruba-speaking population and largest city, Lagos, in this geopolitical zone.

States (alphabetical list)

1 Abia
2 Adamawa
3 Akwa Ibom
4 Anambra
5 Bauchi
6 Bayelsa
7 Benue
8 Borno
9 Cross River
10 Delta
11 Ebonyi
12 Edo
13 Ekiti
14 Enugu
15 Gombe
16 Imo
17 Jigawa
18 Kaduna
19 Kano
20 Katsina

21 Kebbi
22 Kogi
23 Kwara
24 Lagos
25 Nasarawa
26 Niger
27 Ogun
28 Ondo
29 Osun
30 Oyo
31 Plateau
32 Rivers
33 Sokoto
34 Taraba
35 Yobe
36 Zamfara

Territory
Federal Capital Territory - Abuja

Preface

My experience as a social work student, social worker, and researcher in Nigeria revealed a profession still finding its feet, struggling to prove its value, and gain legitimacy and acceptance in Nigerian society. There are those who understand social workers' contributions, among them researchers, academics, practitioners, government officials, and clients, who have worked with social workers. While most social work practitioners are committed to improving the social conditions of undervalued and marginalised groups in society, there are many who remain sceptical of what social workers can achieve. There is a prevailing understanding among social workers that social work is of recent origin and a lack of awareness of the profession's rich history and multiple contributions across Africa, and more broadly than that. There is also a paucity of understanding of social work's international structures and activities. This insular view results in pessimism about social workers' potential beyond micro-level practice. Hence, there is little macro-level engagement to effect change at a structural level. This scepticism prevents assertive professional action to correct misconceptions and doubts about social work's commitment to marginalised groups. There is a need for professional leadership to raise the image of the profession, instil high professional practice standards, and quality service provision. This extends to professional education and ongoing professional development. Educators frequently lament the dearth of local literature and absence of social work texts directly related to Nigeria's peoples, services, issues, and problems. The idea for this book arose to provide a text drawing mainly on local literature, from a wide range of disciplines, and applying it to enhance understanding of the position of social work in Nigerian society and the many issues the profession aims to address. It seeks to provide optimism about social work. Regardless of the President's mystifying tardiness in legitimising the profession, social work is well-embedded in the social fabric of Nigeria and bureaucratic state structures. With support, social work could do a lot more; without support, it does a lot. This book shows what social workers in Nigeria are doing and could do with enhanced understanding of broader political, economic, and sociocultural issues in Nigerian society. By providing a postcolonial perspective, it seeks to encourage debate on issues relating to indigenisation, decolonisation, and culturally responsive practice. It seeks to take the best of international social work, while building local knowledge for culturally relevant social work education and practice. It takes a critical view of these objectives, rather than provide romanticised conceptions of cultural purity and a utopian precolonial existence. Nigeria is a country riven with difference. It is ethnically and religiously diverse. Social class and gender discrimination is rife, though not often talked about in academic literature, where the major emphasis is on ethnoreligious differences. Applying a social work perspective, we see a nation riven with conflict, struggling for a national identity, for social solidarity, while honouring this rich ethnoreligious diversity, battling corrupt political elites, and seeking to find its common humanity. Nigeria is a fascinating country. It is historically interesting and culturally rich.

We hope policy makers read our book and see social work's value to Nigerian society. We hope social workers read it and appreciate their strengths and contributions. We hope students read it and gain a better understanding of the context of their chosen discipline and profession. We have tried to showcase the work of local authors from diverse disciplines, as well as social work. Social work academics are working hard to contribute to knowledge production and dissemination, and collegial scholarship. We hope our book sparks a sense of professional accomplishment and satisfaction, for Nigerian social work has much to contribute to the international social work landscape. We hope our book will reach a global audience and that social workers from all corners of the globe will join Nigerian social work's quest for professional recognition. We have engaged with the profession's *Global Agenda* as the best international social work has to offer countries from the Global South (International Association of Schools of Social Work (IASSW), International Federation of Social Workers (IFSW), and International Council on Social Welfare (ICSW), 2020). It elevates social solidarity, transformative change, and an emancipatory identity in foregrounding social development and a developmental perspective. However, it also affirms the importance of human relationships at all levels and the value of psychosocial approaches in micro-level casework interventions with individuals and families.

As we note throughout this text, social work in Nigeria is a work in progress. We attest its enormous potential in progressive change as it negotiates the peculiarities of Nigerian society and the lived experience of its people. We hope our account of social work, social welfare, and social development in Nigeria will enhance this potential as the profession continues to contribute to people's wellbeing and strive for social justice for marginalised groups. Understanding past struggles with competing professional interests, the preponderance of Western models, and colonial legacies puts social workers in a strong position to negotiate a better future. Recent developments give cause for optimism. There is a concerted effort from social work academics to indigenise the curriculum. The President approved the Social Work Bill. The professional association gained UNICEF's support for its professionalising mandate. We hope our book inspires confidence in social workers and motivates them to engage in political policy-making processes, at all levels. They can accomplish much in their agencies and communities, and at national, local government, and village levels of decisionmaking.

Solomon Amadasun

1 Introduction

This introductory chapter provides an overview of Nigeria and postcolonial scholarship in social work highlighting the importance of history in shaping present predicaments. It argues that, to understand Nigeria's social problems, it is necessary to examine historical antecedents to its poor social development record, traceable to precolonial times when the country comprised unconnected diverse regionally defined ethnic and religious groups. Masked by British unification in 1914, these regional differences have led to prolonged periods of political instability and ethnoreligious divisions that have hampered development post-independence.

The chapter ends with an introduction to the chapters that follow, which collectively examine social work, social welfare, and social development in Nigeria from a postcolonial perspective. Recognising the importance of history in shaping present predicaments, postcolonial accounts examine and reinterpret literary texts, by focusing on the contexts of their production, and revealing the colonial ideologies concealed within them.

Nigeria: Overview

Siollun's (2021) recent postcolonial analysis noted that 'perhaps no question makes Nigerians disagree as much as why Britain created their country. Nigerians looking for deeper meaning for their country's existence may be disappointed to find that there was none. Nigeria's existence is little more than the outcome of balancing the colonial accounting books' (p. 319). The north and south constituted two colonies with 'different colonial personnel, legal systems, land tenure laws, educational policies and systems of governance' (p. 319). As Falola and Heaton (2008) observed, 'when Nigeria became an independent sovereign state in 1960, in many ways it was a state without a nation' (p. 159). Hence Siollun's (2021) observation that, following independence from Britain in 1960, Nigeria continued to grapple with north-south divisions and each region's paranoia about the other. It endured decades of conflict with the 'most spectacular eruptions of instability' (p. 324) emerging between the north and south. They included the 1966 military coups, the 1967–1970 civil war (one of many attempts to repeal the 1914

DOI: 10.4324/9781003382126-1

amalgamation), the 1993 annulment of the presidential election and ensuing political conflict, as well as 'the crisis over Sharia law in the early 2000s' (p. 324). Though artists, poets, writers, and sculptors tried to forge a common national cultural identity, 'it was difficult to build patriotism and emotional loyalty to a country created by a foreign invader and inhabited by people whose prior loyalties had never extended beyond their family, village or kingdom' (Siollun, 2021, p. 325).

With over 214 million people, Nigeria is Africa's most populous country and the sixth most densely populated country in the world. With its population projected to exceed 400 million by 2050, it is poised to surpass the United States as the world's third most populous country after China and India (United Nations (UN), 2019). Situated in West Africa, Nigeria is an influential economic and political player in Sub-Saharan Africa (SSA), through its membership on key regional bodies, including the African Union (AU) and Economic Community of West African States (ECOWAS). The economic output of its commercial hub, Lagos, one of the world's largest cities, exceeds that of many African countries (Husted & Blanchard, 2020). Having surpassed South Africa as the largest economy in Africa, it is the 26th largest in the world, with a GDP of USD510 billion, 14% stemming from resources (Leke et al., 2014; World Bank, 2020). With its rich oil resources, the petroleum sector accounted for 'roughly half of state revenues and a large share of foreign exchange earnings, though services, agriculture, and manufacturing together employ a much larger segment of the labour force and contribute most of GDP' (Husted & Blanchard, 2020, p. 12). As a consumption-driven economy, retail and wholesale trade were the biggest drivers of GDP growth, with 40 million Nigerians in consuming-class households earning more than USD7,500 per annum. Nearly 70% of its population was economically active; many engaged in entrepreneurial activities (0–14 years, 41.7%; 15–24 years, 20.27%; 25–54 years, 30.6%; 65 years and over, 3.3%). With its relatively youthful population, huge consumption base, and abundant natural resources, Nigeria is set to emerge as a global economic powerhouse (Husted & Blanchard, 2020; Leke et al., 2014). Yet, available data suggest otherwise as the country's economy continues to underperform, especially in industrial production and foreign and domestic investment (Onyeiwu, 2021). As Ayobade and Agugua (2020) noted, a decline in industrial production has led to the compensatory rise of a dynamic entrepreneurial sector. However, there is a downside to deindustrialisation. It has led to the dislodgement of a once stable, contracted workforce, leaving many workers in precarious, transitory jobs, forced to function independently in an increasingly competitive and risky informal service sector.

Precolonial state formation involved a mix of centralised authorities over jurisdictions controlled by the Yoruba, Hausa, Kanuri, Edo, Jukun, and other groups. As Iweriebor (1982) noted, 'a distinguishing feature of this system is the existence of one ruler as the focus of power and source of authority' (p. 507). In the Nigerian States, these hereditary rulers – variously referred to as Sarki, Oba, Obi, and Aku – were Nigeria's natural or traditional leaders. However, the Nigerian states have never remained static. For example, by the end of the 19th century, the Hausa states in the north of Nigeria had already developed centralised state systems, when the Jihad of Usman dan Fodio brought a new political order grounded on Islamic principles of government (Iweriebor, 1982). Several communities, including the Igbo, Ibibio, Annang, Idoma, and Tiv, did not have formal state structures but carried out the regular functions of the state.

Unlike other countries in Africa, colonisation in Nigeria did not involve significant white settlement, due to the inhospitability of its climate and geographic terrain. Under colonial rule, there were two tiers of government, a centralised state authority and provincial (or regional) system of indirect rule comprising a mix of colonial and preexisting political traditional institutions. In effect, Britain established an authoritarian administrative state that lacked political, social, and customary legitimacy (Iweriebor, 1982). Powerful elites that had benefitted from the colonial system maintained these colonial structures and continued to dominate in the post-independence era from 1960 onwards.

Following the failure of the first republic (1963–1966), four decades of military rule, and repeated disruptions in governance, due largely to coups and counter coups, vehement calls for constitutional reform and the entrenchment of civil rule led to Nigeria's first multiparty democracy with the election of General Olusegun Obasanjo as its new civilian president in 1999. With its 36 states, 774 local government areas, and centrally situated Federal Capital Territory (FCT) of Abuja, the Federal Republic of Nigeria (FRN) is a representative democracy with centralised power vested in the Federal Government. As Husted and Blanchard (2020) observed, 'its political structure shares similarity to that of the United States, with a bicameral legislature comprising a 109-member Senate and a 360-member House of Representatives' (p. 2). Its state structure aimed to reduce 'massive cultural, political and religious differences between the north and south' (Siollun, 2021, p. 325). Other home-grown innovations included a people's accord that made way for the rotation of federal powers across the country's six geopolitical zones, 'an affirmative action quota system and the alternation of the presidency between northern and southern holders' (Siollun, 2021, p. 325). Its three tiers of government spread responsibility for social development across national, state, and local levels of governance, again to accommodate ethnic and regional variations.

The World Factbook (2022) estimated that Nigeria comprised more than 250 ethnic groups: Hausa 30%, Yoruba 15.5%, Igbo (Ibo) 15.2%, Fulani 6%, Tiv 2.4%, Kanuri/Beriberi 2.4%, Ibibio 1.8%, Ijaw/Izon 1.8%, and other 24.7%. Collectively, the Hausa–Fulani, Yoruba, and Igbo constituted about 70% of the population and occupied most political leadership positions (Ugiagbe & Eweka, 2014). Most of Nigeria's population is Muslim (53.5%) or Christian (45.9%; 10.6% Roman Catholic and 35.3% other Christian) with other religions comprising a mere 0.6% (World Factbook, 2022). The northern regions were mainly

Muslim, populated by the politically dominant Hausa–Fulani (Onyeiwu, 2021) and southern regions predominantly Christian. While religious and ethnic variations have affected the development of social provision, generally, economics influences social development. Hence, most services began in the Christian south around Lagos, Nigeria's commercial hub, as people, especially young men, and women, flocked to the cities for work and other income-generating activities. As we will see in Chapter 2, for the colonial government trying to confront resistance to colonial rule, controlling Nigeria's adventurous youth presented a major challenge, as shown by its construction of the juvenile delinquency problem that Christian providers proved all too willing to support throughout the colonial period as part of their ongoing conversion mission.

The postcolonial period saw many structural changes as the government struggled to hold the nation together. Ongoing political unrest and ethnic division made it difficult to develop a strong public sector with formal social provision, though this might be evidence of Nigeria's reluctance to hold onto the colonial welfare system, initially linked to work, e.g., contributory benefits. Responsibility for social provision is spread across three tiers of government with the federal government responsible for national policy and infrastructure development and local government – the tier with the least financial and human resources and capacity – responsible for essential basic service provision. However, social protection coverage is extremely limited, social sector expenditure very low, and service delivery poor (Holmes & Akinrimisi, 2012). Other postcolonial initiatives, discussed in Chapter 2, included the introduction of social work education, the professionalisation of social work, the ratification of human rights charters, and enactment of corresponding social policies. All these changes bore the hallmarks of Western constructs of social service provision, professionalisation, social policy development, and human rights. They all required adaptation to local governance systems and cultures.

Social work theorists have reviewed this adaptation through the lens of indigenisation (Gray et al., 2008, 2014; Osei-Hwedie, 1993, 2007; Osei-Hwedie & Rankopo, 2008; Shawky, 1972; Walton & Abo El Nasr, 1988), social development (Gray, 2010, 2017; Gray & Ariong, 2017; Patel, 2005), and, more recently, decolonisation (Gray et al., 2013; Harms-Smith & Nathane, 2018; Ibrahima & Mattaini, 2019). These waves of postcolonial scholarship in African social work all highlighted the deleterious impacts of colonialism on social work and social development.

Postcolonial scholarship in social work

The first indigenisation wave began in Egypt in the 1970s when a professor (Shawky, 1972) encouraged his young students to think through their questions about the relevance of imported social work. Ragab (2017) reflected on this history, remembering his first encounter with young academics from 11 African countries at a 1974 Association for Social Work Education in Africa workshop on social work teaching and fieldwork, who, when they compared notes, realised that they were unknowingly grappling with the same issues. So began the first wave of postcolonial scholarship sparking the indigenisation debate (Ragab, 1978; Shawky, 1972). At the time, indigenisation was a vague concept, rooted in colonial discourse about adjusting imported models to fit local practice contexts (Gray & Hetherington, 2008; Gray et al., 2014). Ragab (2017) recounted how the limits of the indigenisation approach appeared, when, at the time, the object of adaptation to local contexts was always US social work. It carried condescending, patronising colonialist overtones and evoked 'images of primitiveness and backwardness, of natives cut off from the civilised world' (Ragab, 2017, p. 36). African scholars realised they were calling for a comprehensive *reconceptualisation* of social work, one that not only transcended indigenisation, but also reversed its direction, and constituted a complete break from it. Thus, the *authentisation* of social work began (Ragab, 1982, 2017). Rather than adapting imported knowledge, authentisation sought 'authentic, local determinants of practice' (Ragab, 1990, p. 44). It asked:

> What are the prerequisites and … components of a genuine local practice which is embedded in a particular country's cultural values, congruent with its historical development, relevant to its economic, political and social realities, and tuned to its future aspirations?
>
> (Ragab, 1990, p. 44)

However, rather than a complete break with imported models, an in-built requirement of authentic models was the inclusion of compatible elements that had proved useful in models developed elsewhere (Ragab, 2017). In time, it became clear, especially in Muslim countries, that religion played a pivotal role in shaping sociocultural realities and authentisation in the Arab world became 'an Islamic reorientation of social work' (Ragab, 2017, p. 38).

Elsewhere, however, scholars would embrace authentisation as an aspect of indigenisation. As Gray and Coates (2008) recounted, two other Egyptian scholars, Walton and Abo El Nasr (1988), produced a seminal paper in which they described 'indigenisation' as a three-stage process of adaptation starting with *transmission*, to *indigenisation*, to *authentisation*. At this point, Ragab (1990) reiterated the need to return to the roots of the debate for direction.

Though Midgley's (1981) influential *Professional Imperialism in the Third World* provided support for indigenisation scholars, he would later take the discourse in a different direction, heralding a second wave of postcolonial scholarship in the social development perspective (Midgley, 1995). Authentic social work in developing contexts would respond to developmental problems, the root cause of which was poverty, and it would fill the gaps in economically defined development by attending to its equally important social aspects (as discussed in Chapter 3). South Africa embraced Midgley's (1995) developmental perspective and Southern African scholars began to write about the challenges surrounding its integration in social work education and practice (Gray & Simpson, 1998; Gray et al., 1996; Hutton & Mwansa, 1996; Louw, 1998; Muzaale, 1987; Ntusi, 1998;

Osei-Hwedie, 1990, 2007; Rankin, 1997). Though progress was slow, other African countries, eventually aided by international social work's Global Agenda on Social Work and Social Development (IASSW, IFSW, & ICSW, 2010), began to embrace a developmental social work perspective, discussed in Chapter 9.

Nevertheless, indigenisation scholarship in Africa grew through the 1980s and 1990s, spurred on by the influential work of Osei-Hwedie (1993, 1995, 1996) and others (Mupedziswa, 1992, 1993; Silavwe, 1995; Walton & El Abo Nasr, 1988). *Localisation* became a major theme of this discourse as social work writers argued for relevant education and practice to fit to the needs of unique local sociocultural contexts. At the time, international social work scholars were beginning to write about culturally sensitive social work and culturally competent practice.

Gray et al. (2008) attempted to shift the discourse on indigenisation to cultural relevance as attempts to indigenise social work had failed. They argued that indigenisation was an outmoded concept and believed a culturally appropriate approach was a better alternative. They attributed indigenisation's failure *inter alia* to the durability of Western ties and ideas, the supremacy of the English language, inability of indigenous scholars to devise locally relevant academic models and curricula, and lack of publications in local languages on indigenous contexts and local practice (Coates et al., 2006; Gray et al., 2008, 2013).

Local writers began to see this as a call for cultural relevance and culturally appropriate social work education and practice (Gray & Allegritti, 2002, 2003; Gray et al., 2008; Osei-Hwedie, 2002a, 2002b; Osei-Hwedie & Rankopo, 2008). It meant accessing culturally genuine values and practices by going back to people's cultural and spiritual roots to seek direction and distancing from Western social work theory and practice (Gray et al., 2008). Osei-Hwedie and Rankopo (2008) recounted their attempts to develop culturally relevant models and indigenise the social work curriculum in Botswana. One of the biggest obstacles was the social work team's cultural diversity. All the senior academics were expatriates, who found 'western theories and techniques comfortable, not only because of their own social work training but also because of the ready availability of western textbooks and teaching materials' (Osei-Hwedie & Rankopo, 2008, pp. 213–214). Another obstacle was the university's desire to be competitive internationally, which worked against the localisation of curriculum content.

Initiatives such as this kick-started the reclamation-of-culture discourse calling for Afrocentric approaches that subsequently crystallised around ubuntu, a precolonial concept expressing the individual's dependence on the community that heralded a return to collective traditional ways of being (Mabvurira, 2020; Mugumbate & Chereni, 2019; Mugumbate & Nyanguru, 2013; Mupedziswa et al., 2019; Sekudu, 2019) (discussed in Chapter 2). Woermann and Sanni (2020), however, argued that an uncritical uptake of this African philosophy in South Africa and Nigeria might inadvertently support negative racial and ethnic divisions, paradoxically fostering disunity between communities, though several Nigerian scholars painted a more positive picture for Nigeria's embrace of ubuntu (Eke & Onwuatuegwu, 2021; Iyayi, 2017). Common to this discourse was the presumption of an Afrocentric perspective. Afrocentrism was a decolonising ideology that differed markedly from indigenisation in that it called for African standpointism, as its vantage point was African epistemology, and African people's understanding and experience of reality.

The third wave of decolonisation argued for a much more radical transformation of social work. As Harms-Smith and Nathane (2018) noted, it was not about domestication (localisation) or indigenisation (adaptation), because these oppressive discourses kept social work rooted in Western modernism and 'the ideological project of colonialism and racist capitalism' (p. 1). Hence, 'claiming that indigenisation is decolonisation fails to acknowledge the oppressive and racist nature of colonisation' (Harms-Smith & Nathane, 2018, p. 8). Crucially, then, decolonisation foregrounded a critical analysis of the imperialist discourses of colonialism, apartheid, neoliberalism, and underdevelopment by engaging with issues of ideology, power relations, and oppression. As Harms-Smith and Nathane (2018) observed, the 'postcolonial' was not about the end of colonial rule; it was 'a form of analysis exposing the violence of colonialism … [that] extends to the intrapsychic level through the intergenerational transmission of trauma and feelings of inferiority' (p. 5), as paternalistic colonialism entrenched racist hierarchies and denigrated indigenous knowledge and ways of being. Rather than a chronological period, it was 'a critique of the colonial conception of reason, humanism and universalism … [that called for] the identification of and resistance to all forms of domination and oppression' (p. 6). Decolonising social work involved reclaiming truths and narratives about, and rewriting, its history; identifying and critiquing colonialist ideologies permeating its discourse and knowledge; and learning from anticolonial, postcolonial, and decolonisation theorists (Harms-Smith & Nathane, 2018). Gray et al. (2013) conceptualised decolonised social work in terms of theory (thinking about indigenous social work), practice (from the bottom-up), education (facilitating local relevance), and research (using decolonising methodologies). They argued that awareness of the decolonisation discourse would enable social workers to resist or withdraw from colonising projects, since it began with recognising Western colonisation as 'a cultural project with very destructive consequences' (Crampton, 2015, p. 10).

The decolonisation scholarship suggested radical social work approaches that called for political engagement, emancipatory practice, and transformative change through the transformation of power relations. We are not sure Nigeria is ready for radical decolonising practice, given its struggle for recognition. The government is unlikely to sanction the actions of revolutionary social workers. However, that does not diminish the importance of a decolonisation-theory informed knowledge for education and practice, though we believe indigenisation remains important in Nigeria, given, among other things, it is about the reclamation of indigenous culture (Osei-Hwedie, 1993). As Osei-Hwedie (1996) observed, indigenisation involved 'finding new ways or revisiting local ideas and processes of problem solving and service delivery ... understanding and articulating local indigenous resources, relationships, and problem-solving networks; and the underlying ideas, rationale, philosophies or values' (p. 216). In this vein, enhancing the profession's relevance in Nigeria requires culturally appropriate practice (Chapter 8) and the integration of indigenous knowledge in social work education (Chapter 9).

Chapter overview

Gray et al. (2018) noted that 'the shaping of relevant, culturally appropriate and socially responsive social work practice in Africa rests crucially on the extent to which future practitioners understand the context in which their work is conducted' (p. 974). Chapter 2 examines the development of social welfare and social work to provide an understanding of the historical context and insights into the dynamics shaping social welfare and social workers' role within it. Similarly, readers unfamiliar with Nigeria cannot fully appreciate recommendations relating to social work education and practice without some understanding of the context to which it is responding. Social workers practising in this complex milieu face many challenges. Most important is the role of social work education (discussed in Chapter 9) in ensuring they are prepared with appropriate knowledge, skills, and interventions to provide culturally relevant services that address the needs of poor and vulnerable people.

Chapter 3 examines Nigeria's social development record and notes social work's push toward developmental responses that address poverty and injustice. The next three chapters examine traditional areas of social work practice drawing on local literature as illustrative examples of locally relevant knowledge to inform practice in child welfare (Chapter 4), disabilities (Chapter 5), and mental health and ageing (Chapter 6). Following these in-depth studies of social work practice contexts, Chapter 7 discusses a new area of practice in response to human trafficking. Chapter 8 examines contemporary social work practice within the context of minimalist public service provision and lethargic policy implementation. It discusses issues hampering social work practice and social workers' ability to respond to pressing social issues and problems, such as those discussed in prior chapters. It concludes with suggestions that contemporary social work adopts strategies at various levels to enhance professional recognition and embeds the profession in Nigerian society as an essential provider of human social services, while Chapter 9 examines social work education as pivotal to enhancing social work's relevance and preparing practitioners to work with vulnerable groups in Nigerian society. Chapter 10 concludes with a reiteration of social work's importance and appeals for government to recognise the profession's valuable contribution to Nigerian welfare and social development.

2 Revisiting the development of social welfare and social work in Nigeria

This chaper begins by reiterating the importance of history for Nigerian social workers struggling to understand why the achievement of government recognition for their profession and its contribution to society has proved so difficult. In the belief that knowledge of Nigeria's welfare history might aid understanding of the profession's struggles in the present, this chapter revisits the historical literature in and outside social work and, using a postcolonial lens, seeks to provide further insight on why social work's attempts to professionalise have failed to produce desired results and establish its legitimacy in Nigerian society. By adopting a postcolonial lens, the chapter seeks to go beyond descriptive historical accounts of social work and social welfare to extend understanding of social workers' struggle to gain professional recognition, discussed in Chapter 8. Revisiting history, it examines precolonial indigenous support systems and the reclamation-of-culture discourse in social work before reviewing precolonial, colonial, and post-independence developments in welfare and social work.

Orikpe (2013) stated that 'a poor knowledge of our national history will hinder informed citizenry which is required for rapid development of the nation. A citizen who does not know his country cannot really situate himself within the effort to build a better nation' (p. 49). This is a sterling reminder for Nigerian social workers struggling to understand why the achievement of public recognition for their profession and its contribution to society has proved so difficult. This chapter seeks to go beyond descriptive historical accounts to extend understanding of social workers' struggle to gain professional recognition, discussed in Chapter 8.

There have been several historical accounts of the development of social work and social welfare in Nigeria (Amadasun, 2021a; Ekpe & Mamah, 1997; Irele, 2019; Jinadu, 1985; Mbah et al., 2017; Ogbonna, 2017). Amadasun's (2021a) chronological account highlighted significant events in this development, while Irele (2019) examined the key agencies involved. Jinadu's (1985) historical analysis of the development of the conceptual and structural landscape of public social services provided some explanation of their ineffectiveness in stimulating social development. Mbah et al. (2017) sought to add to this sparse historical literature by examining social work's development through the

DOI: 10.4324/9781003382126-2

pre-colonial, colonial, and post-colonial eras. They highlighted the way in which it evolved from the indigenous practices of traditional societies to modern (Western) practice in contemporary Nigeria.

Revisiting history

Precolonial indigenous support systems

Most discussions of the development of social welfare begin with an account of indigenous support systems prior to European contact and colonisation. These accounts depict a system that met the needs of families and communities through collective coexistence. Folaranmi and Tope (2013) described a well-organised social welfare system founded on a long tradition of communal care and concern for the needy that predated colonialism: 'The major aspects of indigenous social welfare were traditional charity, respect for elders, communal living system, extended family system, widow inheritance, apprenticeship system, traditional medicine and health care, [and] traditional education' (p. 325).

Focusing on family support, Ekpe and Mamah (1997) described how responsibility for raising children and preparing them for adulthood in traditional societies went beyond parents to the extended family and community at large. Ekpe (1983) described traditional life as 'a type of unlimited co-responsibility' (p. 485). Kinship implied a mix of security and obligation. There was total reliance on the family group that transcended the individual and accorded importance, status, and position in society, and in history, providing for 'physical necessities or even wealth' (p. 485). Family largesse extended to all in need of care and protection, including the young, aged, sick, and disabled.

Ekpe (1983) explained that ancestors provided the basis for social solidarity, order, stability, and submission to authority. They were the source of life, the origin of laws and customs, and continued to protect their descendants. The living consulted and prayed to ancestors and made offerings to them believing they were close to God. As His collaborators and intermediaries, ancestors were able to influence, support, and punish the living.

The family was the main pillar of indigenous support. As Mboto et al. (2021) observed, it was the major vehicle of child socialisation, playing 'a vital role in character formation, ethical and moral upbringing ... [and] all other equally important economic and political functions' (p. 19). In indigenous society, a sound family upbringing offered a genuine antidote to myriad social ills. There were harsh measures to ensure the inculcation of strong values in traditional African society, where 'a child could be flogged for refusing to greet his parents in the morning' (p. 22). As Mboto et al. (2021) noted, there were no modern inventions like child rights preventing parents from disciplining their children in keeping with ethnocultural mores. They highlighted the impact of modernisation, including the advent of human rights that undermined the authority structure within the family and eroded traditional methods of social control.

Land was the second pillar of traditional existence that drew its importance in community life from the necessity of farming or other uses. Its farming use was periodic and brief, with rights limited to the time it was under cultivation. As Ekpe (1983) explained, 'once the farm returned to fallow, the rights lapsed' (p. 486). This worked in a system of group – family or clan – ownership, where patrilineality guaranteed male rights to farm tenure. As an aspect of kinship, every man had the assurance of land to meet his needs.

The third pillar, not 'as an individual affair but as a collective concern' (Ekpe, 1983, p. 486) was marriage, because it enlarged groups, multiplied alliances, and reinforced economic capacity. This meant divorce caused 'a great rupture' (p. 486) that, over time, degraded traditional social structures. There were complex rules governing marriage that forbade incest. Once married, women moved to their husband's household. The bride price paid by the man entitled him to claim the children from the marriage as his own, irrespective of paternity. The bride price and marriage ceremony bound the woman to the husband's family even after his death. Thus, widows frequently cohabited with the deceased husband's kin and any further children that ensued from this relationship remained his. Nevertheless, women maintained their connections with their own kin and these wider attachments formed 'part of the cohesion of the larger society' (Ekpe, 1983, p. 487).

As discussed in Chapter 4, children were extremely important in traditional society, as they contributed to household labour, cared for their parents as they aged, and ensured family longevity. This meant childlessness and infertility impacted heavily on traditional family life and caused problems for women (Makinde, 2016; Makinde et al., 2016, 2017a, 2017b). In all traditional societies, when problems of suffering, deprivation, want, deviance, and death occurred, they were handled by the family or extended family network, that provided support, cared for the sick, handicapped, elderly, orphaned, and destitute. With little understanding of psychological, emotional, physical, and social problems, a fatalistic attitude and belief in supernatural causes prevailed. These culturally embedded beliefs endure. They lead to social solidarity and cohesion, and stigmatisation and discrimination, in equal measure. This is borne out by studies of child witchcraft confession (Isangha et al., 2020; Secker, 2012) and child abuse (Ehigbie & Omorogiuwa, 2022; Nnama-Okechukwu et al., 2020), as discussed in Chapters 4 and Chapter 5, respectively, in relation to people with disabilities. Nevertheless, this indigenous support system provided for the welfare of families and communities in precolonial times and differed vastly from Western individualistic welfare systems.

Postcolonial reclamation-of-culture discourse

The precolonial period is important in light of contemporary scholarship calling for the reclamation of culture and a return to traditional ways of being, as embraced in the philosophy of ubuntu, where members work together for the welfare and prosperity of the family and the extended family takes collective responsibility for the wellbeing of all. This notion of interdependence stressed that the welfare of all superseded the welfare and interests of the individual (Obidi, 2005). Scholars advocating cultural reclamation described traditional African families as well served by their customs and traditions. In advancing this traditional Afrocentric perspective, postcolonial scholarship presumed a common African worldview, despite the multiplicity and diversity of African cultures, languages, and ethnicities. (The same applied to a Western perspective and worldview, despite the multiplicity of Western cultures.) It required the identification of commonalities within African cultures. Usually these included a spiritual dimension expressed variously through interconnectedness and unity of mind, body, and spirit; a clan or tribally based collective identity based on a consanguineous family structure and belief in the authority of elders; and a spiritual connection to the land and environment. Traditional religious beliefs and cultural practices, such as ancestral reverence, supernatural causes, spirit mediums, divination, witchcraft, and a reliance on traditional healing rituals, grounded most African cultures. Indigenous approaches integrated cultural, communal, collective, and familial perspectives, and sacred African traditions – built on an understanding and awareness of African religious and spiritual beliefs – undergirded by ubuntu.

However, it was important not to romanticise this malleable philosophy of African humanism, which Praeg (2014) believed was a response to the tension between collectivism and individualism found in modern societies (Oduor, 2014). He distinguished between ubuntu (precolonial communalist praxis) and Ubuntu (contemporary political and philosophical discourse on that praxis) noting that the very nature of postcolonial societies, with their liberal Constitutions, rendered a return to a precolonial communalist praxis (ubuntu) virtually impossible. In any event, there was no such thing as pristine precolonial communalism free of political cleavages. At best, Ubuntu was part of a discourse on the possibility of using indigenous African communalism as an ideological foundation on which to 'create humanistic contemporary African societies' (Oduor, 2014, p. 87). As an ideological or philosophical position, Ubuntu fell squarely in the tradition of political and scholarly discourses advocating the creation of contemporary societies founded on indigenous African communalism. Hence, the meaning of Ubuntu changed to fit the socio-historical and political context and was 'constantly reproduced in the complex space between the local need for cultural identity and a global demand for the expansion (and naturalisation) of human rights' (Praeg, 2014, p. 11). Essentially, it did this by 'infusing the meaning of these rights with local understandings' (Praeg, 2014, p. 11). Since the onset of decolonisation in Africa, the constant intersection of these local and global imaginaries reproduced different meanings of ubuntu, first as a form of humanism, then as African socialism and, more recently, as 'a quasi-Christianised theology of reconciliation and forgiveness' (Praeg, 2014, p. 12; see Tutu, 1999). Different framings of ubuntu 'as a form of humanism, as an African communitarianism, as an Aristotelian virtue ethic, as an African Socialism and so forth' (Praeg, 2014, p. 12) were merely a symptom of the one-way relations between postcolonial African societies and the West. Referring to ubuntu as a glocal phenomenon, Praeg (2014) noted that:

> Global discourses (Christianity, human rights and so on) give a particular expression to the meaning of local traditions such as ubuntu ... that also allows the resulting Ubuntu to feed back into the global discourse as a locally based critique and expansion of those very discourses (p. 37).

This was evident in global social work discourse, where the first theme of the recently revised Global Agenda (2020–2030) is *Ubuntu: Strengthening Social Solidarity and Global Connectedness* (IASSW, IFSW, & ICSW, 2020). Importantly, for decolonisation theorists, Praeg (2014) asserted that, in a complex and important sense, the problem of Ubuntu was irreducible to the problem of colonialism. In its most fundamental form, the ideological discourse of Ubuntu represented 'a confrontation with modernity and the dual fragmentation of individual and social' (pp. 197–198) consistent with Western philosophies that were indistinguishable from and essential to it, including 'post-Cartesian under-standings of personhood, such as ... Martin Heidegger's ontological hermeneutics and various forms of communitarianism, particularly [the] feminist ethics of care' (Praeg, 2014, p. 208).

This is an important point for social workers, who need to realise that social work's modernist roots and notions put it at odds with many indigenous cultural concepts and practices that the recent appeal to ubuntu – as African humanism – in social work invokes. Social work theorists frame ubuntu as an indigenous concept rooted in: (i) ideals of personhood centred on human interconnectedness, that is, a person is a person through other people, and (ii) collective responsibility, expressed in maxims like 'it takes a village to raise a child' (Mugumbate & Chereni, 2019, p. 28) and 'your neighbour's child is your own' (Mugumbate & Nyanguru, 2013, p. 86). Hence, social workers seeking to develop an African framework for decolonised social work practice turn repeatedly to ubuntu as a source of mutual aid through which people helped one another 'in a spirit of solidarity' (Van Breda, 2018, p. 438). The framework suggests non-materialist forms of culturally relevant intervention that fit well with conformist expressions of developmental social work. It places the onus of development and empowerment on people rather than call out government failures in social provision and protection (Gray, 2010; Harms-Smith, 2017). However, the ubuntu 'desire for consensus also has a potential dark side in terms of which it demands an oppressive conformity and loyalty to the group' (Louw, 1998, n.p.). To be meaningful in Nigeria's divided society, ubuntu would need to move beyond an identity politics based on in-group (tribal or clan) solidarity to embrace ethnic diversity. It would require a strong 'commitment to eliminating division and othering, and to championing unity across diversity (in terms of race, language, culture, religion, gender, sexuality, age and so on)' (Van Breda, 2018, p. 443).

Several writers have attempted to articulate an ubuntu-based theory for social work practice (Mabvurira, 2020; Mugumbate & Chereni, 2019; Mugumbate & Nyanguru, 2013; Mupedziswa et al., 2019; Rasheed & Rasheed, 2011; Sekudu, 2019; Van Breda, 2018). Sekudu (2019) noted that colonisation had eroded ubuntu as the social glue holding the village together prior to colonisation and no longer existed in its precolonial form. In his theorisation of ubuntu, Van Breda (2018) sought to stretch the concept beyond a focus on present social relations, that is, 'respectful relationships with wider and more diverse groups of others (ethics), to accountability to past and future generations (sustainable development), and a commitment to the Earth (ecological or eco-spiritual social work)' (p. 439). The idea that people needed 'to come together in mutually supportive and respectful ways' (Van Breda, 2018, p. 439) was consistent with social work's ethics of care and values of 'human solidarity, empathy, and human dignity' (Mupedziswa et al., 2019, p. 29).

Ubuntu's consensus-oriented philosophical stance and appeal for unity calls for another set of theories to make social work's transformative emancipatory aims explicit and harness them to broad social change goals at the institutional level. Decolonisation theory aids understanding of what it would take for Ubuntu as an ideological discourse to serve the broader aims of decolonised social work practice. As Lawal and Oluwatoyin (2011) observed, to achieve community cooperation and participation in the country's development agenda, Nigeria would need to promote citizenship over indigeneity, nation over locality. Thus, social workers would need to harness the solidarity that Ubuntu engendered to serve broader social change goals for those who remained disconnected from the benefits others in society enjoyed. This meant harnessing social solidarity (ubuntu) to pressurise government to take development seriously, provide essential services to lift people out of poverty, and give them access to the resources they needed to enjoy a decent quality of life. Decolonisation theorists hold that only radical, conflict-oriented, revolutionary measures would institute a more just social system and thus suggest Ubuntu as an ideological discourse.

Precolonial Nigeria: 1472–1850

The seeds for the breakdown in indigenous support systems were sown in the precolonial era with the arrival of the European missionaries, British opportunists, the reshaping of economic interests, the fluidity of sociopolitical structures, and the initial thrust of welfare focused on dislocated children and young people.

Economic interests, political fluidity, and slow mission creep

Siollun (2021) dated Nigeria's precolonial era to 1472–1830 attributing the breakdown of indigenous systems to 'slow mission creep' (p. 5) following European contact through waves of British visitors from slave traders to explorers, businessmen, colonial officers, and missionaries. Yet, the Portuguese developed first contact with Nigerians, establishing trade links with the Benin kingdom and starting the slave trade to work the plantations on the island of St Thomas. The first British ships arrived in the Bight of Benin in 1553, with their captain surprised to find that the Benin *oba* (king) spoke Portuguese. Though Britain entered the slave trade later than Spain and Portugal, in 1663, it eventually surpassed them, establishing major slave-trading ports, and exporting a staggering number of slaves, who endured a great deal of cruelty at the hands of their slave masters (Siollun, 2021). Britain's abolition movement not only ended slavery in 1808 but also provided 'humanitarian grounds' (Siollun, 2021, p. 13) on which Christian missionaries justified their involvement in West Africa and established the first mission (of the Church of England) in Nigeria in 1842.

Later British explorers, fascinated by the River Niger, would venture inland looking for its source. These explorations, though unsuccessful, would produce 'a huge repository of knowledge about the lands and people' (Siollun, 2021, p. 26) – willingly provided by locals in good faith – the British would subsequently conquer. Precolonial states to the north and south of the River Niger included the Muslim states of Kanem-Borno and Lake Chad to the north-east and north-west, respectively, and the interrelated kingdoms of Oyo and Benin (home of the Edo people) to the south-west (modern-day Yoruba country). They also comprised 'several decentralised societies without a paramount ruler to the south-east and north' (Siollun, 2021, p. 27) home to Igbo, Annang, Ibibio, and Ekoi, among other ethnic groups.

Siollun (2021) highlighted several features of these precolonial societies, including the accuracy of their oral traditions and multi-ethnic character, though ethnic groups were geographically spread and unknown to each other prior to British colonisation (Ayatse & Akuva, 2013; Salawu & Hassan, 2011). Further, the three largest contemporary ethnic groups – Hausa, Igbo, and Yoruba – did not self-identify as a single ethnic group in precolonial times; three of the four largest precolonial kingdoms had rulers who exercised political and religious authority; and many exhibited democratic characteristics. The British commenced their colonising project, starting with unscrupulous business dealings, when most states were experiencing internal problems and disputes. Years of military conflict from 1851 to 1920, mainly to protect British business economic interests, laid the groundwork for Britain's occupation and eventual conquest of the colony it would form. The British built an army of Nigerians to serve their colonising interests, drawn largely from northern Hausa men. Over a period of approximately 60 years, through wars and resistance, the British 'changed Nigeria's cultural, educational and religious identity … Britain transplanted to Nigeria its own cultural and religious complexities, and Nigeria became a convergence point for multiple cultural, economic and ethnic interests and rivalries' (Siollun, 2021, p. 249).

Against the backdrop of contemporary scholarship calling for a reclamation of culture and return to traditional ways, this historical examination of precolonial society paints a picture of division and difference, rather than harmony and solidarity. While the cultural reclamation scholarship seems to present traditional societies as uniform havens of collective responsibility governed by beneficent elders and united by common traditions, there were, in fact, diverse sociopolitical forms in precolonial Nigeria. Rather than static traditional societies, the fluidity of precolonial 'Nigeria' produced diverse governance systems, including 'kingdoms, empires, statelets, principalities, city-states and acephalous [headless] societies' (Iweriebor, 1982, p. 507). Iweriebor (1982) grouped these political systems into centralised states (CS) and stateless societies (SS) divided along ethnic lines. For example, the Yoruba, Hausa, Kanuri, Edo, Jukun, and the peoples and societies they influenced or conquered, had CS, in which a single, often hereditary ruler was the source of authority acquired 'either through the manipulation of peoples' religious and spiritual beliefs or because they had economic power' (Iweriebor, 1982, p. 507). Kings and their councils constituted the apex of CS with their hierarchical monarchical structure. SS without formal, elaborate, highly visible state structures, leaders, and functionaries were common among the Igbo, Ibibio, Annang, Idoma, and Tiv. Though considered less developed than CS, community assemblies or broadly representative councils made important political and social decisions in SS. Subsequent scholarship noted their democratic nature and structures that carried out the regular functions of a state, as compared to autocratic CS (Iweriebor, 1982; Siollun, 2021). These traditional leaders came to play a part in the British system of indirect rule, which worked better in CS in the north than in the south, as discussed later in this chapter (Riddick, 1966).

The British began to occupy the resource-rich land of the Igbo in the southeast from 1889 onwards. The Igbo had well-established democratic village-governing procedures and local economies interwoven with complex cultural traditions, including honorific Ozo titles, abomination cleansing, and slave trading (Isichei, 1978). Its 'political institutions in the community – the masquerade, the age grades, the village meetings – gave different forms of political weight to different sections of the community' (Isichei, 1987, pp. 71–72). Thus, the British encountered a traditional system of governance and social support based on collective values and tribal identities. The clan formed 'the mainframe of social organization and ... kin the bedrock of social protection' (Amadasun, 2021, p. 3). The Igbo provided for those in need through their autonomous filial system and age-grade, gender-based, and community self-help structures. Atuonwu (2021) described age grades as organisations comprising people within the same age band, usually born within three to five years of one another. Age-grade fellowship was a sociocultural institution operating at the village level that effectively created peer groups to foster unity, solidarity, loyalty, responsibility, and, if necessary, resistance.

Missionary education

Christian missionaries formed an important part of the precolonial civilising mission in the south as early as 1842. They caused revolutionary change to the southern region's 'religious life and created a Western-educated cadre ... anxious for independence, while the north had little interest in rushing into union with a southern region ... so radically different in religious and social ethos' (Siollun, 2021, pp. 323–324). For a century, missionaries transformed people steeped in traditional religion and indigenous beliefs and practices, converting them to Christianity, while providing education and literacy as their 'most potent weapons' (Siollun, 2021, p. 257). By the end of 1914, the year of amalgamation, 97% of Nigeria's school enrolments and 95% of its schools were in the south. In the first 50 years of the country's existence, most literate Nigerians had received a Western-style mission-school education with its dual function of education and conversion. Islamic resistance in the north and the southern embrace of mission-school education, as well as the absence of a colonial education system, 'increased the cultural differences between north and south by transforming the culture of one region, while preserving that of the other' (Siollun, 2021, p. 265). Ironically, this helped the north emerge from colonialism with much of its 'cultural and religious heritage intact' (Siollun, 2021, p. 275). The south embraced British education seeing it as superior to local school systems. While a southern education was for the masses, a northern education targeted aristocratic elites far removed from local peoples and cultures, with elitist schools and colleges producing 42% of post-independence government leaders. British education gave Nigerians 'a new national language, a new religion practised by half of its citizens, and a new cultural and societal ethos for advancement' (Siollun, 2021, p. 280). It shaped future political leaders out of touch with traditional cultures (Boahen, 1987). It also reshaped African childhoods, as the following discussion shows.

Troubled children

African historians have long recognised the importance of children to Africa's historical development. Children were crucial to the familial, communal, and social fabric of African societies. They were a highly valued source of labour, whose activities sustained families through poverty and 'during the colonial era in particular, real efforts were made to control, remake, and/or manipulate African childhoods' (Diptee & Klein, 2010, p. 3). As Aderinto (2018) observed, 'scholarship on child labour, Boy Scouts and Girl Guides, the representation of children in the newspapers, child prostitution and abolition of domestic slavery, to mention but a few, is all influenced (in varying degrees) by the idea of modern colonial childhood' (p. 733), for which mission education laid the foundation (Aderinto, 2015). Not only did the British modernising thrust undermine traditional structures and disrupt children's lives, it also constructed pejorative labels problematising culturally acceptable behaviour, such as hawking and street trading, that contravened English norms and standards. The construction of juvenile delinquency was a means of social control modelled on English poor laws that brought a system of juvenile reform, which emulated class-based welfare and divided recipients into deserving and undeserving categories, the former deserved charity, the latter punishment (Ogunniran, 2015). It paved the way for child welfare legislation, such as the Guardianship of Infants Act of 1886, modelled on English laws (Ekpe & Mamah, 1997).

Thus, the first thrust of Nigerian welfare during the precolonial period remade childhood based on Christian values enforced through missionary education and child welfare interventions for non-conforming children and young people. The British brought organised social services that missionaries and their charity model proved happy to provide (Irele, 2019), while Nigeria established its ongoing reliance on charitable faith-based organisations and community self-help traditions. Unlike other African countries, it did not develop a system of public service provision, possibly because it was never a white settlement (due to, as already indicated, to the inhospitability of its climate) (Heldring & Robinson, 2012; Siollun, 2021). This was significant because, in most countries, social work developed in tandem with public welfare provision. In colonial administrations, this meant social welfare services for white settlers. Thus, colonialism in Nigeria did not produce a welfare environment that produced the need for formalised social work services within the colonial administration.

Colonial Nigeria: 1850s–1960

Britain's interests in Nigeria were always economic. Aided by Christian missionaries as 'the most effective catalysts of social change' (Siollun, 2021, p. 253), its modernising civilising thrust and attempts to impose a liberal democratic state showed its 'priority was not to create a new nation with a common ethos' (p. 326). To an extent, claimed Siollun (2021), 'colonialism made Nigeria a copy-and-paste version of Britain' (p. 4) with its structures of governance and Christian religions extremely disruptive to precolonial indigenous systems of social organisation. So effective were Christian missionaries in convincing local people to renounce their traditional religions and indigenous beliefs and practices that 'much of pre-colonial Nigerian culture was lost and will never be recovered' (Siollun, 2021, p. 264).

Authoritarian administrative state

Less effective was the colonial government that effectively remained 'an authoritarian administrative state' (Iweriebor, 1982, p. 510). This was due *inter alia* to class and regional franchise restrictions, the absence of universal adult suffrage, and lack of formal rights, all of which constituted essential elements of liberal democracy. As an imposed structure seeking to embed capitalist socioeconomic policies and practices, the colonial state lacked political, social, and customary legitimacy and was met with ongoing resistance set in train by its coercive institutions, especially the police and military, tasked to enforce compliance. It created social classes and power elites with *inter alia* merchants, traders, business and property owners, lawyers, doctors, and journalists constituting the upper classes. Though hungry for independence, these powerful post-independence elites were reluctant to change many aspects of the colonial order that had proved beneficial to them. As Mimiko (1998) observed:

> Decolonization allowed the crop of leaders that aligned with colonial power to take over Nigeria. This ensured the sustenance of a neo-colonial economy even after political independence. These leaders on assumption of power quickly turned up the repressive machinery of the colonial state rather than dismantling it. Significantly, they have no vision of development to accompany the efficient instrument of repression they inherited. All they were interested in was access to power and privileges and not development (p. 163).

Ultimately, colonialism fostered autocratic governance at odds with its liberal democratic ideals. This led to protracted 'political instability, economic mismanagement, social incoherence and the mobilisation of ethnic consciousness (or "Tribalism") – all of which eventuated in the collapse of that experiment in neocolonial parliamentary democracy' (Iweriebor, 1982, p. 512) post-independence.

Indirect rule

Lacking in personnel, the British capitalised on Nigeria's traditional social organisation in its system of 'indirect rule', a form of governance that coopted local indigenous rulers and appointed them Britain's rulers by proxy, although they often played a subsidiary role within the colonial administration. In effect, it was a system of indigenous rule under British supervision. The British delegated these indigenous rulers to carry out day-to-day responsibilities in keeping with their edicts and instructions (Siollun, 2021). In the north, the Hausa-Fulani *emirs*, familiar with well-established political and judicial systems and the Muslim theocracy, proved ideally suited to indirect rule. Hence, the British selected the Hausa-Caliphate system 'as the de facto proxy colonial Government' (Ukelina, 2021, p. 41). It suited the self-funded colonial government to delegate unpopular functions, like tax collection, to these proxy rulers. The model worked best in indigenous cultures with traditional chiefs, and so worked in the north and the Yoruba-speaking south-west. However, in the south-east, among ethnic groups like the Igbo, it generated a great deal of tension, when the British appointed warrant chiefs, selected for their leadership potential, and gave them autocratic powers beyond those of natural traditional leaders. The colonial government also created Native Courts over which warrant chiefs presided. The system was ripe for abuse as warrant chiefs and court officials enriched themselves from a system funded by fees and fines levied by the Native Courts. The system's legacy was a culture of entitlement among warrant chiefs' descendants, claiming hereditary title that had no precolonial existence (Siollun, 2021).

Colonial constructions of social problems

Postcolonial scholarship has 'focused on the question of how development discourses and ideologies intersected with labor control and trade union politics' (George, 2011, p. 839). This focus was indistinguishable from child welfare policy and practice that made children and their street work sites of reformative activity under the developmentalist colonial state of the 1940s and 1950s (George, 2011). However, as Chapdelaine (2020) noted, 'attention to colonial Nigerian children did not occur in a vacuum' (p. 11). It was due, in part, to the 'Save the Children Fund, whose work later encouraged the adoption of the 1924 Geneva Declaration of the Rights of the Child' (p. 11), ensuring social development programs followed the British colonial government's dual focus on community development (largely missionary work) and welfare (mainly recreational clubs and educational activities). They focused on infant, maternal, and family welfare; mental health care; prison visiting; and poor relief. Initially, however, the main focus was aberrant youth through probation and remand schools.

Colonial officials constructed the problem of juvenile delinquency. They saw children and youth as an 'insurrectionary unemployed class' (Burton, 2006, p. 365), hence their project to change young people's aspirations and trading activities by undermining traditional support structures. Rather than seeing families and clan networks as the backbone of community wellbeing, the colonial authorities portrayed them as potentially harmful environments that thwarted their goals. Controlling young people, especially child labour, was one way of altering traditional conceptions of family and collective social values. By problematising their behaviour, the colonial government delivered a strong message on the failures of family and community structures reconstructing them as unsafe environments for children. Fourchard (2006) observed three important features of this constructed youth-crime milieu between the 1920s and 1960s: 'the increase in the number of young offenders, the affirmation of the existence of male offender youth groups and the emergence of an organized network of juvenile prostitution' (p. 122).

The colonial administration's introduction of punitive reform schools to reeducate youth, isolated from their families and traditional networks, into social conformity found support from the welfare pioneering Salvation Army that had established itself in Nigeria in 1920. It played a key role in this social control experiment, which dovetailed with its Christian values and ideals. First landing in Yoruba-dominated Lagos in the southwest, it progressed to Igbo land in the 1920s and later moved southeastwards to Akwa Ibom, home to the Ibibio (majority), Anang, Oron, Eket, and Mbo. Between 1925 and 1944, it ran the first industrial home for delinquent boys built by the colonial authorities in Lagos's market area of Yaba in 1923, which could only house a few eligible convicted juveniles each year (Heap, 2010). A group of concerned Christian men formed the Green Triangle Club to provide community services and accommodation for children trading on the streets of Lagos, opening its hostel at Yaba in May 1942 to accommodate 23 children (Heap, 2010).

Beyond Lagos, pickpockets (*jaguda*) were common in Ibadan in the south-western Oyo State, Nigeria's largest city after Lagos and Kano, from the 1930s into the 1950s. As Heap (1997) reported, founded in 1829 'as a war camp following the collapse of the Oyo kingdom, Ibadan quickly became the largest Yoruba city-state during the period up to its incorporation into the British Empire in 1893' (p. 327). It attracted adventurous, enterprising young people, who 'resisted powerful attempts to inculcate conformist modes of behavior through indigenous and colonial agencies of control and manipulation' (Heap, 2010, p. 50).

To stem its juvenile (children up to the age of 17 years) problem, the colonial government introduced the *Native Children's (Custody and Reformation) Ordinance* in 1928 that applied mainly to orphaned children, deserted by their relatives or sold as slaves, rather than juvenile offenders (Fourchard, 2006). Without services for juvenile offenders at the time, most received corporal punishment or imprisonment with adults. With the introduction of the *Colonial Development and Welfare Act* in 1940 came the employment of the first social welfare officer and pioneer of official social work in colonial Nigeria, Donald Faulkner, in 1941 and the establishment of a social welfare department under the Ministry of Labour. Faulkner established the first government children's home in Lagos to complement voluntary Christian child and adolescent clubs and hostels. These interventions followed a European trend of establishing clubs and groups, such as girl guides and boy scouts, through which adults supervised children's and young people's leisure activities to guide them towards conforming behaviour. Reformists, scholars, and clinicians believed the colonial authorities had to manage young people through reform and indoctrination to prevent them from engaging in street trading, hawking, and petty crime now labelled as delinquent behaviour. Thus, services removed street children under the *Children and Young Person's Ordinance* of 1943 modelled on the 1933 British *Children and Young Persons Act* and juvenile justice system, with Faulkner establishing the first juvenile court in Lagos in 1942. The British social welfare office, in concert with these various Christian services, 'dislocated numerous children from their trading activities, where at times, no criminal activity existed, in the name of "saving" them' (Chapdelaine, 2020, p. 6). Chapdelaine (2020) argued that 'the British Colonial Office ultimately denied children and their guardians certain forms of economic agency by deploying child labour in ways aimed to "save" the colonial economy through agricultural reform' (p. 6).

Outside of Lagos, there was only one juvenile court in Calabar in southeast Nigeria (Fourchard, 2010). Chapdelaine's (2020) analysis of the personal papers of the colonial welfare officer in Calabar from 1949 to 1958, Margaret Belcher, revealed the history of the Calabar remand home, a juvenile correctional institution, which, throughout the 1950s, provided semi-permanent residence for numerous children.

Initially, the colonial administration focused on boys and young men, training them in accordance with British cultural ideals of 'the breadwinner form of masculinity' (George, 2014, p. 171). This changed to include an equally punitive focus on girls with the employment of female welfare officers. The first female welfare officer appointed as Faulkner's assistant in 1946, social worker Alison Lizzett (1955, 1973), focused on girls and young women. Her prohibition of girl street trading led to the arrest of hundreds of young girls, despite older female traders' protests. The Lagos Women's League (LWL), an educated elite group of Christian African women, who valued the ideal of female domesticity and dependence, supported the attention to girl street hawkers, most of whom were Yoruba, thus highlighting differences in Yoruba and Christian lifestyles (George, 2014). These women did not see themselves as colonial subjects but as individuals with the status and power to have a positive influence on young girls whose trading activities they averred (George, 2011). These social reformers and colonial social workers shaped the idea of the 'modern girl … [through] strategies of self-improvement like western style education, job training in clerical and technical fields, and laboring in the western colonial economy' (George, 2011, p. 838). Drawing on welfare office, women's organisation, and court records, oral sources, and newspaper reports, George (2011) argued that 'the struggles over the application of street trading regulations to children in Lagos provide insight into statist attempts to programmatically develop a new culture of girlhood in late colonial Lagos and legitimize developmentalist governance in late colonialism' (p. 840).

The church missionary society of Nigeria in Lagos established a hostel for girls that later became a girl's remand home along these lines. Charlotte Obasa, secretary of the leading multicultural elite LWL in the 1920s, established an orphanage for girls from 1956 to 1967 that later became an approved girl's school named after its founder. However, these loosely organised voluntary initiatives had limited funds and could only cater for a small minority of girls. With few services available for them, the authorities repatriated most to the country. Despite all efforts, Milner (1972) observed that, in the early 1960s, female street trader offenders comprised 75% of juvenile crime in Lagos.

Fourchard (2006) noted that official discourses attributed juvenile delinquency to two inter-related developments, the first social welfare officer's appointment in 1941 and the post-war administrative and judiciary machinery mobilised to address the new social problem that, through legislation, criminalised urban youth, especially female hawkers. Faulkner's comprehensive enquiry in 1941 brought continuing attention to child destitution and street children, whose livelihood activities contravened predominant definitions of appropriate economic engagement. The response was removal to reform schools and remand homes under the *Provisions for the Welfare of the Young and the Treatment of Offenders*. By 1945, there was a juvenile court and police force in Lagos and Calabar, which, due to wartime budgetary restrictions, only became operational in 1946 (George, 2011). A 1948 report extended this discourse attributing this growing social problem to the breakdown of family and tribal ties, and a lack of parental control or punitive disciplinary measures that drove them onto the streets (Marris, 1966). As Heap (2015) explained, 'when children display an increasing complexity of "challenging" behaviors then adults respond with increasingly complex and penetrating means of control, conducted through an ideology of care' (p. 50). By 1956, approved schools accommodated

238 boys and 24 girls convicted of juvenile offences (Fourchard, 2006). Among them, the first reform school for girls in Lagos, established in 1956, sought to provide girls involved in prostitution new career and job skills and the young women's and men's Christian associations began their services. By criminalising the activities of young girls, the social welfare service missed its main target, organised prostitution, and juvenile gangs.

However, as Fourchard (2006) noted, young people migrated to cities attracted by employment opportunities because of poverty. Youth crime was a feature of rapid urban expansion, persistent poverty, unemployment, and inadequate housing. In the absence of colonial social welfare organisations, Christian missions and voluntary organisations, of which there were few, provided limited services, while local rural communities continued to draw on familial and customary traditions. Hence, the problem of juvenile delinquency occupied social welfare services throughout the colonial period. Although some went to reform schools and others received help from voluntary organisations, a return to their families or rural areas from whence they came was the solution for most. Thus, 'a whole set of social workers, probation and police officers had clearly identified a recurrent "youth crime problem" and implemented new policies that dramatically changed the perception of youth' (Fourchard, 2006, p. 131). Fourchard (2006) concluded that 'juvenile delinquency remains one of the idiomatic expressions of the *Bibliothe'que coloniale* and, as far as the literature on youth and street children is concerned, it has not yet been decolonized' (p. 137).

Young men provided a malleable group for the assertion of colonial control. Paddock's (2015) comparative analysis of Igbo (southeastern) and Yoruba (western) participation in the boy scouts showed these 'African subjects … would become the future British colonial employees' (p. 137). Iliffe (1987) noted the colonial office's desire to eliminate cruel forms of child labour, delinquency, and poverty was exacerbated by colonisation's destabilisation of the social environment and economic activities of children and young people, while modernisation and urbanisation created new social problems. Christianity introduced a new morality that enforced conformity to authority. Summarising Belcher's contribution, Chapdelaine (2020) noted that, by:

> Decrying local customs, which incorporated child labour and the movement of children between guardians, as a way to remain economically solvent, Belcher ensured that the BSWO [British Social Welfare Office] gained and maintained authority over able-bodied laborers reproducing indigenous methods of controlling the productive labour of minors (p. 37).

In effect, remand schools trained young people in farming (indigenous methods) and food production. Together these forces constituted a resocialisation project that sought to civilise children by distancing them from their families and communities. Few children in remand schools returned to their families (Chapdelaine, 2020). As in other colonising contexts, child welfare played a key role in resocialising young people. In Nigeria, the focus was on antisocial young men, due to their high visibility and, only later, girls, as awareness of their street-trading activities grew. As Burton (2006) observed, this gendered interpretation throughout the colonial period 'associated employment and unemployment with men, though women had long entered urban centres' (p. 365). Without options for waged employment, their significant contribution came through their informal-sector activities.

Post-independence Nigeria: 1960s onwards

Post-independence, there were numerous structural changes to welfare provision, though the Nigerian government was never overtly pro-welfare, despite its ratification of human rights charters and enactment of corresponding social policies. As Ekpe and Mamah (1997) noted, there were inconsistencies between welfare policies and their administration. The period also saw the development of social work education. These changes reflected Nigeria's response to diverse external influences and its desire to remain within the international fold.

Postcolonial welfare and social development

Within Nigeria's minimalist public service structure in 1960, the placement of social welfare services in the Federal Ministry of Labour reflected colonial links between welfare and work, shown in attempts to transform the activities of economically active young people already discussed. Further, the colonial *Social Security Act* introduced in 1961 provided, among other things, Invalidity and Survivors' Grants for the families of people injured *at work* (Ekpe & Mamah, 1997). However, the Civil War (1967–1970) disrupted social welfare provision and exacerbated poverty, leaving most without social protection. Jinadu (1985) reported that, following the war, the Federal Military Government turned to the UN Economic Commission for Africa requesting advice on social welfare policy and training that led to a visit by Dr A. H. Shawky. His subsequent report did not define, or establish goals and criteria for, social development, though it did outline the respective roles of the Federal, State, and local government and voluntary agencies, and institutions and training conducive to development (Jinadu, 1985). Following his recommendations, social development became Nigeria's welfare model, and the government established the Federal Ministry of Social Development, Youth, and Sports in 1972. The subsequent Social Development Act (No. 12 of 1974) (FRN, 1974) established a Social Development Division within the Ministry of Employment, Labour and Productivity showing enduring links between welfare and work. The government added a fourth sector to the renamed Ministry of Social Development, Youth, Sports, *and Culture* in 1975. Thereafter, 'vacillating social policies and problems of departmental loyalties and rivalries … among state officials resulted in the amendment of the Decree in 1976' (Akintayo, 2021, p. 12) and the government did not release another Social Development Policy for Nigeria (SDPN) until 1989. The policy focused narrowly on social welfare and the ministry that produced it – the Federal Ministry of

Culture and Social Welfare – dissolved in the same year. As Akintayo (2021) observed, the government did not implement the SDPN, which contained explicit social welfare provisions, and 'the concept of social development disappeared from the ministry's nomenclature for many years' (Akintayo, 2021, p. 12).

Jinadu (1985) attributed the lack of social development to conceptual confusion and an absence of culturally relevant social services, noting that the 'strategies goals, processes and functions of the social development sector have never been clearly identified and conceptualized in the context of an overall determination of the rich cultural heterogeneity of Nigeria' (p. 866). Drawing on this analysis, Akintayo et al. (2017) noted a 'lack of ethno-cultural specific references related to social welfare' (p. 21), which they equated with social work, in the SPDN. Kazeem (2011), too, equated social welfare with social work.

Ogbonna's (2017) study of published sources on Nigerian social welfare services found that underdeveloped and poorly funded services posed a threat to public health. Others have blamed Nigeria's 'slow development' (Iloh & Bahir, 2013, p. 323) on the government's failure to build a strong infrastructure, while an administration spread across three levels of government had not helped the situation and had led to a lack of coordinated service delivery and resource wastage. As Holmes and Akinrimisi (2012) observed, social protection coverage was extremely limited, social sector expenditure very low, and service delivery poor. Thus, Nigeria already had a weak state-supported welfare system when international agencies called for structural adjustment in the mid-1980s. The subsequent entrenchment of neoliberal economic management led to further government disengagement from direct social service delivery and infrastructural provision and the introduction of public–private partnerships that, for most countries in the Global South, was a major departure from the traditional practice of state-financed infrastructural development. However, these neoliberal market-economy arrangements required a business environment, regulatory framework, and efficient public sector management, all of which were lacking in Nigeria's service-delivery system. Ministries concerned with welfare and social development were 'either merged with another or renamed ten times between 1976 and 2019' (Akintayo, 2021, p. 12). Another major change came in 2021 with the bifurcation of emergency humanitarian intervention and ongoing social development, when the government split welfare and social work between the Ministry of Women Affairs and Social Development and the Ministry of Humanitarian Affairs, Disaster Management and Social Development. This change was in keeping with international policy mandates and the work of international non-government organisations providing emergency child protection and services to vulnerable groups as part of their humanitarian response.

'Vacillating social development policy' (Akintayo, 2021, p. 13) had not helped social work's cause. As Akintayo (2021) observed:

> Since 1970, successive Nigerian governments have demonstrated ignorance of the dignifying roles of the social work profession in sustaining both

individual and collective well-being in societies, particularly in family and child welfare, as practiced in all developed countries of the world (p. 12).

This contributed to two successive Presidents dragging their heels on supportive legislation for social work. Hence, social work's lack of legal status rendered social casework 'in schools, family, probation, hospitals, psychiatry, institutional care, etc., ineffective' (Akintayo, 2021, p. 14). As discussed in a later section , various education programs developed to provide trained welfare and development administrators, including social work education, though, despite its professionalising initiatives, the evolving profession struggled to receive government recognition.

Nigeria became a signatory to the Convention on the Rights of the Child (UN, 1989), in 1991 and, with its history of juvenile justice, also followed the Guidelines for Action on Children in the Criminal Justice System (UN, 1997). Article 24 stated that everyone in contact with, or responsible for, children, including social workers, should receive education and training in human rights and the principles, standards, and norms of juvenile justice as an integral part of their professional preparation (Ugbe et al., 2019).

Social protection policy has remained in draft without supportive legislation since 2016. The Draft National Social Protection Policy (FRN, 2016) did not mention social work services or social workers. It defined social protection from a life-cycle perspective, defining its goals to prevent and reduce poverty and socioeconomic shocks throughout the lifecourse. It was an umbrella policy encompassing the following eight categories of provision:

1   *Health and education*, including free school meals; free healthcare, education, special services, and assistive devices to people with disabilities; and healthcare for pregnant women, lactating mothers, children under 5, and older persons above 65.
2   *Social welfare and child protection* comprising 'psychosocial support and counselling to survivors of violence against persons, child labour, child abuse, child rape, and human trafficking' (FRN, 2016, p. 13).
3   *Social housing* for homeless and poor people and those living in overcrowded conditions.
4   *Livelihood enhancement and employment*, including unemployment insurance and non-cash benefits to job seekers; labour-based cash transfers, public works program for youths, persons with disabilities, and the unemployed; support for sustainable livelihoods; and affordable childcare services for children under 5
5   *Social insurance* comprising contributory pensions for older people (60 and above).
6   *Social assistance*, including cash transfers; cash-for-work schemes activated at the onset of emergencies; non-contributory pensions for older people (60 and above); cash and food grants for poor families, orphans, street children, and others vulnerable to harmful cultural practices.

7   *Traditional family and community support* comprising support for family and community-based systems for beneficiaries responding to shocks and extreme poverty.

8   *Legislation and regulation* refer to a legal framework that protects beneficiaries, including children through inheritance rights, birth registration, childcare services, and breast feeding.

In conclusion, from 1995 to 2021, the Ministry of Women Affairs and Social Development was responsible for social welfare programs. This and the Federal Ministry of Health employed most social workers in the public services, until the government split the social work desk between the Ministry of Women Affairs and Social Development and the Ministry of Humanitarian Affairs, Disaster Management and Social Development, where they were responsible for providing emergency services for women, children, and other vulnerable groups requiring humanitarian assistance, including internally displaced persons (IDPs).

Introduction of social work education

As we have seen, social work began in Nigeria in the colonial era, following young people's migration to the city of Lagos, ostensibly in response to the difficulties they experienced in adjusting to urban life (Ojanuga, 1985). Its earliest functionaries were missionaries, social reformers, and colonial administrators, who displayed an aptitude for this work. Following the Second World War, the United Nations became a major motivating force and source of guidance for the establishment of social welfare services and schools of social work in colonial administrations across Africa. It promoted the idea that these administrations required formal welfare services staffed by professionally trained personnel. In most colonial administrations, social workers had received their training overseas and lent their expertise to embedding social work in the local development milieu. George's (2011) analysis of female hawkers in Lagos highlighted that female social reformers, social workers, and colonial officers constituted an influential educated Christian multicultural elite with recognised social status, who identified with the colonists' modernising values and deemed them preferable to traditional practices. It also provided a clue to early social workers' role. Ojanuga (1985) noted that most colonial administrators carrying out social work functions had a secondary school education or diplomas with three- to six-month in-service training. Professionals with a university education had trained in the United Kingdom and no state had more than 10 professionally trained social workers in the mid-1980s, all of whom received lower salaries than other professions. Given most had received their social work education overseas, it followed that they had received training in Western models and methods.

These models and social welfare policies developed under British colonial rule tended to overlook long-standing traditional social structures and supports for vulnerable Nigerians (Anucha, 2008a, 2008b; Ogundipe & Edewor, 2012). As Ugiagbe (2017) observed, the colonial administration superimposed its structures on 'naturally occurring, informal extended family and tribal networks, communalistic lifestyles, and collectivist responses to the welfare of children, orphans, widows, widowers, and the elderly' (p. 271). Social work, too, modelled itself on British systems and helping methods that overlooked local sociocultural mores and complexities and ignored precolonial structures founded on the 'traditions, values, and norms of the Nigerian people' (Amadasun, 2021a, p. 261). Anucha (2008a) believed this stemmed from the prevailing belief that 'anything that came from the West was superior and therefore was worthy of inclusion in Nigeria's social and economic system' (Anucha, 2008a, p. 151).

The first Nigerian social work education program began at the University of Nigeria, Nsukka (UNN) in 1976 and the second at the University of Benin (UNIBEN) in 1979. Both institutions located social work in Departments of Sociology and Anthropology giving it a heavy sociological bent. The Guidelines for the Fourth National Development Plan 1981–1985 (Federal Ministry of National Planning, 1981) stressed the government's commitment to strengthening training programs for social workers, as discussed in Chapter 3. There followed a dramatic increase in the number of social work programs, most in sub-units attached to other departments. All based their programs on imported models, the relevance of which became a major issue in postcolonial social work education in Nigeria.

Nigeria's embrace of international professionalising standards and definitions and professional organisational structures, including university-based education and professional associations, was necessary for its acceptance into the international social work fold. The first Nigerian Association of Social Workers (NASoW) established in 1975 was an umbrella body of professional social workers across the education, welfare, community development, medical social work, NGO, private, and student sectors. Given Nigerian social work's struggle to receive internal recognition, its membership of international social work organisations provided external validation. Internally, NASoW's ongoing professionalisation thrust that began in 1975 culminated in the 2017 Nigerian Council of Social Work (Establishment) Bill 2017, known as the Social Work Bill. Following its failure in successive legislative assemblies, it received provisional Senate approval in January 2018, though failed to receive presidential approval. Tabled again in 2019, the Senate once again called for further information giving rise to concerted efforts to clarify contentious issues prior to the Bill's resubmission. Without professional recognition, social workers struggled to meet immense challenges of poverty, unemployment, pressing issues for women and children, and AIDS and HIV exacerbated by poor healthcare services (Amadasun, 2021). Despite the growth in social work education and establishment of curriculum standards through the National Universities Commission's (2017) Benchmark Minimum Academic Standards (BMAS) for undergraduate bachelors and masters' courses in social work, curriculum change to enhance social work's relevance remains a project in progress.

Ratifying human rights charters and enacting corresponding social policies

Nigeria's legal system is a mix of Islamic law, English common law, and customary law. However, as a signatory to international and regional human rights charters and a member of the African Union (AU) and United Nations (UN), Nigeria promotes its identity as a modern liberal democracy. Its ratification of human rights charters and conventions down the years is indicative of its obligations in this regard (Minnesota University Library, Human Rights Library, n.d.). Foreign aid and international humanitarian assistance are also contingent on Nigeria's commitment to its human rights obligations. Further, the increasing focus on rights-based practice in social work means social workers in various practice contexts need to be cognisant of the international (UN Treaty Body Database, n.d.) and African conventions Nigeria has ratified to address core social issues, ranging from refugee and human trafficking to forced labour and child rights issues. The following charters have relevance for social workers:

Employment and forced labour

1960	Convention concerning Forced or Compulsory Labour (ILO, 1930)
	Abolition of Forced Labour Convention (ILO, 1957)
1974	Equal Remuneration Convention (ILO, 1951)
2002	Discrimination (Employment and Occupation) Convention (ILO, 1958)

Human rights

1967	Convention on the Elimination of All Forms of Racial Discrimination (UN, 1965)
1983	African Charter on Human and Peoples' Rights (African Commission on Human and Peoples' Rights, 1981)
1993	International Covenant on Civil and Political Rights (UN, 1966a)
	International Covenant on Economic, Social and Cultural Rights (UN, 1966b)
1999	Constitution of the Republic of Nigeria (FRN, 1999a)

Human trafficking

2001	Convention against Torture and Other Cruel, Inhuman or Degrading Treatment or Punishment (UN, 1984)
2010	Convention for the Protection of All Persons from Enforced Disappearance (UN, 2010)
2018	Convention against Transnational Organized Crime and Protocols to prevent trafficking in persons, especially women and children (UN, 2018)

Migrants, refugees, and displaced people

1983	Convention Governing Specific Aspects of Refugee Problems in Africa (OAU, 1969)
2009	International Convention on the Protection of the Rights of All Migrant Workers and Members of their Families (UN, 1990)
2012	Convention for the Protection and Assistance of Internally Displaced Persons in Africa (Kampala Convention) (AU, 2009)

Rights of the Child

1991	Convention on the Rights of the Child (UN, 1989)
2001	African Charter on the Rights and Welfare of the Child (AU, 1990)
2002	Convention Concerning the Prohibition and Immediate Action for the Elimination of the Worst Forms of Child Labor (ILO, 1999)
2010	Optional Protocol to the Convention on the Rights of the Child on the sale of children child prostitution and child pornography (UN, 2000a)
2012	Optional Protocol to the Convention on the Rights of the Child on the involvement of children in armed conflicts (UN, 2000b)

Rights of People with Disabilities

2010	Convention on the Rights of People with Disabilities (UN, 2006a)
	Optional Protocol to the Convention on the Rights of Persons with Disabilities (UN, 2006b)

Torture

2001	Convention against Torture and Other Cruel, Inhuman or Degrading Treatment or Punishment (UN, 1984)
2009	Optional Protocol of the Convention against Torture (UN, 2002)

Women's rights

1985	Convention on the Elimination of All Forms of Discrimination against Women (UN, 1979)
2004	Optional Protocol to the Convention on the Elimination of All Forms of Discrimination against Women (UN, 1999)
	Protocol to the African Charter on Human and Peoples' Rights on the Rights of Women in Africa (African Union, 2003)
2018	Convention against Transnational Organized Crime and Protocols to prevent trafficking in persons, especially women and children (UN, 2018)

Ugwuanyi and Chukwuemeka (2013) noted that, with human rights conventions as their guide, political leaders had formulated 'brilliant policies' (p. 59) but had fallen short of their stated aims by failing to institute corresponding monitoring mechanisms to oversee their implementation. Hence, the major issue in Nigeria was not policy formulation but rather ineffective implementation, since 'only effectively implemented policies can bring about national development' (Ugwuanyi & Chukwuemeka, 2013, p. 59). Nigeria has instituted policies and laws that have a significant bearing on social work practice to support the international and regional conventions to which it is a signatory. These conventions are as follows:

1995	National Human Rights Commission Act (FRN, 1995)
1999	National Policy on Women (FRN, 1999b)
2003	Child Rights Act (NHRC, 2003)
2004	Compulsory, Free Universal Basic Education Act (FRN, 2004)
2006	National Gender Policy (Federal Ministry of Women Affairs and Social Development, 2006; FRN, 2006)
2007	National Guidelines and Standards of Practice on Orphans and Vulnerable Children (Federal Ministry of Women Affairs and Social Development, 2007)
2008	National Gender Policy on Education (Federal Ministry of Education, 2006)
2010	National Human Rights Commission (Amendment) Act (NHRC, 2010)
2013	Nation Action Plan for the Elimination of Child Labour (2013–2017) (FRN, 2013a)
	National Policy on Education (FRN, 2013b)
2014	HIV and AIDS (Anti-Discrimination) Act (FRN, 2014)
	National Standards Policy for Improving the Quality of Life for Vulnerable Children in Nigeria (USAID ASSIST Project, 2014)
2015	Trafficking in Persons (Prohibition), Enforcement, and Administration Act, as amended (FRN, 2015a)
	National Migration Policy (FRN, 2015b)
	Violence Against Persons (Prohibition) Act (FRN, 2015c)
	Administration of Criminal Justice Act (FRN, 2015d)
2016	Draft Social Protection Policy (FRN, 2016)
2017	Anti-Torture Act (FRN, 2017)
2018	Discrimination Against Persons with Disabilities (Prohibition) Act (FRN, 2018)
2019	National Guidelines and Referral Standards Policy on Gender-Based Violence Prevention and Response: Nigeria (GBV Sub-Sector Nigeria, 2019)
2021	National Policy on Internally Displaced Persons (IDPs) (FRN, 2021
	National Action Plan for the Promotion and Protection of Human Rights 2022–2026 (NHRC, 2021)

Nigeria introduced its first Child Rights Act in 2003 (NHRC, 2003). It covered all aspects of child welfare, child protection, and juvenile justice. Table 2.1 provides a chronology of social policy, social welfare, and social work's development. The merits of these legislative and policy frameworks notwithstanding, critics have drawn attention to human rights violations and lacklustre

Table 2.1 Chronology of social policy, social welfare, and social work development

	Colonial welfare
1842	Thomas Freeman established the first Christian mission. Early missionaries provided medical care and initiated child welfare and women's programs.
1886	*Guardianship of Infants Act.* The Salvation Army Church and Green Triangle Group established industrial schools for delinquent children. Boys' and Girls' Clubs formed to address issues of juvenile delinquency.
1923	Lagos Women's League (LWL) supported the development of welfare services.
1925	Salvation Army established the boys industrial home - a reform school for young boys
1928	*Native Children (Custody and Reformation) Ordinance* to stem the influx of migrants and juveniles to the cities
1929	*Colonial Development Act*
1932	First government reform school in Enugu State
1934	Assistant Superintendent of Prisons, Donald Faulkner, headed the juvenile reform school in Enugu that provided technical training for convicted juveniles, under the aegis of the Prisons Department.
1935	Unemployment Inquiry Commission
1940	*Colonial Development and Welfare Act*
1941	Alexander Patterson, Commission of Prisons for England and Wales and Chairman of the Colonial Penal Administration Committee appointed the first Social Welfare Officer, David Faulkner
1942	Women's Welfare Council formed by the LWL
1943	*Provisions for the Welfare of the Young and the Treatment of Offenders* including the establishment of Juvenile Courts and Juvenile Court Police Force *Children and Young Person's Ordinance (CYPO)*
1944	Government assumed responsibility for the Green Triangle Club and Salvation Army homes
1945	*Colonial Development and Welfare Act* provided a significant extension of the 1940 Act
1946	Ten-Year Plan of Development and Welfare for Nigeria and Juvenile Courts in Lagos and Calabar established
1955	Inception of adult probation
1956	First girls' rehabilitation school in Lagos; Young Women's Christian Association (YWCA) and Young Men Christian Association (YMCA) formed
1958	*Children and Young Persons Act*, enacted as a colonial ordinance in 1943, amended in 1945, 1947, 1950, 1954, and 1955 made provision for the welfare of children and young people, the treatment of young offenders, and for the establishment of juvenile courts; the Lunacy Ordinance, 1916, amended and renamed the *Lunacy Act of 1958* (still the only mental health act)
	Postcolonial welfare
1960	Convention concerning Forced or Compulsory Labour (ILO, 1930); Abolition of Forced Labour Convention (ILO, 1957); Federal Ministry of Labour charged with social welfare provision

(Continued)

Table 2.1 (Continued)

	Postcolonial welfare
1961	*Social Security Act* for older adults and Invalidity and Survivors' Grants for people unable to work
1962	First National Development Plan 1962–68 (Federation of Nigeria, 1962)
1966	Nigerian Civil War began; International Convention on Civil and Political Rights (UN, 1966a)and International Covenant on Economic, Social and Cultural Rights (UN, 1966b) ratified
1967	International Convention on the Elimination of All Forms of Racial Discrimination (UN, 1965)
1968	First International Conference of Ministers for Social Welfare at UN in New York (for social welfare ministers from developing countries)
1970	Nigerian Civil War ended; Dr A H Shawky (United Nations Regional Adviser on Social Welfare Policy and Training) invited to study social welfare services; and Second National Development Plan 1970–74 (FRN, 1970)
1971	Shawky's report marked an important turning point for social work and social development in Nigeria
1972	Federal Ministry of Social Development, Youth, and Sports formed
1974	Equal Remuneration Convention (ILO, 1951); *Social Development Decree No. 12* (FRN, 1974)
1975	Third National Development Plan 1975–80 (Federation of Nigeria, 1975); Ministry of Social Development, Youth, Sports, and Culture;Nigeria Association of Social Workers (NASoW) founded
1976	Social Work Education and Training started at the University of Nigeria, Nsukka
1979	UNIBEN approved the training of social workers
1981	Fourth National Development Plan 1981–85 (FRN, 1981)
1982	Federal School of Social Work, Emene, Enugu State and Social Development Institute, Iperu, Ogun State introduced certificate courses in social work
1983	African Charter on Human and Peoples' Rights (African Commission on Human and Peoples' Rights, 1981); Convention Governing Specific Aspects of Refugee Problems in Africa (OAU, 1969)
1985	Convention on the Elimination of All Forms of Discrimination against Women (UN, 1979)
1986	Structural adjustment brought cuts in social infrastructure, protection, and welfare services; cessation of five-year development plans
1989	*Social Development Policy for Nigeria* placed social welfare under the Federal Ministry of Culture and Social Welfare; Federal government established the People's Bank of Nigeria (PBN) modeled on India's Grameen Bank
1991	Convention on the Rights of the Child (UN, 1989) ratified; National Mental Health Policy for Nigeria (FRN, 1991)
1992	NASoW registered with the Corporate Affairs Commission (CAC)
1993	International Covenant on Economic, Social and Cultural Rights and International Covenant on Civil and Political Rights
1995	*National Human Rights Commission* Act (FRN, 1995); Ministry of Women Affairs and Social Development established; five-year undergraduate degree in social work introduced at UNIBEN

(*Continued*)

Table 2.1 (Continued)

	Postcolonial welfare
1999	*Constitution of the Republic of Nigeria* (FRN, 1999a); *National Policy on Women* (FRN, 1999b).
2001	Convention against Torture and Other Cruel, Inhuman or Degrading Treatment or Punishment (UN, 1984); African Charter on the Rights and Welfare of the Child (AU, 1990); PBN dissolved and merged with Nigeria Agricultural and Cooperative Bank to become the Nigeria Agricultural and Rural Development Bank
2002	Discrimination (Employment and Occupation) Convention (ILO, 1958); Convention Concerning the Prohibition and Immediate Action for the Elimination of the Worst Forms of Child Labor (ILO, 1999)
2003	National Economic Empowerment and Development Strategy (NEEDS), 2003–2007 (NPC, 2004) and the National Agency for the Prohibition of Trafficking in Persons (NAPTIP) created
2004	*Child Rights Act* replaced the Children and Young Persons Act; *Compulsory, Free Universal Basic Education* Act FRN, 2004); Optional Protocol to the Convention on the Elimination of All Forms of Discrimination against Women (UN, 1999); Protocol to the African Charter on Human and Peoples' Rights on the Rights of Women in Africa (African Union, 2003)
2006	National Gender Policy (Federal Ministry of Women Affairs and Social Development (FRN, 2006); Social Work in Nigeria Project (SWIN-P) at UNIBEN to improve the quality of social work education in Nigeria
2007	National Guidelines and Standards of Practice on Orphans and Vulnerable Children (Federal Ministry of Women Affairs and Social Development, 2007); First students for the professional Masters of Social Work (MSW) at the UNIBEN; National Universities Commission (NUC) introduces Benchmark Minimum Academic Standards (BMAS) for undergraduate programs
2008	National Gender Policy on Education (Federal Ministry of Education, 2006)
2009	International Convention on the Protection of the Rights of All Migrant Workers and Members of their Families (UN, 1990); Optional Protocol of the Convention against Torture (UN, 2002); Vision 20:2020 (NPC, 2009)
2010	*Employee's Compensation Act* (FRN, 2010); National Human Rights Commission (Amendment) Act (NHRC, 2010); Convention on the Rights of People with Disabilities (UN, 2006a); Optional Protocol to the Convention on the Rights of Persons with Disabilities (UN, 2006b); Convention for the Protection of All Persons from Enforced Disappearance (UN, 2010); Optional Protocol to the Convention on the Rights of the Child on the sale of children child prostitution and child pornography (UN, 2000a); SWIN-P Project launches a platform to create the Nigerian Association of Social Work Educators
2011	First edition of the *Journal of Nigerian Social Work Educators* issued; Independent Department of Social Work established at the UNIBEN (outcome of SWIN-P Project)
2012	Convention for the Protection and Assistance of Internally Displaced Persons in Africa (Kampala Convention) (AU, 2009); Optional Protocol to the Convention on the Rights of the Child on the involvement of children in armed conflicts (UN, 2000b); National Policy on Internally Displaced Persons (IDPs) (FRN, 2012)

(*Continued*)

Table 2.1 (Continued)

	Postcolonial welfare
2013	Nation Action Plan for the Elimination of Child Labour (2013–2017) (FRN, 2013a); National Policy on Education (FRN, 2013b); National Policy for Mental Health Services Delivery in Nigeria (FRN, 2013c) and National Mental, Neurological and Substance Use Programme and Action Plan (FRN, 2013d)
2014	*HIV and AIDS (Anti-Discrimination) Act* (FRN, 2014); National Standards Policy for Improving the Quality of Life for Vulnerable Children in Nigeria (USAID ASSIST Project, 2014)
2015	*Trafficking in Persons (Prohibition), Enforcement, and Administration* Act, as amended (FRN, 2015a); National Migration Policy (FRN, 2015b); *Violence Against Persons (Prohibition) Act* (FRN, 2015c); *Administration of Criminal Justice Act* (FRN, 2015d)
2016	Draft Social Protection Policy (FRN, 2016)
2017	*Anti-Torture Act* (FRN, 2017); Economic Recovery and Growth Plan (ERGP) (2017–2020); Nigerian Council of Social Work (Establishment) Bill 2017, known as the Social Work Bill; National Universities Commission (NUC) Benchmark Minimum Academic Standards (BMAS) for undergraduate and postgraduate social work curriculum
2018	*Discrimination Against Persons with Disabilities (Prohibition) Act (Disabilities Act)* (FRN, 2018); Convention against Transnational Organized Crime and Protocols (UN, 2018)
2019	National Guidelines and Referral Standards Policy on Gender-Based Violence Prevention and Response: Nigeria (GBV Sub-Sector Nigeria, 2019); Re-tabling of the Bill for an Act to establish the Nigerian Council for Social Work to Regulate the Practice of Professional Social Work in Nigeria, and for Related Matters; Minister of Humanitarian Affairs, Disaster Management and Social Development established; Mental Health and Substance Abuse Bill (FRN, 2019) still not passed into law
2020	Vision 20:2030 aims to make Nigeria one of the world's top 20 economics by 2030
2021	National Policy on Internally Displaced Persons (IDPs) (FRN, 2021a); National Development Plan (NDP) 2021–2025 (FRN, 2021b); National Poverty Reduction with Growth Strategy (FRN, 2021c); National Action Plan for the Promotion and Protection of Human Rights 2022–2026 (NHRC, 2021); parts of the Social Work Desk in the Ministry of Social Welfare moved to the Ministry of Humanitarian Affairs; Social Work Desk split between this and the federal Ministry of Women Affairs and Social Development; AU Draft Policy Framework and Action Plan on Ageing (AU & HelpAge International, 2021); National Policy on Ageing for Older Persons in Nigeria (FRN, 2021d)
2022	National Action Plan on Human Trafficking in Nigeria 2022–2026 (FRN, 2022a); Chartered Institute of Social Work Practitioners (Establishment) Act, 2022 (FRN, 2022b); African Protocols on Ageing and Disabilities as part of AU Social Agenda 2063 (AU, 2022)

policy implementation marring Nigeria's development agenda. Policies have failed due *inter alia* to the lack of government accountability for the wellbeing of its citizens. Other problems affecting policy implementation include widespread corruption, excessive red tape, inadequate budgets, human resource shortages, ethnic and religious differences, patrimonialism, and overbearing political interference. The government's recent National Action Plan for the Promotion and Protection of Human Rights 2022–2026 (NHRC, 2021) shows recognition of the need to improve its human rights record.

Conclusion

For the most part, external forces have dictated the direction of Nigerian social development policies and welfare provision. This chapter has examined the historical literature in and outside social work on the development of social welfare and social work and construction of social problems through the pre-colonial, colonial, and post-independence eras. It provides further insight on why social work's attempts to professionalise have failed to produce desired results and establish its legitimacy in Nigerian society. By adopting a post-colonial lens, the chapter went beyond descriptive historical accounts to extend understanding of Nigeria's welfare system and social workers' struggle for recognition, discussed in Chapter 8. Chapters 3–7 discuss areas of policy and services mentioned in this chapter in further detail. Chapter 3 covers social development, Chapter 4 child welfare, Chapter 5 women and disability, Chapter 6 mental health and ageing, and Chapter 7 human trafficking.

3 Nigeria's social development record

This chapter examines Nigeria's poor social development record in the face of vast human and natural resources. It proposes that the persistent paradox of poverty amid plenty, despite successive development policies and national development plans, was due to a range of factors, including violent conflict and institutional failures, especially poor leadership and governance, corruption, an incompetent civil service, shortage of services and resources, and a lack of political will. Though the changes required to correct these problems lay far beyond social workers' purview, the authors' attest the profession's responsibility to contribute to social development through relational interventions at all levels, including engagement in community development initiatives to enhance people's educational and employment opportunities.

Nigeria has vast human and natural resources, including crude oil, natural gas, coal, tin, and iron-bearing columbite yet, given the dismal social conditions of large sections of its citizens, it is a country of persistent paradox (Dauda, 2019). Despite its natural wealth, Nigeria's ranking of 161 on the United Nations Development Program's (UNDP) Human Development Index of 189 countries reveals its appalling social development record; amid unprecedented wealth, half the population lives in extreme poverty (UNDP, 2020). Real-time data from the World Data Lab's (2022, July 28) World Poverty Clock indicated that more than 83 million Nigerians (39% of the population) lived in extreme poverty earning less than USD1.90 a day, with 53% in rural areas and 9% in urban areas. Thus, Nigeria accounted for just over 12% of the global population living in extreme poverty. The NBS (2019) household survey showed that four out of 10 Nigerians (89.2 million) spent less than N137430 (USD324) per year, the equivalent of N376.5 (USD1) a day, especially in the north. It reported an income inequality rate of 35.1 (with 100 meaning perfect inequality of expenditure distribution and 0 perfect equality). Gender wise an equal number of men and women lived in extreme poverty (41%). Over 70% of the population earned less than USD3.20 a day. Thus, Nigeria accounted for the largest extremely poor population in the world that exceeded 'the total population of South Africa, Namibia, Botswana, Lesotho, Mauritius and Eswatini combined' (Onyeiwu, 2021, n.p.).

Poverty and inequality in Nigeria have a strong spatial dimension and are considerably higher in rural areas. The National Bureau of Statistics' (2020)

DOI: 10.4324/9781003382126-3

Poverty and Inequality in Nigeria report gave an official urban poverty rate of 18.04% and a rural poverty rate of 52.1%, while the World Bank (2021) reported that 84.6% of the rural population was poor. Rife inequality exacerbated disproportionate acute poverty rates for households across the country's regions. In an Oxfam commissioned report, Mayah et al. (2017) noted that:

> The scale of economic inequality has reached extreme levels, and it finds expression in the daily struggles of the majority of the population in the face of accumulation of obscene amounts of wealth by a small number of individuals (p. 4).

Based on their estimations, 'the amount of money that the richest Nigerian man (sic) earns per annum could be sufficient to lift 2 million people out of poverty for one year' (Mayah et al., 2017, p. 4).

There were striking differences between regions. The incidence of poverty – and associated high illiteracy and low education rates – was highest in the 19 northern states with an average poverty rate of 58% compared to an average of 24.3% in the 17 southern states (NBS, 2019). The World Bank (2021) reported that 76.3% of people in the northern region were poor: North Central (60.7%), North East (69.1%), and North West (71.4%). The North East is home to Boko Haram, one of the largest Islamist militant groups in Africa, attempting to establish an Islamic state based on sharia law (Mentone, 2018). Recurring insecurity has hampered productivity in the north, where there are few commercial enterprises (Ani & Adams, 2020). Ijiaya et al. (2016) reported that Niger State in the North Central region had a poverty rate of 61.2% in 2014 resulting from high levels of 'adult illiteracy, lack of access to … food, shelter, drinkable water, health, sanitation, [and] electric power' (p. 289). Most people in Niger State (over 80%) were on-farm or non-farm agriculturists. Sokoto State in the extreme North West was the country's poorest state, with an 87.73% poverty rate, followed closely by Taraba (87.72%) in North East, and Jigawa (87.02%) in North West, Ebonyi (79.76%) in South East, Adamawa in North East (75.41%), and Zamfara in North West (73.98%) (NBS, 2019). High birth rates, coupled with low household income, had exacerbated poverty in the north. Jigawa had the highest birth rate, followed by Kano and Kebbi in North West. Poverty rates were lower in the south, where higher literacy rates and investment in education led to lower birth rates: South East (59.5%), South South (55.5%), and South West (49.8%).

Lagos, Nigeria's richest state, had a poverty rate of 4.5% (NBS, 2019). It is the most populous and developed state though is smallest in area. It is the major economic hub in Nigeria and the fifth largest in Africa even though 65% of the people living in Lagos were urban poor and resided in slums and settlements (Nwogu, 2021).

Health indicators revealed that Nigeria had made notable progress in combating fatal diseases in recent years, scaling back HIV and AIDS prevalence and declaring itself free of polio in 2020 following a prolonged immunisation campaign. Nevertheless, data from the World Bank (2019) showed that the government had to do much more to ensure healthy living standards and eliminate malnutrition. The data showed that 30% of Nigerians lacked access to improved water, while 70% lacked access to basic sanitation. At the same time, roughly 37% of children younger than five had stunted growth (a risk indicator of impaired development), with the highest proportions in the Northern regions. Among Nigerians aged 15–49 years, 35% of women and 22% of men lacked a formal education with literacy lowest in the North East and North West (National Population Commission (NPC) and International Classification of Functioning, Disability and Health (ICF), 2019).

Due to widespread poverty and underdevelopment, and social work's ethical commitment to working with poor and vulnerable groups in society, it is important to bring social work into the social development fold, especially given its institutional location in the Ministry of Social Development since 1989. It is, therefore, important that social workers are aware of Nigeria's development record and ways in which they might facilitate social development. Included in the social development portfolio are issues pertaining to:

- The environment, including water resources, sanitation, and disaster management
- Women and gender equity
- Population and identity management (statistical data collection mechanisms)
- Poverty alleviation and social protection
- Humanitarian affairs, addressing issues relating to irregular migrants and internally displaced and trafficked persons
- Youth and sport development
- Employment and job creation
- Persons with disabilities (FRN, 2021b).

The following discussion examines Nigeria's post-independence planning for national development, factors hampering progress, ways forward, and international initiatives tilting social work towards increased engagement in social development to promote the welfare of vulnerable groups in society.

National Development Plans (NDP)

1962–1968 NDP1

Interrupted by the 30-month civil war (1966–1968), the first National Development Plan (NDP) (Federation of Nigeria, 1962) comprised a list of uncoordinated regional projects to meet the colonial government's objectives rather than a conscious effort to advance the Nigerian economy's performance. Ukelina (2021) provides a detailed account of the drafting of NDP1 in which the Center for International Studies (CIS) at the Massachusetts Institute of

Technology played a pivotal role, appointing economist Wolfgang Stolper to lead the planning team. Funded by the Ford Foundation, Stolper was the plan's leading architect. He arrived in Nigeria soon after independence in 1960 and was in for a bumpy tide with ethnic differences and political tensions almost torpedoing the plan. Introduced in 1962 for a period of six years, it came to an abrupt end, due to the collapse of the first republic and the subsequent civil war in 1967. However, the political compromises made led to a plan that was bigger than the resources available for its execution, which rested heavily on international funding that did not fully materialise and thus its failure (Ogwumike, 1995; Ukelina, 2021). Ultimately, the planning process exposed Nigeria to external economic interventions in ways that bound its economy and development to global multilateral financial institutions, which pushed policies in 'their economic interests at the expense of Nigeria's development' (Ukelina, 2021, p. 40). Ukelina (2021) delineated three problems in the planning process that shaped the plan's outcomes: 'Regional (ethnic) differences, reliance on international experts over local Nigerian economists, and economic prescriptions that favored short-term gains over long-term investments' (p. 40). The plan's failure showed that economic progress could not resolve political and ethnic conflicts (Ukelina, 2021). The Kainji hydroelectric dam project was the largest project in NDP1. Despite its failure, other achievements included the Port Harcourt refinery, the Jebba paper mill, the Bacita sugar company, and the bridge across the River Niger linking Western and Eastern Nigeria (Anah, 2014).

1970–1974 NDP2

The formulation of the second NDP (FRN, 1970), which began at the end of the civil war in 1970, came at a time when Nigeria's sale of crude oil and other products was on the increase and the nation needed restructuring in the aftermath of the war (Adah & Abasilim, 2015). The plan prioritised agriculture, industry, transport, manpower, defence, electricity, communication, and water supply and essential social services (Ogwumike, 1995). However, fluctuations in the international oil market led to a shortfall in anticipated revenue highlighting the negative impact of Nigeria's mono-economy and its heavy reliance on oil, which, at the time, provided 90% of government revenue, from which the financing of development planning flowed (Anah, 2014).

1975–1980 NDP3

The third NDP (FRN, 1975) covering 1975 to 1980 heralded a return to rural development, especially agricultural improvement (Adah & Abasilim, 2015). However, the agriculture and social development scheme that included education, housing, health, and welfare for the rural population received only 5% and 11.5% of the development budget, respectively (Okigbo, 1989), which was 10 times higher than that for NDP2 and 15 times higher than the budget for NDP1 (Obi, 2006). This raised questions about the government's commitment to rural development (Akinbowale, 2018). Instead, allocations to the manufacturing sector led to the fastest recorded growth rate of an average of 18.1% per annum, with accompanying growth in the building and construction sector, and government services (Okowa, 1991). Thus, as with prior plans, NDP3 did not achieve its planned targets, despite these achievements (Akinbowale, 2018).

1981–1985 NDP4

The fourth NDP (FRN, 1981) was the first under a civilian government, following 15 years of military rule beginning in 1966 (Akinbowale, 2018). With expectations of funding from oil exports, it was the largest and most ambitious plan of the four (Adedeji & Senghor, 1989). NDP4 recognised the importance of health and social development in improving living conditions and their pivotal role in increasing income, improving income distribution, and reducing unemployment (Ogwumike, 1995). Its focus on primacy healthcare (discussed in Chapter 6) involved, among other things, the training of a new cadre of community health officers, as well as nurses and specialist doctors being lost due to the brain drain. It stated that:

> Intermediate and aide cadres of health professionals such as community health assistants, nursing assistants, and health aides will be trained at the schools of Health Technology. A crash programme of training for these cadres of health personnel and their trainers as well as nurse tutors is imperative … to produce the manpower for the Basic Health Service Programme.
>
> (Federal Ministry of National Planning, 1981, p. 77)

NDP4 dissolved the division of social welfare situated in various ministries and signalled a greater focus on social and community development to strengthen local communities' capacity for self-help. As regards welfare, the plan mentioned private-public engagement and, as discussed in Chapter 2, the expansion and strengthening of university-based training programs for social workers for employment as *inter alia* community development officers, social work educators, and social welfare workers, in community development, vocational training, and rehabilitation, respectively. Structural changes to social welfare at the Federal level included the planned dissolution of the Ministry of Social Development, Youth and Sports and placement of welfare under a single government agency; the reorganisation of the National Advisory Committee on Social Development, established by the *Social Development Decree, 1974*, into a National Advisory Council to compile national guidelines for social welfare functions; and the repositioning of existing councils as standing Committees of the National Advisory Council constituted by representatives of government agencies and voluntary organisations working in the sector. The proposed Council would spearhead improved social development activities involving:

- Services for the family and child, women, and aged
- Services for the indigent and for the socially, physically mentally handicapped, as well as those affected by emergencies and natural disasters
- Community services designed to harness the latent qualities of community spirit among citizens towards self-help programmes
- Youth and sports development (Federal Ministry of National Planning, 1981, p. 87)

It called for a broad focus on social welfare as 'a vehicle for promoting social development aimed at improving the quality of life of the people' (Federal Ministry of National Planning, 1981, p. 97). However, the expected level of revenue to fund the plan did not eventuate. Though it looked good on paper and had much appeal for social workers, Alapiki (2009) described NDP4 as the most dismal in the economic history of Nigeria, while the Punch Editorial Board (2020) believed NDP4 marked 'the beginning of a lack of political will, incompetence, poor implementation, and policy somersaults' (n.p.).

1986–2020

Successive policies and programs over the next 34 years until NDP5 included structural adjustment (1986–1990), the rolling plan era (1990–1998), the National Economic Empowerment and Development Strategy (NEEDS) (2003–2007) (NPC, 2004), Vision 2010, and Vision 20:2020 (NPC, 2009) and its seven-point agenda (Udoudo & Ubu-Abai, 2016). The structural adjustment period set an agenda of restructuring and diversifying the economy. It aimed to achieve a stable fiscal environment and balance of payments and lay the foundation for non-inflationary and private sector growth (Adah & Abasilim, 2015). However, instead it led to further government withdrawal from service provision in an already weakened public service infrastructure (Iloh & Bahir, 2013; Todowede, 2013). Nigeria did not have the efficient marketised services, business environment, and regulatory frameworks to support a neoliberal service-delivery system (Iloh & Bahir, 2013).

Subsequent initiatives also failed to generate meaningful development. The Punch Editorial Board (2020) described Vision 2020s woeful failure: The poverty rate increased from 52% in 1999 to almost 70% by 2019 and Nigeria became the world's poverty capital in 2018. Unemployment increased from 7.7% in 1990 to 23.1% in 2019. The over-staffed, indolent, corrupt civil service got worse, not better (Punch Editorial Board, 2020). Analysts attributed development failure to poor governance (Okoye & Yugu, 2009) and the lack of clear implementation plans and competent functionaries to ensure program delivery (Lawal & Oluwatoyin, 2011). Also, foreign aid did not necessarily support national development plans with donors tending to fund and implement predetermined projects and programs without local consultation or adaptation. For example, Monye et al.

(2010) showed that in the period between 1999 and 2007, almost 50% of foreign aid totalling USD6 billion went to health for HIV and AIDS, malaria, maternal health, family planning, and immunisation programs, followed by poverty alle-viation and education, with agriculture, energy, and women's empowerment lower on the list of donor priorities. Despite international declarations on participation and partnership, donors led programs that matched their, rather than the gov-ernment's, priorities, possibly due to the ineffectiveness of the National Planning Commission that, nevertheless, received a large proportion of funding (Monye et al., 2010). The northern states (67%) received more aid than the southern states (33%) though some centres, e.g., Kano, Kaduna, Abuja, and Bauchi in the north and the Cross River and Edo States in the south, benefitted more than others. Monye et al. (2010) attributed the ineffectiveness of foreign aid in Nigeria to a lack of institutional and individual capacity, corruption, and a lack of recipient transparency and accountability.

2021–2025 NDP5

NDP5 builds on the prior Vision 20:2020 and the Economic Recovery and Growth Plan (ERGP) (2017–2020). It sought to accelerate sustained, inclusive private sector-led growth to achieve an economic growth rate of 5%, add 21 million jobs, and lift 35 million people out of poverty under the National Poverty Reduction and Growth Strategy (FRN, 2021c). Besides economic growth, the plan focused on infrastructure, public administration, human capital (edu-cation and health), and social and regional development. NDP5 acknowledged the structural discrimination against women in Nigerian society as follows:

- Patriarchal cultural norms causing economic, legal, political, and social discrimination against women and girls within households and at the community level.
- High prevalence of child marriage, particularly in the Northwest and Northeast regions, where 48% of girls are married by age 15.
- Poor maternal and reproductive care with women's limited access to education and health services increasing maternal and infant mortality rates.
- Exceedingly low political representation of women, with no state having more than one woman elected to the state house of assemblies in the 2019 elections.
- Inadequate enforcement of existing laws and policies.
- Historically gender-neutral approach to development planning overlooking biases against women, girls, and children in policymaking.
- Low remuneration compared to men doing the same work.
- Low land-ownership among women, who accounted for most of Nigeria's agricultural workforce (women represented only 13% of agricultural land-owners).
- Women accounted for most of Nigeria's unemployment and underemploy-ment with many trapped in poverty, due to a lack of access to career opportunities (FRN, 2021b, p. 139).

In response, NDP5 aimed to increase gender parity by focusing on women's economic development, especially in agriculture, and addressing violence against women. Nigeria has adopted a peace-and-security approach to addressing the latter given rising insecurity arising from the violent extremist organisation, Boko Haram, that subjected 'women and girls to kidnapping, domestic servitude, forced labour and sex slavery' (FRN, 2021b, p. 139). Ugwu (2021) reported that more than 70% of displaced persons in northeast Nigeria were women and children. Hence the comprehensive legal framework for combating terrorism and violence against women (FRN, 2021b) included measures designed specifically to deal with Boko Haram, including the National Counter Terrorism Strategy (Office of the National Security Advisor, 2016) and Policy Framework and National Action Plan for Preventing and Countering Violent Extremism (Office of the National Security Advisor, 2017). The Office of the National Security Adviser played a coordinating role with the Nigerian military primarily responsible for combating terrorism (Mentone, 2018). As regards women affected by violence and conflict, the National Action Plan on UNSCR1325 on Women, Peace and Security (including State and Local Action Plans) Federal Ministry of Women Affairs and Social Development (2017); National IDP Policy (FRN, 2021a); National Emergency Framework (National Emergency Management Agency, 2010); National Disaster Response Plan (FRN, 2002), State Anti-Human Trafficking Taskforces, and Nigeria Sexual Offenders Register were all measures to improve security for women. In addition, 22 of Nigeria's 36 states had established shelters for women fleeing violence. The government prioritised policies to address violence and abuse against children and ran an intensive campaign to end child marriage, especially in northern Nigeria (where 48% of girls were married by the age of 15 years) and promote girls' education. However, despite its comprehensive legal framework, policy implementation remained a problem. For instance, the government recently acknowledged its inadequate enforcement of the Violence Against Persons (Prohibition) Act (FRN, 2015c) and National Gender Policy gender-parity benchmarks (FRN, 2021b). Still, there were no dedicated national instruments for the protection of women in IDP camps in Nigeria, despite ongoing reports of rape and sexual exploitation, and HIV and other sexually transmitted infections (Ugwu, 2021). There were reports that violence against women perpetrated by camp administrators and humanitarian workers exacerbated their situation (Ugwu, 2021).

Factors hampering development

Violent conflict

Adegbami and Adeoye's (2021) insightful analysis highlighted the central role violent conflict played and its impact on development in Nigeria to the extent that the government's inability to quell violent groups and instil peace and security has led to labels like failed state and a loss of trust in political leaders.

They discussed the interacting reasons for, and causes of, ongoing violent conflict (also discussed elsewhere in this text) as follows:

- *Insurgents' activities*: Besides Boko Haram, several extremist groups were responsible for violent attacks on Nigerian communities, including the Movement for the Survival of Ogoni People (MOSOP), Movement for the Actualization of the Sovereign State of Biafra (MASSOB), Niger Delta People's Volunteer Force (NDPVF), Movement for the Emancipation of the Niger Delta (MEND), and Niger Delta Avengers (NDA).
- *Armed banditry*, included cattle rustling, village raids, highway robberies, and kidnappings, especially in Zamfara, Katsina, Kaduna, Sokoto, and the Niger State in the North West.
- *Farmers-herders' conflicts*, where pastoralists largely of Fulani ethnic extraction from northern Nigeria attack local farmers in agrarian communities in the central and southern parts of Nigeria. Recent co-ordinated and sophisticated ethnic-religious attacks led the Global Terrorism Index's (2016) ranking of the Fulani herdsmen as a militant group and the 'fourth most deadly terror sect in the world after the Boko Haram, ISIS, and al-Shabaab, in that order' (Adegbami & Adeoye, 2021, p. 7).
- *Poverty and inequality* between and among different groups, and corrupt public officials, fuelled aggression and conflict between individuals and groups.
- *Unemployment*, especially among the youth, led to their engagement in violent conflict and illicit activities, such as trading in arms and ammunition and hard drugs, the ingredients of violent conflict.
- *Ethnoreligious diversities and differences* were the root cause of most conflicts in Nigeria around struggles to gain economic, social, and political power.
- *Failure of the social contract*, due to the government's refusal or inability to devote budgetary resources to the provision of essential social services.
- *Culture of impunity among public officers* whose abysmal performance has sparked public protests that end in conflict from the officials' security people.
- *Activities of religious extremists* fuelled by Islamic-Christian resentment led to the use of religion as weapon for fomenting conflict, due to the narrow-mindedness, ignorance, misunderstanding, fundamentalism, and fanaticism of religious adherents. Religious extremism was also due to, among factors, socioeconomic differences, poverty, parochial interpretations of religious beliefs, and fear of domination by religious majorities.

These violent conflicts hampered development. They damaged the economy and people's livelihoods, especially in conflict-affected areas. They are responsible for the decline in people's welfare and health and have increased the number of people with disabilities, displaced people, children engaged in armed conflict, out-of-school children, and people living with mental illness. Conflicts have exacerbated older people's wellbeing, impacted heavily on the country's health system, and increased the incidence of violence against women and children. They have also discouraged local and foreign investment producing dire consequences for economic and social development.

Government's lack of commitment to development

Lawal and Oluwatoyin (2011: 238–239) attributed the failure of Nigeria's successive development plans to the government's lack of commitment to development shown by the following:

1   The absence of, and government's failure to appoint, officials with executive capacity to formulate and execute implementation plans.
2   The lack of public consultation with village decision-making structures and local government agencies excluded from development planning processes.
3   The lack of good governance and leadership, and high-level corruption and indiscipline, with corrupt leaders lacking a commitment to development, making the state an instrument of capital accumulation, rather than of promoting social and economic development and the interests of citizens.
4   A mono-economic base dependent on crude oil that enriched corrupt leaders to the detriment of other abundant natural resources, including natural gas, tin, iron ore, coal, limestone, niobium, lead, zinc, and arable land.

Adah and Abasilim (2015) listed the following challenges: Imposition of policies; lack of adequate human resources or capital to implement development plans/policies; corruption; and lack of credible leadership. Nigeria does not have a nationalistic, patriotic political class or elite (Saliu, 2007). Most agree that failures of leadership have undermined Nigeria's path to economic and social development (Ayodele et al., 2013; Lawal & Oluwatoyin, 2011; Lawal & Owolabi, 2012; Yunusa, 2020). Poverty reports continually hold political elites responsible for widening inequality and unrelenting poverty in Nigeria. Mayah et al. (2017) highlighted that pervasive corruption and rent seeking (i.e., generating economic wealth through shrewd or potentially manipulative use of resources) diverted state resources and discouraged private investment.

Nigeria's ranking on the Global Corruption Perception Index 154/180 does not help its case for increased private investment (Transparency International, 2021). Fatile (2012) noted corruption was responsible for the ineffectiveness and inefficiency of Nigeria's public sector, underdevelopment, and increasing crime, despite successive governments' laws, institutions, and programs to control it. Thus, 'no service is rendered without money exchanging hands' (Fatile, 2012, p. 56). As Fatile (2012) noted, corruption affected foreign investment, economic growth, and government expenditure choices; it also reduced private investment and fuelled inflation.

Mayah et al. (2017) observed that poverty and inequality were not due to the lack of, but to the ill-use, misallocation, and misappropriation of, resources by 'a political elite out of touch with the daily struggles of average Nigerians' (p. 10). Without effective leaders in touch with their citizenry, there would be a mis-alignment between government and donor priorities (Monye et al., 2010). Lawal and Owolabi (2012) highlighted that the paucity of leadership was a longstanding problem:

> The crop of leaders that have attained leadership position since independence had in one way or the other lacked vision, most of them have been engrossed with corruption and political bickering leading to the enthronement of maladministration and mismanagement of public resources, and consequently economic setback and abject poverty as nation (sic) heritage (p. 2).

Among other factors, Lawal and Owolabi (2012) cited leaders' disrespect for the rule of law, lack of commitment to development, disregard of accountability and transparency, and corruption as reasons for the crisis in governance. George et al. (2021) noted that, as an element of good governance, the rule of law hinged on the premise of resolvable conflicts and flexible procedures for amending rules and regulations, when necessary. Instead, Nnamani and Obinna (2013) noted that many local governments within Nigeria's 774 local govern-ment areas carried paid redundant workers, superfluous political officers, and local government councillor's wives. Further, local government councils, from their chairpersons (usually men) to their messengers, did not respect the rule of law or carry out their designated duties and responsibilities. As Nnamani and Obinna (2013) observed, 'in this type of scenario, the government cannot be close to the people and the necessary development at the grass-root cannot take place … This is why virtually all in the country have become a desert of under-development' (p. 291). This was also a problem at state-government levels, where financial mismanagement and fraud within bloated, inefficient bureauc-racies led to misspent resources earmarked for social and economic development in a complex environment, where ethnic-identity conflicts have exacerbated poverty and 'the state's declining capacity for development' (Mbah & Nwangwu, 2013, p. 417).

Way forward

To reverse the trend of slow development in Nigeria, the World Bank (2019b) called for pivotal investments that would stabilise infrastructure gaps, policy uncertainty, chronic power shortages, and years of underinvestment in educa-tion that had impeded productivity and hampered sustainable development. However, the lethal cocktail of resource mismanagement, poor leadership, corruption, and ethnic-identity conflict discouraged foreign investment and fuelled poverty and inequality in Nigeria. Lawal and Oluwatoyin (2011) drew attention to the hallmarks of successful development countries. They focused on the development of the agricultural sector. They had an effective system of mass education. They developed local, indigenous industries. They employed an export-oriented strategy. They enforced a Spartan discipline of their leadership. They had efficient bureaucracies that focused on human resource development and capacity building. They encouraged a dynamic private sector to work in cooperation with the government towards a society-wide vision of development. They emphasised infrastructure development, institutional capacity building, and attended to problems of governance. They encouraged consistency and policy stability. They suggested the Nigerian government should accept that:

1   Development required total commitment from leaders at all levels of government.
2   Wholesale economic liberalisation was not necessarily synonymous with development.
3   Stability and policy continuity encouraged investment and propelled development.
4   An improved agricultural sector was essential.
5   Human resource development was a *sine qua non* to Nigeria's national development.
6   There was a need for attitudinal change to reverse pessimism, encourage a sense of patriotism, and accept that real development came through internal activities rather than from external influences.
7   The government needed to promote citizenship over indigeneity to 'achieve cooperation and participation of all communities in the development process' (Lawal & Oluwatoyin, 2011, p. 240).
8   There was an imperative need to reform electoral processes.
9   The government should not view development plans exclusively as tools for economic growth but as holistic, encompassing national issues cutting across economic, sociocultural, and political divides.

The Punch Editorial Board (2020) called for massive structural change:

> 'The present structure has to give way to true federalism. Government should make way for the private sector and honestly and transparently privatise all state-owned commercial assets, open the space for foreign direct investment and undertake a root-and-branch reform of the public sector … Leaders need to place national objectives above partisan politics' (n.p.). The Board believed the bungled Vision 2020 did not bode well for Vision 2030s 'ambition to free 100 million citizens from poverty over the next decade' (n.p.).

Social work's push for social development

Partly to address criticisms of its Western bias from the Global South, international social work organisations embarked on a program to bring the profession into line with international development agendas, first through the

MDGs and then the SDGs from 2015 onwards. The Global Agenda on Social Work and Social Development (2010–2020), first mooted in 2010, came to fruition in 2012 as a joint project of social work's two premier international organisations and the International Council on Social Welfare (ICSW) (IASSW/IFSW/ICSW, 2012). It aimed 'to strengthen the profile of social work and to enable social workers to make a stronger contribution to policy development' (Jones & Truell, 2012, p. 454). These organisations have since produced reports based on four pillars of social development:

1 Promoting social and economic equalities
2 Promoting the dignity and worth of peoples
3 Promoting community and environmental sustainability
4 Strengthening recognition of the importance of human relationships.

The revised Global Agenda (2020–2030) has thus far produced two themes: Ubuntu: Strengthening Social Solidarity and Global Connectedness and Co-building a new Eco-Social World: Leaving no one behind. In addition, the updated Global Standards for Social Work Education and Training noted 'new developments and innovations … relating to sustainable development, climate change and the United Nation's (UN) Sustainable Development Goals … in the Global South' (Ioakimidis & Sookraj, 2021, p. 163). Jayasooria (2016) noted the SDGs provided social workers 'an opportunity to redefine their role pertaining to people empowerment, socio-economic development, human rights and the environment' (p. 19). The President of the International Consortium for Social Development (ICSD) drew attention to the international definition of social work that committed the profession to social change, social development, social justice, human rights, collective responsibility, and respect for diversity (Pawar, 2019). He argued that social work's ethical codes predisposed the profession to political engagement and action to achieve macro change reiterating Jones and Truell's (2012) claim that the Global Agenda would enable social workers to make a stronger contribution to policy development. Thus, social workers have several frameworks to guide them in contributing to social development in Nigeria. Documenting their experiences in this regard would make a major contribution to international social work literature and deepen understanding of the opportunities and restraints awaiting social workers seeking to influence change through greater political engagement.

Conclusion

This chapter has shown that Nigeria does not have a good development record, despite successive policies and development plans. As Anah (2014) claimed, despite 'abundant crude oil generated revenue, the development plans cannot be said to have sustained development in Nigeria' (p. 100). Factors hampering successful development include violent conflict and institutional failures, including poor governance and leadership, corruption, an incompetent civil service, shortage of services and resources, and a lack of political will. Though the changes required to correct these problems lie far beyond social workers' purview, they have a responsibility to contribute to social development through relational interventions at all levels, including engagement in community development initiatives to enhance people's educational and employment opportunities. Chapters 4, 5, and 6 examine three major development issues facing Nigerian social workers related to child welfare, people with disabilities, and trafficked persons.

4 Child welfare – a system in need of care

This chapter proposes that Nigeria's child welfare system is in urgent need of emergency care, arguing that children's wellbeing rests *inter alia* on an efficient public service infrastructure, dedicated social workers, innovative social protection measures, implementable policies, vocal child rights advocates, and family and community partnerships. Following a review of indigenous childcare practices, child welfare policy, child protection, and child welfare issues, the Nigerian child welfare system emerges as 'good on paper, abysmal in practice'. The government's failure to support overburdened social workers reveals a lack of commitment to building a robust child welfare system with strong child protection measures. The punitive emphasis on juvenile justice, the neglect of children's mental health issues in residential and correctional facilities, ongoing insecurity, baby harvesting, and the trafficking, exploitation, and abuse of children, including statutory rape and child labour, all suggest a system with a dubious commitment to child rights and the best interests of children. This is especially concerning, given Nigeria has one of the youngest populations in the world, with 50% (or 107 million) of its people younger than 19 years of age. Children up to four years old comprised the largest age group, while those between the ages of five and nine years constituted the second largest age band (Statista, 2022). The Federal Ministry of Women Affairs and Social Development (FMWASD) estimated there were 17.5 million orphans and vulnerable children (over 16% of the population) in Nigeria, most of whom had lost their parents through AIDS and HIV and 95% of whom had not received any support or assistance (SPRING, 2016). The FMWSAD was responsible for children's welfare and ensuring a qualified competent welfare workforce. However, State governments were responsible for the deployment of professional staff in local social welfare departments, hospitals, and institutions.

As shown in Chapter 2, due to minimalistic public welfare provision, indigenous communal care through the biological and extended family, and kin and community networks, including indigenous education systems, provided for child socialisation (Uchendu, 2007), wellbeing, and development. Colonial government child welfare interventions for street children and juvenile offenders, mainly in regional capitals, took a predominantly legalistic approach. Western-style education, introduced by missionaries, characterised education in the south,

DOI: 10.4324/9781003382126-4

while, as part of the Zakat Islamic system to provide for the poor, education in Almajiri (Koranic) schools was pervasive in the northern regions. Despite Islamic dominance, however, as in other parts of the country, the northern regions had retained their indigenous sociocultural heritage (Akintayo, 2021).

Indigenous childcare practices

Ekpe (1983) noted that in indigenous society, children grew up 'in an intense situation of kinship, family, and lineage … bound by … family obligation and family histories' (p. 487). From infancy, they were part of an extended family network, where relatives were substitute parents or siblings, with special duties towards them:

> They learn from a very early age to spread their love and regard, their rewards and their worries and concern over larger groups of people. They grow up thus with many affectionate relatives to whom they build up sentimental attachments even if these are not as close as their attachments to their own parents. This may have the effect of lessening the conflict of relationship. For instance, when a child is annoyed with his parents, he can seek refuge with these others; if he is orphaned, they practically take his parents' place … The child is thus brought up with a strong sense of community. This mutual support, community, and sense of kinship are among the qualities of the family.
>
> (Ekpe, 1983, p. 487)

Thus, the strong reliance on informal, unregulated care options for children has a longstanding history supported by strong sociocultural values on the role of extended families and kin networks in socialising children. Most children in alternative care are in informal, undocumented, unregulated arrangements 'with extended family or in unrelated households' (Connelly & Ikpaahindi, 2016, p. 4), where they might be at risk of exploitation and abuse (Anazonwu, 2019; Connelly & Ikpaahindi, 2016; Nnama-Okechukwu et al., 2020; Offiong & Uduigwomen, 2019; Okoli & Udechukwu, 2019; Olaore & Drolet, 2017; Sossou & Yogtiba, 2009; Uzuegbu, 2010). Aruna (2018) reported that family structure had a marked effect on the incidence of child sexual abuse. Children in foster care were 10 times more prone to sexual abuse and those living with a single parent with a live-in partner were 20 times more likely to fall victim to child sexual abuse than children living with both biological parents (Aruna, 2018).

Studies of child abuse have found that most children were abused by people whom they trusted (Aruna, 2018; Ehigie & Omorogiuwa, 2022). One in three abusers were close family members – fathers, brothers, uncles, mothers, aunts, sisters, and cousins, while 6 out 10 were friends, neighbours, teachers, child carers, and babysitters (Ehigie & Omorogiuwa, 2022) and, as Ehigbie and Omorogiuwa (2022) found, most cases of abuse went unreported, due to fear of stigmatisation.

They highlighted the important role of parents in protecting children through open communication and sex education. Mothers, especially, with close relationships to their children, could teach them to 'report any kind of inappropriate touching of their body, especially their private parts' (Ehigbie & Omorogiuwa, 2022, p. 52), named appropriately, and, most importantly, how to say no and protect themselves in situations that made them feel uncomfortable.

Nnama-Okechukwu et al. (2020) focused on the positive and negative aspects of informal fostercare among the Igbo noting the need for culturally sensitive interventions to enhance children's safety. To counter the risks, they saw the need for statutory child welfare intervention to document and monitor informal childcare placements.

Uzuegbu (2010) discussed the cultural practices that contributed to the abuse of children, including ethnoreligious beliefs informing practices like Almajiri, child witchcraft stigmatisation, ignorance about children with disabilities, early marriage, and female genital mutilation, as well as preference for large families and male children. Sossou and Yogtiba (2009) likewise examined the pernicious problem of culturally induced child abuse, including child trafficking, child marriage, *Trokosi*, and neglect of disabled children. Practised in the Republic of Benin and parts of Nigeria, *Trokosi*, known locally as *voodoosi* or *vudusi* (Tubor, 2019) involved sending young female children, particularly virgins as young as 10, to fetish shrines as sex slaves 'to atone for the sins and crimes committed by their relatives, who usually were already dead' (Sossou & Yogtiba, 2009, p. 6). This system, based on traditional religious beliefs, discriminated against women and young girls, denying them access to education and healthcare, and placing them in sexually abusive situations, where they were often impregnated by custodial fetish priests.

John et al.'s (2015) study of indigenous childrearing practices in the Niger Delta Region found pervasive use of cultural preventive measures to ward off evil spirits, protect babies from witchcraft or sorcery, and prevent untimely death, misfortune, and bad luck, all of which could have harmful health implications. They included the following:

- Herbal remedies (oral, bath, enema, and instillation)
- Tying of charms and amulets (made from dried chicken sacrum, cowry, black string, or beads) around the neck, waist, wrist, and ankle
- Use of various oils and ointments for body massage from the third day after birth until nine months, but especially within the first six months
- Application of palm kernel oil and Shea butter ointment mixed with native garlic on the anterior fontanelle
- Making of incisions on the skin of the forehead, side of the face, middle of the chest, and back of the waist, smeared with gun powder or burnt herbs to seal the cuts.

Offiong and Uduigwomen (2019) highlighted the pervasive practice of witchcraft attributed to religious beliefs and values that 'trample on children's rights'

(p. 24). Secker's (2012) in-depth analysis of this practice showed that members of the immediate family or clergy were the primary accusers. Labelling children as witches accounted for the increasing number of street children living in harsh, unsavoury conditions and vulnerable to exploitation, abuse, and trafficking. Sociocultural values and belief systems that support practices like witchcraft stigmatisation contribute to child rights' violations (Offiong & Uduigwomen, 2019).

On the other hand, Ogunniran (2015) noted how legislative provisions were at odds with cultural practices and why states could adapt laws to fit ethnoreligious beliefs and cultural practices:

> In some states, for example, girls are withdrawn from schools for early marriages, even betrothed from childhood. Tattoo on the skin is seen as a form of identification or beatification in some parts of the country. In the Northern part of Nigeria, child beggars or *almajiris* are an endemic feature of that society. Rights conferred on children are regarded as alien to our culture wherein children are to be seen and not heard (p. 58).

Like Akintayo (2021), Ogunniran (2015) supported acceptance of cultural relativity in adapting national legislation to state contexts, even though this might compromise children's rights.

Child welfare policy

Though regional customary and Islamic (sharia) law and other traditional systems made provision for children needing care, national child welfare laws were a recent institution in postcolonial Nigeria with the Child Rights Act only enacted in 2003. It was concerned primarily with four aspects of children's rights: children's *participation* in decisions affecting them; *protection* against discrimination and all forms of neglect and exploitation; *prevention* of harm; and *provision* for their basic needs (Nwanna & Ogunniran, 2019). It prohibited sexual intercourse, betrothal, and marriage with a child (under the age of 18 years) and made forced or exploitative labour, the trafficking of children, and female genital mutilation criminal offences. However, national legislation on issues pertaining to children fell within the residuary legislative category and child welfare issues depended largely on the States' adoption and adaptation of the Child Rights Act (Iguh & Nosike, 2011). This, in turn, depended on dominant ethnoreligious beliefs and practices in various states (Akintayo, 2021).

International and regional laws have had a huge influence on Nigeria's child welfare legislation (Abdulraheem-Mustapha, 2016; Akintayo, 2021; Emelonye, 2020; Iguh & Nosike, 2011; Iguh & Oti-Onyema, 2020). Akintayo (2021) noted that the United Nations Children's Fund (UNICEF), especially, played a major role in improving research and practice in the Nigerian child welfare system, as had the International Labour Organisation (ILO). Hence, Nigeria had adopted the:

- Convention on the Rights of the Child (UN, 1989)
- African Charter on the Rights and Welfare of the Child (AU, 1990)
- International Covenant on Economic Social and Cultural Rights (UN, 1966a)
- International Covenant on Civil and Political Rights (UN, 1966a)
- Convention Concerning the Prohibition and Immediate Action for the Elimination of the Worst Forms of Child Labor (ILO, 1999)
- Optional Protocol to the Convention on the Rights of the Child on the sale of children child prostitution and child pornography (UN, 2000a)
- Optional Protocol to the Convention on the Rights of the Child on the involvement of children in armed conflicts (UN, 2000b).

The International Covenant on Civil and Political Rights (UN, 1966a) articulated special measures of protection and assistance for children without discrimination. The International Covenant on Economic Social and Cultural Rights (UN, 1966b), supported by ILO conventions on child labour, called for measures to ensure children received protection from economic and social exploitation by prohibiting their employment in harmful work that threatened their healthy development (Emelonye, 2020). With assistance from international human rights organisations, these international laws have informed national policies pertaining to children, including the:

- National Guidelines and Standards of Practice on Orphans and Vulnerable Children (FMWASD, 2007)
- Nation Action Plan for the Elimination of Child Labour (2013–2017) (FRN, 2013a)
- National Standards Policy for Improving the Quality of Life for Vulnerable Children in Nigeria (FMWASD, 2014)
- Ending Violence Against Children in Nigeria (2015–2016)
- National Strategic Plan to End Child Marriage in Nigeria (2016–2021)
- National Priority Agenda for Vulnerable Children in Nigeria (2013–2020) (FMWASD, 2013).

The National Priority Agenda (FMWASD, 2013) recognised 'the need to strengthen [the] technical ... child-sensitive capacities of magistrates, prosecutors, police, social workers and other officials in the justice system' (Connelly & Ikpaahindi, 2016, p. 6). However, despite all these efforts, institutional structures to support child and youth legislation have not improved since colonial times. Consequently, Nigeria had 'the highest number of out-of-school children in the world by 2020' (Akintayo, 2021, p. 13), with one in four children engaged in street labour (Omorogiuwa, 2020). This despite free and compulsory basic education for children up to 15 years. Internal conflict hampered children's healthy educational development contributing to the 10.5 million out-of-school children aged 5–14 years in Nigeria (UNICEF, 2020). Thus, most children, who were unable to go to school because of safety issues, were in the north, where the school attendance rate was 53%. In many instances, the government has had to close schools to ensure children's security. The 10 worst states were Bauchi, Niger, Katsina, Kano, Sokoto, Zamfara, Kebbi, Gombe, Adamawa, Taraba, and the FCT of Abuja, with about eight million out-of-school children and an average enrolment rate of 57%. The situation was dire in the northeastern region, where the insurgency had left 2.8 million children in need of emergency-education support across Borno, Yobe, and Adamawa. The security situation in the northeastern states had led to the closure of over 800 schools. Insurgents had destroyed 497 classrooms and damaged 1,392. The kidnapping of children and vandalism of school property left parents and guardians petrified of sending their wards to school. The out-of-school situation was worse for girls in the northeast and northwest, where more than 50% were not in school. According to UNICEF (2020), 29% and 35% of Muslim children in the northeastern and northwestern states, respectively, received a Koranic education that did not include basic literacy and numeracy skills.

Clearly, there have been problems with implementing child rights laws and child welfare policies, with NDP5 (FRN, 2021b) noting inadequate enforcement of the Child Rights Act (NHRC, 2003), which was in force only in the FCT of Abuja and in states that had enacted this legislation (Iguh & Nosike, 2011). Akintayo (2021) noted that 'as of 31 December 2020, only the federal capital territory of Abuja and 27 … of Nigeria's 36 states' (p. 13) had adopted the Child Rights Act. Nine of the 12 sharia states – Sokoto, Bauchi, Kano, Kebbi, Borno, Niger, Gombe, Yobe, and Zamfara – had not adopted or adapted the national legislation. However, even in states that had incorporated the Act into their domestic laws, there were problems relating to their implementation (Connelly & Ikpaahindi, 2016).

In states that had not adopted the 2003 Act, excluding the sharia states, the Children and Young Persons Act 2003 applied (CRIN, 2013). Originally enacted in 1943 and extended to the Northern Region in 1958, it related primarily to juvenile justice. Its major innovations were the establishment of a juvenile justice system and juvenile courts, and restriction of street trading for children under 14 years (Aderinto, 2015). It criminalised street hawking, which was an established sociocultural tradition among Hausa people. As discussed in Chapter 2, it was a response to the problem of juvenile offenders, or rather young people's behaviour that did not fit colonial norms. Thus, it carried a punitive rather than a protective child welfare ethos. It has received heavy criticism over the years, due to its exposure of children to the criminal justice system and failure to promote the wellbeing and welfare of juvenile offenders (Nwanna & Ogunniran, 2019; Ogunniran, 2015). For this reason, Abdulraheem-Mustapha (2016) recommended its abolition.

Akintayo (2021) attributed Nigeria's child welfare challenges to ethno-religious diversity, infiltration of non-native worldviews (Islam and Christianity, especially), colonial legacies, vacillating postcolonial social policies, conceptual ambiguities (as welfare terminology had no indigenous equivalent), and persistent professional rivalries. His solutions included an acceptance of cultural relativity relating to child maltreatment, leveraging the transformative mandates of the social work profession, and using research and systems thinking to transform professional rivalries into multidisciplinary approaches. Akintayo (2021) argued convincingly for the government to accord the social work profession its rightful role in Nigeria, as child and family social workers could reduce many of the challenges in the country's child welfare systems and practices by implementing its child welfare policies and programs.

Child protection

Nwokolu-Nte and Onyige (2020) defined child protection broadly to include family welfare, including informal childcare practices, and legal statutory provision. As already discussed, the major placement option for children in need of out-of-home care was in undocumented, unregulated informal placements with extended family members or in unrelated households, where wards might be at risk of exploitation and denied access to education (Connelly & Ikpaahindi, 2016). The narrower definition used in Western countries, generally encompassed legal adoption (the permanent placement of children with a new family) and out-of-home care (foster care preferably, with residential care as a last resort) under the umbrella of child protection. The removal of children from their biological families involved a complex legal process of child removal following thorough investigation by a child protection officer. Holmes et al. (2012) reported there were too few social workers working in Nigeria's child protection system, which was not a priority for Nigerian policymakers and government agencies. While there were well-developed NGO-supported child protection networks, they depended mainly on the services of *pro bono* professionals and volunteers (Connelly & Ikpaahindi, 2016) and the family court system operated only in Lagos and, to some extent, in the FCT. Also, there was considerable variation in child welfare service provision across the country. NGOs, practitioner networks, and community-based organisations had made inroads in child protection, leading service innovation, but government inertia and overlapping ministerial responsibilities had hampered statutory provision (Connelly & Ikpaahindi, 2016).

A relatively small number of children and families in Nigeria tended to enter the statutory system through police referral and social welfare ministries, with the latter 'bedeviled by a general lack of financial and human resources to effectively deliver services' (Nwokolu-Nte & Onyige, 2020, p. 149). Where available, formal alternative statutory care options included residential placement in overcrowded orphanages and shelters run by NGOs, religious bodies, private individuals, and government. Without a stringent evaluation and monitoring system, orphanages in the south had become baby factories, as discussed below. Although there were legal provisions for adoption and foster care, which were becoming more culturally acceptable, related services, legal supports, and investigatory processes were poor (Onayemi & Aderinto, 2019). There were not enough social workers to carry out child protection investigations and compile court reports with placement recommendations. There were not enough foster care placements or residential places for children in need of care. Due to the shortage of formal alternative fostercare and adoption options, traumatised children removed from neglectful, abusive situations spent prolonged periods in correctional (juvenile justice) or welfare (residential care) facilities, which was not a satisfactory situation (Atilola et al., 2017).

Issues in child welfare

Cultural acceptability of child adoption

The Child Rights Act 2003 made provision for culturally sensitive legal adoption (Ojelabi et al., 2015) and the Children and Young Persons Act 2003 required every State Government to institute adoption services. The law prohibited inter-country adoption. Nevertheless, adoption was a foreign concept in many traditional African societies, even for childless couples, because the extended family and kinship networks provided for children in need of care. This applied in many Igbo communities. Ojelabi et al. (2015) noted that complex ethnoreligious beliefs, values, and practices made child adoption difficult in southeastern Nigeria, the ancestral home of the Igbo. Adopted children were treated as outcasts and bastards, sometimes with hatred, disrespect, and constant reminders that they did not belong to the family. People in the South-West (Yoruba land) were more positively disposed to child adoption though Yoruba still held negative cultural beliefs about adopted children. Rather than adopt, men in infertile marriages were encouraged to marry another woman (Ojelabi et al., 2015). Further, Ojelabi et al. (2015) noted that 'the patrilineal and kinship nature of most Nigerian families make it very essential for a woman to gain the full consent and support of the husband and the extended family in a decision to adopt' (p. 79).

Though sharia law forbade child adoption, Avidime et al.'s (2013) study of the attitudes of women (n=200) of reproductive age (15–49 years) towards child adoption in the Muslim city of Zaria[1], Kaduna State[2], north-central Nigeria, revealed that 89.4% of respondents were aware of child adoption (35% through mass media) and 77% were positive about it. Most (64.2%) expressed preference for adopting girls. The researchers believed this high level of knowledge and acceptability of child adoption suggested it was an option worth exploring for Muslim infertile couples.

Despite the afore-mentioned cultural reservations, adoption was available mainly in the southern states, where it was becoming more widely accepted (Ojelabi et al., 2015). Ohachenu's (2016) study on child adoption in Orlu, in northeast Imo State in southern Nigeria, showed that couples would adopt children to assist in household chores, care for them in old age, and replace them when they died, carry the family name, and take over their inheritance to maintain family lineage and continuity.

Onayemi and Aderinto's (2019) qualitative study involving social welfare officials (n=9), key informants (n=10), orphanage managers (n=5), and legal practitioners (n=5) found several procedural problems in the investigatory processes surrounding adoption that threatened child placement and security, including a lack of synergy between adoption officials, insufficient training and retraining of adoption officials, and an unsupportive legal system.

Child abandonment

While sociocultural values placed a high premium on children, child abandonment was a common phenomenon, related to cultural proscriptions about illegitimate children, unwanted teenage pregnancy, especially ensuing from rape, abuse, or incest, and cultural practices surrounding child witchcraft stigmatisation, such as exorcism, was a common phenomenon (Isangha et al., 2020; Moshood, 2020; Secker, 2012). Child abandonment constituted a serious form of child abuse and neglect, and left abandoned children suffering long-term social, psychological, and health issues. It was also a criminal offence in terms of Section 16 of the Violence Against Persons (Prohibition) Act (FRN, 2015c). The Child Rights Act (FRN, 2003) prohibited child torture and other forms of cruel, inhumane, or degrading treatment or punishment, while Section 34 (1) of the Constitution (FRM, 1999) stated that every child was entitled to respect for human dignity. Aside from state and federal laws, Nigeria was also a signatory to many international conventions aimed at protecting the rights of the child, including the International Convention on Economic, Social and Cultural Rights of the Child (UN, 1976) and the Convention on the Rights of the Child (UN, 1989). Notwithstanding these laws and conventions, cases of child abuse and abandonment were rampant in the country (Moshood, 2020; Offiong & Uduigwomen, 2021; Uzuegbu, 2010).

Childlessness

African societies, generally, placed a high premium on children, with social status and the success of marriages linked strongly to childbearing (Makinde et al., 2017a; Ohachenu, 2020; Ojelabi et al., 2015; Omobowale et al., 2019). African cultures valued children above wealth: 'Children may secure a couple's marriage, and the right of property and inheritance, provide social security and maintain family lineage among other factors' (Omobowale et al., 2019, p. 22). Omobowale et al. (2019) noted that children occupied 'a strategic space among the Yoruba ... and a childless marital relationship is often a source of concern for couples, and it may result in separation, divorce or extra-marital affairs by both parties' (p. 20). The interference of in-laws placed enormous pressures on childless women to produce children or move on so their son could marry another wife (Naab et al., 2019). This led to stress and increased the risk of mental illness (see Chapter 6).

Besides acute emotional distress, some endured psychological and physical torture (Avidime et al., 2013). As Omobowale et al. (2019) observed, 'in a situation of childlessness, the female partner is more affected because childbirth certifies a woman's position in both her nuclear family and among her in-laws and ensures she has a stake in her home' (p. 20). In Igbo and Yoruba society, children provided societal and generational continuity, security in old age, and inherited parental wealth, property, and assets. Therefore, childlessness created social and psychological problems and marital insecurity and generated conflict for childless parents.

Despite advances in assisted reproductive technologies (ARTs) resulting in the improved management of infertility as a treatable condition, relatively few women had access to these costly services (Makinde et al., 2017a; Ojelabi et al., 2015). Makinde et al. (2017a) linked the high cost and low cultural acceptance of ARTs to infertile couples increasingly turning to illegal adoption through baby factories to avoid the stigma of childlessness and alternative methods of conception.

Illegal child adoption and baby factories

Illegal adoption was a widespread problem in Nigeria that had spawned lucrative businesses selling babies and coercing young women into baby-making factories, where their infants were forcibly removed at birth for illegal adoption, trafficking, and, sometimes, cultural sacrificial rituals (Obaji, 2020; Okoli & Udechukwu, 2019; Udechukwu, 2019). Makinde et al. (2016) described baby factories as 'buildings, hospitals or orphanages that have been converted into places for young girls and women to give birth to children for sale on the black market, often to infertile couples, or into trafficking rings' (p. 6). Located mainly in Southern Nigeria, populated predominantly by Igbo and Yoruba people, these baby-harvesting factories had propagated new forms of abuse of infants and their biological mothers, who endured physical, psychological, and sexual violence (Makinde et al., 2017b). They had arisen to meet two needs: Those of desperate teenagers facing the stigma of unwanted pregnancies, who were talked into giving up their babies for financial benefit and, secondly, the needs of their chief patrons, childless couples attracted by issues surrounding the cultural disapproval of ARTs, surrogacy, and adoption (Makinde et al., 2017b). As Makinde et al. (2016) explained, 'the high burden and stigmatization of infertility in Nigeria, and the unwillingness of infertile couples to associate publicly with adoption or surrogacy, contributes to the increased patronage of baby factories' (p. 7).

Hence, their proliferation arose from a complex array of social, cultural, and economic factors. With the high cultural premium placed on children and parenthood and stigmatisation of childless and infertile women, faced with losing their inheritance rights, the situation was rife for this fast-growing phenomenon (Makinde et al., 2017a, 2017b). Udechukwu's (2019) study of illegal child adoption in Enugu State in the southeast found 63% of respondents (n=200 social welfare officers) reported that people sanctioned this practice to save money (44%) and avoid red tape and stigmatisation (40.5%). Some young women and girls wanting to end an unwanted pregnancy were caught up in the baby factory business, while searching for illegal abortion options. They sold their babies to avoid the stigma and shame of an unwanted pregnancy and family persecution, and for financial gain. The Igbos' cultural preference for male children had also had an impact making males more profitable than females.

Medical and health workers also benefitted financially from this business, referring young women entangled in baby making (Makinde et al., 2016). There was little to stop these practices, due to the absence of legislation and criminal sanction, and corrupt law-enforcement agencies. The absence of legislation on surrogacy created the impression that the sale of babies was permissible, while the statutory rape and impregnation of underage girls and the crime of profiteering from their abuse went unpunished (Makinde at al., 2017a, 2017b).

Dealing with this problem was extremely complex. Besides legislation, there was a need for widespread advocacy and education to prevent unwanted pregnancies and enlighten young women about the long-term health risks of baby-factory pregnancy and childbirth (Makinde et al., 2017a). It would also help to remove administrative and legal bottlenecks and cultural barriers for infertile couples wanting to explore options for conception or adoption and increase counseling to help them navigate available options (Makinde et al., 2016, 2017b). There was an urgent need for the regulation of adoption and surrogacy, and the licensing of professionals practising within this arena in Nigeria, including social workers (Makinde et al., 2016).

Children in conflict

With decades of violence and unrest, millions of Nigeria's children and adolescents caught up in the armed conflict have endured sexual violence, forced marriage, and recruitment by armed groups, thus facing double victimisation: 'Not only are they subject to grave violations, but they also face rejection, stigmatization and, in some cases, violence when they try to return to their home communities' (UNICEF, 2016, p. 4). Obikeze (1979) discussed a study of children evacuated to foreign countries, due to the civil war (1967–1970). Evacuating children for security reasons was not new to Nigeria. This was a practice among the Igbo in precolonial times during inter-ethnic conflicts. Based on survey data from the displaced children, their parents, foster parents, or guardians (n=856), and social workers involved in the evacuation (n=35), Obikeze (1979) concluded that evacuation was a culturally appropriate social work intervention for children in conflict situations. However, most of these children ended up in displaced persons' camps, where the living conditions were extremely undesirable, and they were vulnerable to abuse and exploitation.

Child labour

Some researchers highlighted the variance between indigenous and Western notions of child labour (Ajala, 2010; Akintayo, 2021). In most traditional households, the family constituted a unit and children, along with other able-bodied family members, worked the land or herded cattle, while among the Hausas, hawking was an accepted cultural practice. This was at odds with the ILO's International Program on the Elimination of Child Labour (IPEC), also referred to as ILO-IPEC. Thus, numerous Nigerian ethnocultural groups engaged in child labour practices deemed child abuse in international law. Azi and Saluhu's (2016) study of child labour found that 52% of children in Calabar city were victims of abuse. Most researchers attributed the phenomenon of street children to, and described it as, child abuse and neglect (Abari & Audu, 2013; Adeyemi & Oluwaseun, 2012; Clark & Yesufu, 2016). Abari and Audu (2013) described 'the high prevalence of the problem of street children [in Nigerian cities] as … child abuse and neglect' (p. 45) leading children to desert their families to survive on the streets. Adeyemi and Oluwaseun (2012) described street children as 'casualties of economic growth, war, poverty, loss of traditional values, domestic violence, [and] physical and mental abuse. Every street child has a reason for being on the streets' (p. 88), which, in Nigeria, might include economic necessity, conflict, abuse, accusations of witchcraft, and family breakdown. Abari and Audu's (2013) study of street children in Ibadan found most were from poor families with low education and used their street-trading activities to contribute to their family's upkeep. Conditions on the street were harsh and dangerous, potentially robbing a quarter of Nigeria's children of their future (Omorogiuwa, 2020).

Omorogiuwa (2020) highlighted that nearly a third of children between the ages of 7 and 14 years of age in Nigeria and 12 to 15 million children overall, or one in four, were involved in child labour. Given the scale of the problem and its deleterious impacts on children's healthy physical and social development, the government's failure to provide child welfare services and enforce children's legislation was criminal. As with all issues relating to children's welfare, 'providing targeted interventions that meet the needs of street children requires an understanding of who they are, what they need, what they do and how they can be identified' (Adeyemi & Oluwaseun, 2012, p. 88).

Child rape

Iguh and Oti-Onyema's (2020) examination of statutory rape, that is, sexual intercourse with a minor, under the Child's Right Act noted that there was no express mention of the term in Nigeria's legal instruments, even though it was a recognised crime and prohibited act with offenders liable to life imprisonment irrespective of their age. Nevertheless, the Child's Right Act prohibited sexual intercourse with a person younger than 18 years of age labelling it rape. Olatunji's (2012) analysis of Nigerian legislation on rape found several shortcomings that hampered effective prosecution of purveyors of this crime. It limited definitions of rape to male female rape that involved penetrative vaginal sex. It excluded male rape victims and anal sex. It placed the onus on the rape victim to prove that penetration had occurred, provide corroboration of the crime, and proof of non-consent. Few women reported rape, due to the difficulties of proof, mishandling of rape cases, and slim likelihood of legal prosecution. Aruna (2018) noted the lack of stringency in Nigeria's Criminal and Penal Codes on child sexual abuse, with the Child Rights Act not yet enacted in many States. With court delays and police inadequacies, there was little legal protection to prevent the alarming prevalence of child rape and litany of problems that ensued (Achunike & Kitause, 2014; Agbo, 2019; Folayan et al., 2014; Olusola & Ogunlusi, 2020).

Agbo's (2019) study of eight states found child labour, children left alone without care, and male rape of children for ritualistic purposes all contributed to the high incidence of child rape. It left children stigmatised and emotionally traumatised, which sometimes resulted in suicide. Many contracted sexually transmitted diseases and experienced health problem, including physical pain and injury. It also resulted in low academic performance, poor school attendance, and school dropout. Achunike and Kitause (2014) attributed the worrisome epidemic of rape to, among other factors, cultural practices surrounding early marriage, myths surrounding sex, a culture of silence, modernising influences, and peer group pressure. They provided vivid accounts of rape in Nigeria and its impact on victims, including physical injuries, fatigue and chronic headaches, and emotional problems, such as suicide attempts, stress disorders, depression, and sexual dysfunction.

Juvenile justice in crisis

Historically anchored in punitive incarceration, the contemporary Nigerian juvenile justice system was woefully inadequate. Sa'ad (2008) noted the 'virtual absence of trained probation officers and very inadequate number of trained social workers in all the states' (p. 79), while Obidimma and Obidimma (2012) claimed there were 'no well-established and adequately equipped institutions and coherent programs for dealing with juvenile offenders and preventing juvenile delinquency in the country' (p. 94).

Yekini and Salisu (2013) noted it was the Ministry of Youth and Development's portfolio to employ social workers to work as probation officers in the juvenile justice system, preparing court reports for children beyond parental control and in conflict with the law and monitoring the activities of children in remand homes and approved schools. They reported that the Ministry employed 230 social workers in Lagos State, deploying some to work in the juvenile justice system as follows: Juvenile Courts in Ikeja and Yaba; girls' remand home in Idiaraba and boys' remand home in Oregun; and girls' approved home in Idiaraba, boys' approved school in Isheri, and intermediate boys' approved school in Yaba. They found these over-burdened social workers carried heavy caseloads and received poor remuneration. They also reported corruption among probation officers, due to inadequate monitoring of their behaviour and practice.

Atilola et al. (2017) reported that there were only 25 social work probation officers working in youth correctional facilities catering for over 300 residents. Atilola et al. (2019) reported that there were only three overcrowded, over-stretched federal-run youth correctional institutions providing 600 beds for a population of 50 million young people. Most had no prior exposure to, or training in, psychosocial assessment and clinical interventions, though they were working with young people with complex mental health issues.

Atilola et al. (2019) described the Nigerian juvenile justice system as an amalgam of the social welfare and youth correctional systems, dealing mainly with minor offenders, many of whom had complex mental health and behavioural issues. It was a system in crisis, due to, *inter alia*:

- Overcrowded youth correctional facilities and too many young offenders in emergency placements in welfare-run refuges for traumatised abused and neglected youth.
- A lack of community-based diversion programs meaning incarceration was the likely outcome for juvenile offenders, especially those from poor communities for minor offences.
- A high prevalence of ongoing psychiatric, substance abuse, behavioural, and psychosocial problems among residents in youth correctional facilities and absence of mental health policy, strategy, and service provision, effectively making them warehouses for 'troubled and troubling youth … without addressing their psychosocial and mental health needs' (Atilola et al., 2019, p. 20).
- Shortage of youth mental health professionals and overburdened social workers and probation officers in youth correctional facilities.

Conclusion

Effective child welfare rests on *inter alia* an efficient public service infrastructure, dedicated social workers, innovative social protection measures, implementable policies, vocal child rights advocates, and family and community partnerships (Offiong & Uduigwomen, 2021). Nigeria has implementable policies that states can choose not to adopt, adapt, and implement. Even those that adopt them do not implement them uniformly. There is no monitoring of policy implementation or standards of practice. Most services are in regional capitals. The government does not support social workers, who are overburdened and carry heavy caseloads. It appears uncommitted to building a robust child welfare system with strong child protection measures. Child welfare looks good on paper but abysmal in practice. The punitive emphasis on juvenile justice, the neglect of children's mental health issues in residential and correctional facilities, ongoing insecurity, baby harvesting, and the trafficking, exploitation, and abuse of children, including statutory rape and child labour, all suggest a system with a dubious commitment to child rights and the best interests of children. They suggest Nigeria's child welfare system needs emergency care.

Notes

1 Zaria is Kaduna's educational centre. It is home to Nigeria's largest university.
2 Almost all the Hausa and Fulani inhabitants in the north of Kaduna State are Muslims. There are about 30 other ethnic groups in the south of the state. Not all are Muslim. The Gbari (Gwari) is the largest ethnic group in the southern part of the State. The assassination in Kaduna (the old northern region capital city from 1954 to 1967) of Sir Ahmadu Bello, Sardauna of Sokoto and Northern premier, in a purported Igbo military coup in January 1966, led to the Nigerian Civil War (1967–1970).

5 Social exclusion, gender, and disability in Nigeria and the social work response

This chapter explores disability in Nigeria, the country with the highest number of persons with disabilities in Africa. It begins with a discussion of African understandings of disability and international influences promoting social models of disability, despite the predominance of religious-medical conceptions of disability in Nigeria. Following a brief overview of discourses informing perspectives on disability, it continues with an examination of barriers to social inclusion, especially for women with disabilities, before suggesting solutions that might inform a social work response. It suggests a political role for social workers in advocating for social interventions, state services, and strong representation for people with disabilities, while engaging in research and advocacy to demonstrate the benefits of social interventions in disability service provision.

Despite its ratification of human rights charters relating to people with disabilities, the Nigerian government tends to regard disability as a charity and welfare matter rather than a human rights issue. Following disability groups and activists' relentless advocacy since Nigeria's ratification of the international Convention on the Rights of People with Disabilities (UN, 2006a) in 2010, the government passed the *Discrimination Against Persons with Disability (Prohibition) Act* eight years later (FRN, 2018).

Given ongoing claims that women with disabilities endured more poverty and inequality than men with disabilities, it is fitting to highlight policies relating to women's rights in Nigeria. Based on the Convention on the Elimination of all forms of Discrimination against Women (CEDAW) (UN, 1979) and its accompanying protocols, amendments, and conventions, which Nigeria ratified in 1985, the first National Policy on Women was in Chapter 2 of the Nigerian Constitution (FRN, 1999b). Sections 15(2) and 42(1) of the Constitution prohibited sex-based discrimination. However, the policy did not provide a comprehensive definition of discrimination against women seeing it as implicit in all forms of discrimination, including sex discrimination (section 42). Section 17 outlines the elimination of demographically derived disparities, while Section 17(3)(e) focuses on gender-based disparities and states that the state shall direct its policy towards ensuring equal pay for equal work without discrimination on the grounds of sex, or any other ground. Some provisions in Section 26 relating to citizenship, such as those on citizenship rights,

DOI: 10.4324/9781003382126-5

discriminated against women (Nigeria CEDAW NGO Coalition, 2008). They provide for extension of a Nigerian man's citizenship to his foreign-born wife, while making no reference to a similar path for the foreign-born husband of a woman, who is a Nigerian citizen. Section 26(2) provides that the president may confer Nigerian citizenship on any woman who is or who has been married to a Nigerian citizen. By implication, this section limits the right of a Nigerian woman to transmit her nationality to a foreign husband. The Constitution (FRN, 1999a) also called for a 30% representation of women in all tiers of government.

Reinforcing earlier policy, the National Gender Policy 2006 called for the inclusion of women in all spheres of society. It led to empowerment programs for women (FRN, 2006; Ministry of Women Affairs and Social Development, 2006). However, there were formidable structural barriers rooted in Nigeria's patriarchal system, sustained by traditional African and Islamic values, beliefs, and practices that supported early marriage and constrained the educational and economic advancement of young women (Bakare, 2015). These barriers perpetuated continuing inequalities for women in health, education, employment, politics, and social life and their exclusion from full participation in Nigerian society (Ayimoro, 2020; Okongwu, 2021).

Just as gender policy has not brokendown barriers to women's advancement, so too, disability legislation has not led to increased social protection measures for people with disabilities, generally. Impassable barriers hamper service planning and access to economic and social opportunities for people with disabilities. First, the absence of reliable statistical information results in widely varying statistics on the prevalence of disability in Nigerian society. Secondly, public ignorance results in stigma and discrimination keeping people with disabilities from participating fully in education and employment. Thirdly, despite Nigeria's anti-discriminatory policies, society seems to ignore the rights of people with disabilities, making little effort to include them. Finally, Nigeria's reliance on a philanthropic assistance model and biomedical approach to disability has hampered social interventions to remove barriers to the inclusion of people with disabilities in Nigerian society. Literature attests that people with disabilities continue to have limited opportunities to participate in education, employment, recreation, and other aspects of community life open to people without disabilities (Amadasun, 2020; Ayimoro, 2020; Effiong et al., 2018; Eleweke & Ebenso, 2016; Ibekwe & Uduma, 2019). This partly arises from African understandings of disability.

African understandings of disability

Berghs (2017) noted a multiplicity of interpretations of 'disability' in Africa found in ethnic groups' oral histories, music, dance, ritual, and (secret) society practices; colonial and postcolonial histories of medical and institutional segregation and prevention; and religious, evangelical, and missionary services. Also influential in definitions and understandings of disability and public attitudes to people with disabilities were radio, TV, popular culture, music, the arts, and social media. She also noted the influence of international aid organisations that have played a major part in changing African understandings of disability. Ogundola's (2013, 2019) textual analysis of newspapers reports of disability between 2001 and 2010 revealed stereotypically offensive language when reporting disability stories across Nigeria. He concluded that media frames that emphasised frailty, charity, and disparity, and used derogatory labels, facilitated negative stereotyping, prejudice, and stigma.

Most influential has been the widely used World Health Organisation's (WHO, 2001) International Classification of Functioning, Disability, and Health with its demarcation of differences between disease, illness, and impairment and measurement of six core functional domains: seeing, hearing, communication, cognition, walking, and self-care. The WHO (2010) also promotes community-based rehabilitation (CBR) with its focus on rights-based empowerment, equal opportunities, and social inclusion as the intervention of choice in Africa. The promotion of CBR has met with some criticism not least because this model was a product of foreign policy and financing; it conformed to donor interests and excluded local people with disabilities from planning and program development (Colaridge & Hartley, 2010). Schwarz (2014) highlighted the absurdity of knowledge stemming from wealthier countries when most disabled people lived in low and middle-income countries. Furthermore, Bashir et al. (2020) found only 14 peer-reviewed papers on CBR in Nigeria, lamenting the laxity of Nigerian researchers in producing useful knowledge on the usefulness of this intervention for people with disabilities. International organisations have also promoted theories and models of disability that have influenced local academic scholarship and funded research conducted through civil society and non-government organisations (Eleweke & Ebenso, 2016).

International organisations have also had an influence on the Nigerian disability movement, through their involvement in, and advocacy of, international and national policy agendas linked to human rights, social development, and environmental sustainability, including the UN definition of 'persons with disabilities' enshrined in the Convention on the Rights of Persons with Disabilities (UN, 2006b) (Imam & Abdulraheem-Mustapha, 2016). Nigerian disabled peoples' organisations (DPOs) have played a major role in national disability policy formulation to translate this convention into local legislation and embed it into state structures. Further, these local and international influences have popularised social models of disability (Eleweke & Ebenso, 2016) though Johnson (2019) claims medical definitions and treatments of disability prevail in Nigeria, along with religious and cultural superstitions and traditional healing practices. Religious beliefs reinforce patriarchy and cultural practices, like female genital mutilation, that result in disability and injustices against women (Johnson, 2020). Johnson (2019) noted that this religious-medical conception of disability resulted in the ostracism, exploitation, and killing of women with disabilities in Nigeria.

Social models of disability

Social models of disability draw on various theories that advance the idea that socially imposed structural barriers exclude people with disabilities from society's mainstream. These barriers result in, and sustain, inequalities in society. They relate to, or arise from, differences of race, class, gender, ethnicity, religion, and (dis)ability. These theories inform feminist, social exclusion, and disability-is-poverty discourses. However, despite the growing body of international literature on social models of disability, especially on social exclusion and its intersection with gender inequality, there is little research on the social exclusion of women with disabilities in Nigeria. Ibekwe and Uduma (2019) noted an absence of reliable Nigerian statistics on poverty rates among people with disabilities generally, though Aluko and Mbada (2020) claimed poverty was rampant among rural women with disabilities, who were more likely to experience violence and harmful practices than their urban counterparts (Johnson, 2019, 2020; Meyer et al., 2022; Olaitan, 2021; Rohwerder, 2018). Afolayan's (2015) qualitative study (n=40 young disabled women) in southwestern Nigeria showed how stigmatising representations of women with disabilities as 'helpless, incompetent, asexual and intellectually challenged' (p. 54) continued to have a negative impact on their lives. She showed that 'disablist and gender discourses and stereotypes acted to rationalise and reproduce hegemonies of male dominance and able-bodiedness' (Mohamed & Shefer, 2015, p. 12) in Nigerian society.

Social exclusion discourse

Gaining popularity in Third Way social policy in the 1970s, the political social exclusion discourse sought to find neoliberal measures to enhance employment participation and reduce welfare budgets in the UK and promoted activation policies in Europe more broadly. Critical social theorists were quick to counter the political discourse through their structural interpretation of social problems. They highlighted that social exclusion resulted from structurally sanctioned social relations, which perpetuated the marginalisation and exploitation of undervalued groups in society. As Mbah and Nwangwu (2013) observed, social exclusion was 'a function of class and other identity-based distinctions' (p. 417). Structural barriers included negative stereotypes that excluded people from mainstream society and positioned them as second-class citizens. Critical social theorists highlighted poverty as a major source of disadvantage and social exclusion (Burchardt et al., 2002a; Goodwin, 2003), though Birchall (2019) noted not all members of socially excluded groups were disadvantaged economically. Health inequalities discourse demonstrated the relationship between poverty and poor health outcomes that increased the likelihood of premature death (Crisp, 2010). Moore et al. (2010) described research on disability-related discrimination as one of the most significant discussions in critical disability studies contributing to the disability rights movements in the 1970s. Ideologies of ableism and difference laid the groundwork for discriminatory practices.

Burchardt et al. (2002b) identified three core features of social exclusion – relativity, agency, and dynamics. Relativity – the individual or group's status relative to others in society – led to judgments based solely on the socially excluded person's context or situation. Agency implied someone or something doing the exclusion, with excluding agents including political, economic, and social institutions. Dynamics referred to social processes that enforced a sense of powerlessness by denying excluded groups a voice, autonomy, and decision-making power.

Disability-is-poverty discourse

The Institute for Development Studies (IDS) (2020) reported that 90% of people with disabilities lived below the poverty line, 62.5% of adults with disabilities were unemployed, and 30% worked in the informal sector. The UN Monitoring Report (2011) supported the intersecting social exclusion and disability-is-poverty discourses noting:

> A growing body of research now shows that the most pressing issue faced by millions of persons with disabilities worldwide is not their disability but rather poverty. Much of this poverty is the direct and indirect result of exclusion and marginalization of persons with disabilities due to stigma and prejudice about disability (p. 7).

Eide and Ingstad (2013) highlighted problems with poverty-is-disability research because it provided some insights but not the whole story. It failed to unravel the complexity of the relationship between poverty and disability and the myriad intersecting factors contributing to negative outcomes for people with disabilities. They observed that, lifting people out of poverty would:

> Not ... eradicate disability and disabling conditions, regardless of the level of understanding of disability ... disability, discriminatory practice, cultural beliefs, environmental barriers, lack of equitable basic services, etc., are all factors that need to be dealt with or utilised in poverty alleviation efforts ... to ensure that people with disabilities benefit in an equitable manner.
>
> (Eide & Ingstad, 2013, p. 5)

Gureje et al.'s (2006) cross-sectional survey of Yoruba-speaking areas in southwestern Nigeria did not find any relationship between poverty (measured by asset ownership and type of housing) and the occurrence of functional disability in aging adults (n=2152 over the age of 65 years, 52.5% men and 47.5% women). They found that the prevalence of functional disability in older adults was highest among those in urban settings and lowest among rural dwellers. The prevalence of impairment was 9.2%, while 19% of previously non-disabled older adults with disabilities who needed assistance had no access to help.

Feminist discourse

Feminist theorists' gendered perspective highlights the social, economic, and political processes that lead to the social exclusion of women, including the socially sanctioned disenfranchisement and powerlessness preventing their full participation in society (Phillips, 2006; Shelley et al., 2018). Feminists draw attention to the intersecting factors compounding women's exclusion with patriarchy, gender, poverty, and disability cardinal components of discrimination against women in society (Fawcett et al., 2009). They highlight the high incidence of poverty among women, due to their exclusion from income, employment, and education. Pearce (1978) coined the phrase *feminisation of poverty* to describe women's disproportionate representation among the world's poor, due mainly to patriarchy and toxic masculinity. Phillips (2006) noted not only a lack of income but also a deprivation of capabilities and gender inequalities, despite rights charters protecting women's freedom and dignity and promoting female empowerment. Feminist theory suggests that, due to the gendered nature of Nigerian society, women experience social exclusion more than men, especially since they carry the greater share of responsibilities for raising children and taking care of the household (Collings & Spencer, 2020; World Bank, 2012). Feminist literature suggests women's inequality is the 'effect of the oppression of women in society, the gendered operation of [the] labor market, and family responsibilities' (Aluko & Mbada, 2020, p. 86). In support of this theory, Rabbort and Wallace (1990) noted that most African cultures perpetuated women's subservience to men and devalued their roles as 'natural carers' (p. 51).

Common to these discourses informing social models of disability is the notion that structural barriers enforce and maintain inequalities for people with disabilities. The following discussion highlights various barriers, including the absence of reliable statistical information, public ignorance and stigma, persistent discrimination, and lack of measures to enhance the social inclusion of people with disabilities in Nigerian society.

Barriers to the social inclusion of people with disability

Nigeria's six geopolitical regions, political division into 36 states and 774 local government areas, and 450 ethnolinguistic groups makes for a complex and variable system of governance and social provision, with the large urban areas having a greater share of services than rural areas and the northern regions more impoverished than the southern regions (Federal Ministry of Women Affairs and Social Development, 2017).

Absence of reliable statistical information

The absence of reliable statistical information results in widely varying statistics on the prevalence of disability in Nigerian society. This leads to problems in policy implementation and service planning. The World Report on Disability

(WHO, 2011) reported that about 25 million Nigerians (15% of the population) had at least one disability, while 3.6 million had significant difficulties in functioning. The IDS's (2020) situational analysis of disability in Nigeria reported estimates ranging from 3.3 to over 25 million, the latter from the advocacy body, the Joint National Association of Persons with Disabilities (JONAPWD). The World Bank's (2020) rapid assessment report on *Disability Inclusion in Nigeria* estimated that 29 million people experienced disability. However, Nigeria's National Population Commission's (NPC) (2018) Nigerian Demographic and Health Survey found 8% of households in Nigeria had a member – an equal percentage of men and women – living with some form of disability. The survey included a series of questions based on the Washington Group on Disability Statistics, which, in turn, drew on the WHO's (2001) International Classification of Functioning, Disability, and Health and its six core functional domains: seeing, hearing, communication, cognition (remembering or concentrating), walking (and climbing steps), and self-care (washing all over and dressing). The NPC (2018) survey included the household population age five years and over. It found that, overall, 92% of the household population had no difficulty in any domain, while 7% had some difficulty and 1% had significant difficulty or could not function in at least one domain. Among adults aged 15 years and older, an equal percentage of men and women (2%) had significant difficulty or could not function in at least one domain (NPC, 2018). The proportion of household members who had difficulty in each domain generally rose with increasing age: 1% of household members below the age of 40 years had a great deal of difficulty or could not function independently at all in at least one domain, as compared with 9% of those aged 60 years and over. Widowed women and men were more likely to have difficulty in each of the domains than their counterparts in the other marital status categories. For example, 30% of widows and 37% of widowers had difficulty seeing, while 19% of widowed women and 20% of widowed men had difficulty walking or climbing steps (NPC, 2018). Notably, the WHO's International Classification measures functional rather than social disability and the NPC's (2018) statistical findings do not support arguments about the unequal position of women with disabilities nor do they provide measures of poverty among women or people with disabilities generally (Ibekwe & Uduma, 2019).

Public ignorance, stigma, and persistent discrimination

Public ignorance results in stigma and discrimination keeping people with disabilities from participating fully in society. Dominant public discourses in Nigeria portray people with disabilities in derogatory terms as less than human, cursed, and an economic burden on society. The IDS (2020) noted widespread ignorance among Nigerians regarding the causes of disability and deeply entrenched mythical beliefs about its origins. Rohwerder (2018) found a lack of understanding and awareness and misconceptions about the cause of disabilities often resulted from cultural or religious beliefs that attributed disability *inter alia* to misdeeds of ancestors, parents, and the person with disabilities; supernatural forces, such as demons or spirits; witchcraft and wizardry; and fate or divine punishment. This led to the stigmatisation of, and discrimination against, people with disabilities that, in turn, resulted in their exploitation, oppression, and isolation in Nigerian society. Supported by legislation and policies, the segregation of people with disabilities perpetuated negative stereotypes that reinforced prejudice and discrimination (Rohwerder, 2018). Further, ignorance about the nature and abilities of people with disabilities contributed to inhumane and unjust treatment justified by beliefs that they were unable to contribute financially, have a normal relationship, or report sexual abuse. Misconceptions fostered erroneous beliefs that their disability was contagious, or they brought bad luck or, conversely, that their bodies had magical powers, or they were witches; all contributed to the stigma, discrimination, and abuse they experienced (Rohwerder, 2018). Rohwerder (2018) highlighted that stigma varied with the nature and severity of disability with people with intellectual disabilities, complex mental health issues, albinism, and sensory disabilities enduring more stigma than those with physical disabilities. Injustices perpetrated included infanticide and paternal abandonment; registration failures, where counts of people with disabilities were lost in demographic research; violence, abuse, and restricted participation; and segregation and ostracism (Haruna, 2017; Rohwerder, 2018). Johnson (2019, 2020) highlighted the dire consequences for women with disabilities, as borne out by Nwatu et al. (2020), who found false witchcraft accusations biased against women accused of malfeasance against their husbands. This was not only a human rights violation, but also yet another instance of gender-based discrimination.

Nigeria's anti-discriminatory policies seemed powerless against cultural and religious misconceptions, as society ignored the rights of people with disabilities making little effort to include them (Afolayan, 2015; Etieyibo & Omiegbe, 2016; Haruna, 2017; Olaitan, 2021). Though there were three core pieces of legislation to protect the rights of people with disabilities, their variable implementation did little to assuage their harmful treatment. The *Employee's Compensation Act* (FRN, 2010) provided for compensation for employment-related injuries and disabilities. The *Discrimination Against Persons with Disability (Prohibition) Act* (FRN, 2018) required that all public organisations observed a 5% quota for people with disabilities and stated, among other things, that any person or institution should not – in any manner or under any circumstance – discriminate against an individual on the grounds of his or her disability. The act provided for the short-lived ineffectual National Commission for Persons with Disabilities tasked with the full integration of people with disabilities into society (Ibekwe & Uduma, 2019).

Lack of measures to reduce social barriers

Predominant religious-medical conceptions of disability as a product of nature fuelled Nigeria's reliance on a philanthropic assistance model and charitable approach to disability (Johnson, 2019). This has overshadowed under-standings of disability as a cultural product and hampered social interventions to remove barriers to the inclusion of people with disabilities in Nigerian society. The Nigerian household survey (NPC, 2018) was in keeping with the WHO's focus on the functional limitations of people with disabilities. It said little about the social barriers and poor social outcomes confronting people with disabilities in Nigeria though research confirms the presence of social barriers (Amadasun, 2020; Effiong et al., 2018; Eleweke & Ebenso, 2016; Smith, 2011). Smith (2011) found that women with disabilities, especially intellectual disabilities, were more likely to have lower levels of education and employment, lack access to health services, and endure discrimination and abuse than their male counterparts. As Eide and Ingstad (2013) highlighted, research has, thus far, not shed light on the weight of intersecting factors contributing to negative outcomes for people with disabilities. Hence, Smith (2011) presented international sources to support her local study's conclusion that the most vulnerable groups were ethnic minorities, older people, women, children, refugees, and displaced people with disabilities. Likewise, for her conclusion relating to poverty among people with disabilities, she speculated that a person with disability often faced stigma and discrimination through the common practice of arranged marriages, while polygamy brought addi-tional responsibilities and stress for men with disabilities. Studies like this do little to enhance understanding of the nature of the relationship between disability, poverty, gender, age, religion, ethnicity, education, occupation, employment, and economic status or factors contributing to poor outcomes for people with disabilities.

Solutions to inform a social response

There was very little literature or research on the nature and context of social interventions in the disabilities field. Most articles came from academic re-searchers who drew on Western theory and value-based models. While noting an important role for social workers and their past positioning at the forefront of social service delivery to people with disabilities, Amadasun (2020) lamented their absence in contemporary disability services in Nigeria. His study of social workers (n=7) in a not-for-profit non-government organisation found that social workers involved in rehabilitation services offered counselling and organised recreational activities, noting the abandonment of education and empowerment programs to improve the lives of people with disabilities.

Ayodele et al. (2018) described an integrative multidisciplinary team inter-vention based on the Western clinical-diagnostic model in which psychosocial assessments formed the basis of eligibility for community programs for people with disabilities (Ayodele et al., 2018; Olaleye, 2013). Chukwu et al.'s (2019) psychological study of family coping strategies comprised 107 parents and sib-lings of children with learning disabilities from highly educated elite families that were predominantly Christian and for whom support from their religious and spiritual community helped them cope with the difficulties they experienced. Some families, however, also drew on traditional healing methods. Informed by psychological and systems theory, the researchers interpreted their findings on positive problem-focused coping strategies, such as use of appropriate information and professional advice, in terms of psychological theories of resilience and healthy adaptation, which they compared to emotional strategies used by poorer families. Some families in their study fit the avoidant category 'by pretending the problem does not exist, blaming each other or being withdrawn socially' (Chukwu et al., 2019, p. 6). These theories fit the predominantly Igbo-speaking Imo state, where most people were Christian, and few adhered to African Traditional Religions common in other parts of Nigeria. Thus, Chukwu et al. (2019) implied Western theories and models of research and practice were appropriate to modern Nigeria's educated elites.

In keeping with the WHO's (2001) functional model, Chukwu and Idemili-Aronu (2019) described intellectual disability as an 'affliction' (p. 3), 'burden' (p. 10), 'mental disorder' (p. 10), and 'social, educational and health problem … [that] results in substantial limitation' (p. 3). Their study of social services designed to help families cope with the challenges of having a person with intellectual disability in the family found caregiving rested mainly with the family, due to the lack of government social support services. Like Chukwu et al. (2019), they noted the deeply religious values of the Igbo of Imo State and the influence of their belief in spiritually related causes on family health seeking and access to social services. Since the three non-government organisations in Imo State did not employ social workers, Chukwu and Idemili-Aronu (2019) sought to explore family experiences with disability services to inform social work interventions in this area of practice. Rather than sociocultural factors, lack of knowledge of, and geographical distance from, services resulted in little use of community resources. Given the researchers' theoretical orientation, they speculated that Igbo beliefs in supernatural causes resulted in shame and stigma and, therefore, the non-utilisation of services. In suggesting possibilities for social work intervention, the researchers drew on Western sources noting the importance of education, advocacy, and 'a re-focused conceptual framework that will support and promote client self-determination, empowerment, confidentiality, equity and social justice' (Chukwu & Idemili-Aronu, 2019, p. 10). Despite social workers' lack of presence in disability services, Omorogiuwa (2017), too, claimed a crucial role for social workers in 'improving the mental health outcomes and well-being of individuals with mental disabilities' (p. 6) drawing on international sources.

Social interventions and mass education

Rohwerder (2018) highlighted the importance of self-help, empowerment, and social support groups at the intrapersonal and familial levels, all of which were familiar social interventions, as was casework with families to aid the development of positive childrearing practices for children with disabilities for parents, who experienced exhaustion, fear, hope, despair, anger, intimidation, commitment, and love (Omoniyi, 2014). Community-level engagement included awareness raising and education to spread accurate information to counter myths and superstitions about disability, challenge inaccurate stereotypes, and encourage inclusive practices. However, direct-contact interpersonal interventions showed more promise for stigma reduction than public-education approaches signalling the ongoing importance of social casework (Rohwerder, 2018).

Most difficult was broader-level governmental and structural interventions to tackle misinformation and stigma, due to failures of policy implementation and enforcement, and weaknesses in data capture and reporting on the abuse and exploitation of people with disabilities (Ibekwe & Uduma, 2019; Olaitan, 2021). Haruna (2017) observed a lack of 'political will and commitment on the part of the government to ensure, protect and promote the interests of people living with disability in Nigeria' (p. 111). He described disability legislation and policies as nothing more than unbinding statements of intent. Changing social attitudes to women and ethnic and religious minorities, as well as people with disability, required massive public-education campaigns and the buy in of political, business, and traditional leaders reinforcing the rights and fair treatment of people with disabilities in Nigerian society (Imam & Abdulraheem-Mustapha, 2016).

State obligations

Arimoro (2019) highlighted the state's obligation to work towards the inclusion and accommodation of people with disabilities in Nigeria. He called on the government to implement the appropriate measures required to 'protect their rights and guarantee their freedom from discriminatory practices' (p. 89). This required government commitment and funding (Ayodele et al., 2018). Ibekwe and Uduma (2019) reported on restricted resource allocation for disability services in the Federal Ministry of Women Affairs and Social Development that carried official responsibility for policies and programs for people with disabilities. Given the costly responsibility falling on families, Isaac and Tanga (2014) suggested Nigeria follow South Africa's lead and provide social grants to caregivers of children with disabilities. Haruna (2017) saw a place for the biomedical model 'in alleviating or reducing the suffering of disabled people through the provision of training, rehabilitation, technical aids, medical interventions and professional support' (p. 105). These social interventions were all important in promoting independence and were a reminder that appealing to government for increased resources on biomedical grounds might be more effective in the short-term, given the problem of shifting well-embedded public attitudes based on religious-cultural misconceptions of disability. It might lead to better healthcare for people with disabilities in Nigeria (Ugwoegbu, 2016).

Strong representation

Eleweke and Ebenso's (2016) small qualitative study involving five DPO executives and seven individuals with disabilities highlighted problems with DPOs' representation of disabled people's rights. Most participants expressed disappointment that, rather than advocate for people with disabilities, DPO leaders used their access to government contracts to further their own interests, suggesting misuse of public funds. This suggests the need for government regulation and monitoring of the work of civil society and non-government organisations in receipt of international aid and public money through the Corporate Affairs Commission mandated to register these organisations (Haruna, 2017). However, these organisations received very little government funding from federal and state ministries of women affairs and social development responsible for the disability portfolio (Haruna, 2017). Haruna (2017) attributed the lack of people with disabilities' participation in mainstream decision making to public attitudes, given over 90% of the population viewed disability from a charity perspective. They regarded people with disabilities as not 'good enough to receive aids, support and other forms of humanitarian efforts rather than being active citizens in society and national development' (p. 111). Strong representative organisations should play a role in correcting misconceptions about, highlighting injustices against, and promoting the interests of people with disabilities (Smith, 2011). Social workers and community development practitioners could play a role in working with DPOs and consumer advocacy groups to ensure people with disabilities have a voice in Nigeria.

Research and advocacy

Despite its continued use in Nigeria, Bashir et al. (2020) highlighted the dearth of Nigerian CBR research noting the 'need for comprehensive intervention studies, case reports and descriptive studies to better inform practice' (p. 160). They found 14 peer-reviewed publications, mostly authored by academics with little direct contact with people with disabilities. Research involving people with disabilities could contribute greatly to understanding of the intersecting factors in poor disability outcomes. Schwartz (2014) highlighted five challenges for disability-related research in SSA. First was the need for qualitative studies of insider experience drawing on first-person accounts, as highlighted in feminist research, to balance quantitative surveys and statistical measures (Gray et al., 2015). Secondly, she suggested participatory research drawing on the expertise of people with disabilities. Schwartz (2014) believed that people with disabilities had the expertise to set the research agenda; the best scenario would be to equip them with skills to research themselves. Thirdly, she called for exactness on what the research measured without conflating one construct with another. Fourthly, she saw the need for greater use of epidemiological methods and quality research noting 'the quality of evidence depends not on who is providing the evidence but on the quality of the research work' (Schwartz, 2014, p. 5). Finally, it is important to have realistic expectations about research. Despite the desirability of evidence-based policy, most often people judged policies on their utility rather than their research base. Noting these challenges, social workers could make a significant contribution through their direct engagement with people with disabilities and their observations of the effects of intersecting barriers hampering access to education, employment, and social services. Collecting these data at an organisational level could enhance their advocacy potential and power to influence policy and service development.

Conclusion

Despite calls for social responses, the influence of the WHO's (2011) functional definition and dominant medical-religious model has led to a greater focus on health and education in disability interventions. CBR has brought allied health professionals into the frame, while the absence of social services has left social workers without a presence in disability provision. This chapter has suggested a political role for social workers in advocating for social interventions, state services, and strong representation for people with disabilities, while engaging in research and advocacy to demonstrate the benefits of social interventions in disability service provision.

6 Mental health and ageing

This chapter discusses mental health and ageing as contexts that demonstrate the importance of cultural relevance given traditional conceptions of mental illness and indigenous practices surrounding older people and widowhood. It examines the institutional, legal, and policy context of mental health and cultural conceptions of mental illness. Turning to ageing, it examines the policy and services context, sociocultural practices surrounding ageing, and the social work role. It shows how an absence of legislation to provide a framework and standards for the protection and promotion of the rights of people living with mental health conditions and older persons leads to problems in service provision to two highly vulnerable sectors of the population. It highlights the importance of a cultural understanding to understand barriers to treatment or the inhumane treatment of widows and childless women, for example. It proposes that social work can play a crucial role and, as in other contexts of practice, highlights the need to educate policy makers and the general public on social workers contribution to human wellbeing.

Mental health

Institutional, legal, and policy context

Authors writing about mental health in Nigeria uniformly express concerns about the government's neglect of this public health issue and its outdated legislation (Wada at al., 2021). Nigeria enacted its first mental health legislation - the Lunacy Ordinance - in 1916. Amended in 1958, the renamed *Lunacy Act of 1958* gave medical practitioners and magistrates the power to detain an individual suffering from mental illness. With no amendments since then, this archaic piece of legislation reflected a period of history in which there was very little understanding of mental illness and the treatment of people with mental health-care needs was inhumane and ineffective.

Thirty-three years later, the National Mental Health Policy for Nigeria (FRN, 1991) called for the integration of mental health in general health services at the primary, secondary, and tertiary levels of healthcare, placing responsibility for comprehensive access to mental healthcare on primary care, hence local

DOI: 10.4324/9781003382126-6

government (Ryan et al., 2020). The National Policy for Mental Health Services Delivery in Nigeria (FRN, 2013) set out the principles for the delivery of care to people with mental, neurological, and substance abuse problems (Ugochukwu et al., 2020). It reaffirmed the 1991 commitment to mental health service provision through primary healthcare. It recommended the transfer of tasks relating to mental healthcare to non-specialist providers in primary care settings and encouraged public-private sector partnerships in healthcare delivery (Gureje et al., 2015). Table 6.1 summarises these policy developments.

Although non-government partners – comprising for-profit and not-for-profits, including faith- and community-based organisations – filled some gaps in primary care, services remained woefully inadequate, as did the shortage of mental health professionals. Jidong et al. (2022) said there were only 50 psychologists to every 150,000 citizens (1: 3000), while the Association of Psychiatrists in Nigeria (2020) reported there were 250 practising psychiatrists and 200 psychiatry trainees in the country. Besides the shortage of psychiatrists, psychiatric treatment was inaccessible, due *inter alia* to the prohibitive cost of medicines or transport, and lack of accessible clinics and specialist practitioners, as well as a lack of knowledge about, or belief in the value of, medical treatment (Jack-Ide & Uys, 2013).

Table 6.1 Mental health policy

Legal status	Legal document	Action
LAW	Lunacy Act of 1958	Outdated
POLICY	National Mental Health Policy for Nigeria (FRN, 1991)	Called for integration of MH in general health services; placed responsibility on primary healthcare, hence local government (Ryan et al., 2020).
	National Policy for Mental Health Services Delivery in Nigeria (FRN, 2013a)	Reaffirm the 1991 commitment to mental health service provision through primary care and encouraged public-private sector partnerships, though not implemented fully
LEGISLATION	Mental Health and Substance Abuse Bill (FRN, 2019)	Awaiting enaction
PLAN	National Mental, Neurological and Substance Use Programme and Action Plan (FRN, 2013b)	Under revision
INSTITUTIONAL BODY	National Mental Health Action Committee of the Federal Ministry of Health (FMOH)	Expert think tank, advocacy group and implementation monitoring body (Abdulmalik et al. (2016)

Community health workers with two to three years post-high school training in community healthcare were at the forefront of primary care, but most were unable to identify mental health conditions, such as psychosis, depression, and epilepsy (Gureje et al., 2015). Ultimately, the policy, like its predecessor, failed through lack of implementation, due to the inadequate training and supervision of primary (community) healthcare workers, insufficient funding, absence of essential resources, inequitable, inefficient, poorly coordinated services, and lack of political will (Gureje et al., 2015; Jack-Ide et al., 2012; Ryan et al., 2020).

This lack of political will was evident when the Mental Health Bill submitted to the National Assembly in 2003 met with little support. More than six years without progress led to its withdrawal in 2009 and resubmission in 2013. However, like many other policies, it had yet to become law and improvements in the quality of life and care for people living with mental health issues remained negligible. Funk and Drew (2015) highlighted the importance of mental health legislation as it:

> Provides a framework and standards for the protection/promotion of the rights of people with mental health conditions and to codify the principles, values, aims and objectives of mental health policies and plans. It is crucial that mental health legislation promotes integrated, community-based care and support and acts to improve the quality of services and promote the rights of people with mental health conditions (p. 527).

In the absence of appropriate Nigerian legislation, Ugochukwu et al. (2020) referred to the state of mental health in Nigeria as a global human rights emergency. Due to negative societal attitudes and inadequate resources, facilities, and staffing, approximately 80% of individuals with serious mental health issues could not access care. With the 250 psychiatrists – for a population of 214 million – working mainly in urban areas, a shortage of care facilities and poor knowledge of mental disorders at the primary healthcare level, in the main, left families to care for family members with complex mental health needs.

Anyebe et al.'s (2019) study of the availability of mental health services at primary healthcare centres (n=47) in three northern Nigerian states involved in-depth interviews (n=13) and field observation. They found that *none* of the mental health units on the service-delivery charts of the primary healthcare centres studied provided any formal mental healthcare. As Obianuju et al. (2020) observed, with limited or non-existent community-based primary healthcare services, only the most severe cases had access to psychiatric in-patient care in hospitals or informal institutions. However, Gureje et al. (2015) found that poor coordination between the three levels of intervention led to a disproportionate number of less seriously mentally ill patients receiving specialist care, while those with more severe conditions received inadequate primary care. As a result, this chronically and dangerously under-resourced mental health system could not cater for the needs of the estimated one in eight Nigerians suffering from serious mental illness. Ignorance of the causes of mental illness, widespread stigma and discrimination, and poorly equipped services led to the abuse and exploitation of people with mental health problems (Gureje et al., 2015; Onyemelukwe, 2016).

Following international pressure and the WHO's (2013a) Mental Health Action Plan, the Nigerian Senate held a public hearing for the Mental Health and Substance Abuse Bill (FRN, 2019) in February 2020, with widespread consultation in train. Ugochukwu et al. (2020) called for legislation to accord with:

1   The WHO (2013b) Checklist on Mental Health Legislation to ensure it met international standards.
2   The International Covenant on Economic, Social and Cultural Rights (UN, 1996b) and the African Charter on Human and Peoples' Rights (African Commission on Human and Peoples' Rights, 1981) to ensure cultural sensitivity and human rights standards.
3   The national health insurance scheme mandate and include mental health cover to ensure accessible, affordable care.
4   Best practice and include additional support for outpatient, primary, and community care services for people with mental illness.
5   The National Mental Health Service Delivery Policy of Nigeria and provide integrated mental health training, responses, and psychoeducation within primary healthcare settings.

If passed, the Bill would make provision for much-needed budgetary allocations for mental health facilities and mental healthcare providers to protect individuals suffering from mental illness from gross human rights violations, including degrading treatment and destitute living conditions. In the interim, Anyebe et al. (2019) suggested the need for local, community-based primary mental healthcare to provide community education and disseminate information about mental health services and available treatments for people living with mental illness. Aspects of such provision to which social workers could contribute included:

- *Psychosocial and livelihood support*, especially self-help groups providing peer support. Again, social workers were well-placed to run psychosocial support groups, education groups, and income-generating initiatives.
- *Advocacy and awareness-raising* conveying accurate information on mental illness and securing commitments from government officials at different levels to resourcing mental health services. With few advocates for mental health issues in Nigeria (Onyemelukwe, 2016), this was a role social workers could play with their training and skills.
- *Monitoring and evaluation*: Although the Mental Health Policy (FRN, 2013) called for efficient auditing of service provision and delivery, mental health was not part of the national health management information system. Thus, many mental health program were unable to report on basic indicators, such as service use (Ryan et al., 2020).

Cultural conceptions of mental illness

As discussed in Chapter 4, African cultures placed a high premium on children. They were also intolerant of childlessness and placed a great deal of pressure on married couples to produce children. Childlessness, then, had catastrophic consequences, especially for women. As Ukpong and Orji (2006) noted, husbands and in-laws despised, neglected, abused, and isolated women with fertility problems, who frequently experienced high levels of depression and anxiety. In their Nigerian study, they found that 'the predictors of poor mental health outcomes were not having at least one child, lack of supporting relationship with spouse, attitude towards adoption, age and financial burden of treatment' (p. 264).

Cultural understanding of health affected receptivity to treatment and practices that prevented mental illness and promoted mental health treatment. Besides childlessness, cultural childrearing practices could have detrimental health consequences for women and children. Omigbodun and Olatawura (2008) believed that understanding traditional childrearing practices, and the way in which they had changed over time, was important in the context of rapid social transformation and concerns about the breakdown of traditional structures and practices. Health policy and education should promote healthy traditional childrearing practices, such as confinement following delivery, breastfeeding, carrying the child on the back, and sleeping with the child. Conversely, healthcare providers should correct *misinformation* preventing pregnant women from eating nutritious foods, encouraging delivery in traditional healers' homes, and unhygienic care of the umbilical cord, as well as hierarchical or gender-biased food distribution. Other aspects with a negative effect on children's mental health, included child fostering and child labour, though, as discussed in Chapter 4, these required structural changes and mass education campaigns.

There has been a revival of traditional healing and traditional medicine. Reverence for, and trust in, traditional healers make them the first port of call for Nigerians, given the nature of the contemporary mental health system in the country (Jidong et al., 2021) and prevalent belief that mental illness has supernatural causes (Ojua et al., 2013; Onyemelukwe, 2016). As Ojua et al. (2013) observed, given cultural interpretations of illness as a spiritual (evil) attack, people turned to traditional healers believing in their spiritual healing powers. Jidong et al. (2022) described traditional healing as 'useful, effective, affordable, [and] culturally and linguistically compatible with indigenous Nigerians' (p. 505). It is also compatible with Pentecostal Christian religious healing practices involving prayer and fasting to cast out the malicious spirit causing mental illness and other health afflictions (Eaton, & Agomoh, 2008; Jidong et al., 2022; Ojua et al., 2013). Jidong et al.'s (2022) study of the Berom people in the Jos Plateau State of Nigeria, most of whom were farmers, revealed the important part Christianity and ATR played in their rich cultural heritage. For them, diviners played an important role in mental health healing and protecting individuals, families, and the entire community from evil spirits.

Like the Berom people, the Igbo, an ethnic group constituting 60% of Nigeria's population, adhered to prevailing beliefs that attributed mental illness 'to a spiritual attack, often in the form of a curse placed by enemies through a traditional healer (using either incantations or poison)' (Eaton & Agomoh, 2008, p. 2). People usually approached traditional healers or 'prayer houses' (Pentecostal churches that specialised in exorcism common in the south). Treatment usually involved herbal remedies, chaining, beating, cutting of the skin, acid burning, or starvation (fasting) as a means of containment. These abusive practices were extremely harmful, and the visibility of the injuries caused marked mentally ill people and led to their social isolation or negative stigmatisation. Onyemelukwe (2016) foregrounded stigma as a negative aspect of cultural beliefs that manifested itself in widespread discriminatory practices against mentally ill people:

> There are places in Nigeria where mentally ill persons are chained and left outside in all conditions of the weather, and then beaten up from time to time ... to 'heal' them, where mentally ill persons are beaten by their spouses to exorcise the evil spirits, where some unscrupulous mental health professionals give out diagnoses without due investigation (p. 64).

Jegede (2005) described *were* as a Yoruba notion or idea representing cultural perceptions of mental illness resulting from:

1   *Natural* sources that led to natural illness (*aare*), such as conditions resulting from accidents or drug use, though traditional healers often attributed these to supernatural causes.
2   *Supernatural* or mystical sources, such as those resulting from the anger of the gods (*orisa*), enemies (*ota*), or ancestors (*ebora*), the province of a traditional healer known as a diviner (*babalawo*).
3   *Preternatural* or mystical sources, usually caused by witchcraft (*aje*) that might call for rituals and sacrifices (*etutu*) and were preventable through use of charms (*oogun*), including amulets (*onde*), bangles (*ide*), rings (*oruka*), scarification (*gbere*), and oral concoctions (*abuje*).
4   *Genetic* sources or incurable hereditary diseases (*arun idile*) (Jegede, 2002, 2005).

Jegede's (2005) study of Yoruba perceptions of mental illness involved interviews with traditional healers (n=10), who revealed that *were* was a derogatory concept that equated behavioural aberrations, especially those on the extreme, with mental illness depicting social instability and a pathological condition that affected social and interpersonal relationships, therefore marital stability. The stigma of illness led to social ostracism and isolation. The Yoruba viewed the body as a system of interacting parts regulated by the brain and saw changes in bodily processes, such as eating, drinking, and sleeping, as pathological, though restlessness was a primary indicator of mental illness. Most people did not seek help until the illness had reached a critical stage, due to the negative stigma of *were*. Thus, Jegede (2005) suggested the need for appropriate education on problems relating to mental health, especially the importance of prevention and early intervention to avoid the terminal stage of *were*. Accurate knowledge might lead to appropriate health-seeking behaviour and reduce the high levels of vagrancy and homelessness among people with mental health conditions (Jegede, 2005).

In a study of mothers' perceptions of illness, i.e., mothers with children under five years of age (n=50), Jegede (2002) found that most people sought traditional healing prior to going to hospitals (*ile-iwosanl*) as a last resort. This led to high mortality rates since most cases were terminal when they reached the hospitals. Thus, people referred to hospitals as houses of death (*ile iku*).

Anyebe et al.'s (2021) study in northern Nigeria showed that the primary barrier to mental health service provision at the community level was poor funding, a lack of skilled mental health workers, and inadequate training of available personnel, while sociocultural factors, such as community rejection of services, stigma, and misconceptions were secondary barriers. The implication of findings like these is that, despite sociocultural and ethnoreligious beliefs, people in local communities would use primary healthcare services if they were affordable and accessible, and even more so, if they were culturally responsive to their needs and concerns.

Social workers could play a much greater role in mental health service provision as part of interdisciplinary community health teams, linking people to resources and providing culturally appropriate counselling and support. Social work professional associations, too, could play an important advocacy role, not only for people living with mental illness, but also in placing the profession at the forefront of mental health promotion by highlighting what social workers could contribute and pushing for social work positions in community-based mental health services. Social workers could contribute as service providers, in training community mental health workers and volunteers, through research, and by contributing to local mental health knowledge. Finally, universities could run professional development programs for mental health social workers in conjunction with NASoW.

Ageing

Traditionally, older people were well-integrated into, and enjoyed high status in, Nigerian society with supportive cultural systems valuing their knowledge and experience and the extended family system providing for their social and economic needs (Adeleke et al., 2017). This was typified in the Yoruba-speaking people of southwestern Nigeria's dictum that 'without the elderly people, communities and villages will collapse' (Ajala, 2006, p. 181). Older people played an indispensable role in traditional societies. However, as recounted elsewhere in this text, the breakdown of traditional support systems has compromised the status and wellbeing of older people leaving them isolated and vulnerable (Ajala, 2006; Okoye, 2013). The social changes leading to diminishing informal support has placed enormous pressures on families caring for their ageing relatives, especially those with declining health and dementia (Ogunniyi et al., 2005). Changes in family structures have left older people with increasing commitments to care for children, due, among other things, to the impact of rural-urban migration and HIV and AIDS, with many facing loneliness, anxiety, depression, dementia, and abuse (Ajala, 2006; Ebimgbo et al., 2021; Ekoh et al., 2020a; Ojagbemi & Gureje, 2019; Ojembe & Kalu, 2018, 2019). The distance between older people and their adult children and lack of social engagement exacerbated these problems (Togonu-Bickersteeth & Akinyemi, 2014). Research to date showed that income insecurity, lack of social security and healthcare, declining health, depression, and loneliness were major issues associated with ageing in Nigeria (Ebimgbo et al., 2021; Ojagbemi & Gureje, 2019; Ojembe & Kalu, 2018, 2019). Clearly, growing old in Nigeria was fraught with challenges (Agunbiade, 2016) for the relatively small proportion of the population (about 5%) that reached old age (60 years), given the average life expectancy for Nigerians of 55 years (NBS, 2019). Nevertheless, Nigeria had the highest number of people aged 60 years and over in Africa (Ebimgbo et al., 2021). The World Bank (2021) estimated that 2.75% of Nigerians reached the age of 65 years in 2021. Statista (2022) put the number of the population over 60 years of age in 2022 at 9,370,131: 5,023,895 men (54%) and 4,346,236 women (46%). Given that they constituted a relatively small proportion of Nigeria's population, policies and services for older people were not a government priority.

Policy and service context

Nigeria lacked effective national policies to safeguard the care and welfare of older persons. Adegbite et al. (2020) attributed this situation to the government and political leaders' belief that the provision of care for older people was a family responsibility. Hence, due to changing demographics, diminishing family support, and the absence of social security, social services, and free comprehensive healthcare, older people in Nigeria faced numerous challenges (Araromi, 2015; Ayegboyin & Salami, 2019; Ibiezugbe, 2018; Tanyi et al., 2018). Exclusive contributory pension schemes and low pension coverage, due to high illiteracy and unemployment rates, left most older people without a social security safety net; even government workers received minimal and irregular payments, while disability benefits were available only to people in paid employment injured on duty (Araromi, 2015; Uwakwe et al., 2009). According to Araromi (2015), 'a lack of adequate provision for workers after their retirement has caused many aged civil servants to die in active service' (p. 133). Nigeria has not followed the lead of other countries in Africa, where old-age pensions produced widespread societal benefits keeping many older people out of extreme poverty (Togonu-Bickersteeth & Akinyemi, 2014; Uwakwe et al., 2009).

Hence, the Federal and state governments and policymakers needed to make social reforms for older people an urgent priority and address the absence of legislative provision for older people. They needed to ratify and follow the AU Draft Policy Framework and Action Plan on Ageing (AU & HelpAge International, 2021) and the African Protocols on Ageing and Disabilities developed by the African Union Commission as part of the AU Social Agenda 2063 (AU, 2022), as well as the National Policy on Ageing for Older Persons in Nigeria introduced in 2021. Ayegboyin and Salami's (2019) delineation of Nigerian categorisations of four stages of ageing might be helpful to policymakers and providers considering targeted services for older people as they aged as follows:

- *Agba* (young elderly) 60–69 years, encompassed the ideal period of retirement in Nigeria (60–65 years), though many older persons worked beyond this age out of necessity. Cadmus et al. (2022) emphasised the need for employment opportunities for older people, other than subsistence, to foster social relationships and positive health effects. Older persons in rural communities also required changes to make their physical environment more age-friendly.
- *Agbalagba* (old elderly) 70–79 years characterised by depreciating (mental and physical) capacity and diminishing participation in social activities, therefore, decreased social engagement and opportunities for support.
- *Agbalagbakejekeje* (older elderly) 80–89 years characterised by increasing dependence on family and social support, due to disability and difficulty performing, or an inability to perform, important activities.
- *Arugbo* (oldest elderly) above 89 years characterised by complete dependence on family and social support, due to diminished capabilities.

Mojoyinola and Ayangunna (2012) believed it was vitally important that social workers were knowledgeable about policy and legislation surrounding aged care and ensuring older people had access to the resources and services to which they were entitled. However, government policy and service provision and social support was grossly inadequate leaving the onus of care on the family and informal networks (Ebimgbo et al., 2019).

Tanyi et al.'s (2018) small exploratory study involving interviews with government officials (n=3) found that developing policies and services, with personnel capable of understanding and responding to the social priorities and complex needs of older people, was a major challenge for the government. In the absence of targeted services, a great number of older persons did not receive any services and support, while most were unable to cater for their health, hygiene, and nutritional needs (Ayegboyin & Salami, 2019; Ibiezugbe, 2018; Salami, 2016). Ayegboyin and Salami (2019) saw the need for specialised healthcare and social services for older people delivered through partnerships between government and viable private community health providers to enhance ease of access to healthcare services for older persons. The Ibadan study of (successful) ageing (Gureje et al., 2014) identified the potential value of health promotion in older people promoting a healthy lifestyle, good nutrition, and overall wellbeing.

In the absence of formal services and informal support for older persons, especially the largest number living in rural communities, the family continued to provide care and support for older family members (Ekoh et al., 2021; Ibiezugbe, 2018; Tanyi et al., 2018). In the absence of familial support, many relied on community and church charity (Uwakwe et al., 2009). However, there was little research on the way in which families and charities helped or the quality of care received (Togonu-Bickersteeth & Akinyemi, 2014). Akinyemi (2009) noted that previously held beliefs about care guaranteed by having many children had proved erroneous. Instead, empowering a child through education was the pivotal factor in securing wellbeing in old age, especially since care frequently equated to financial assistance. Material care became the responsibility of adult children with low incomes or income-earning potential (Togonu-Bickersteeth & Akinyemi, 2014). However, that, too, was changing, due to high unemployment levels among young people, with parents having to support their children for longer periods. Young people had also become more materialistic and consumer driven, again reducing the likelihood of familial care in old age (Togonu-Bickersteeth & Akinyemi, 2014). Without familial support or a welfare safety net, the incidence of older people begging had risen in Nigerian cities.

Sociocultural practices surrounding ageing

Though many rural communities had preserved the cultural tradition of familial care for older family members (Cadmus et al., 2022), most studies attested diminishing informal support. Besides problems associated with inadequate support and ageing generally, the literature on sociocultural practices surrounding ageing (Ajala, 2006), widowhood (Durojaye, 2013; Iwobi, 2008), end-of-life planning (Agbawodikeizu et al., 2018, 2019), burial (Azeez & Salami, 2020), and dementia (Adebiyi et al., 2016; Ekoh et al., 2020b; Wahab & Ikebudu, 2014) provided valuable guidance for culturally relevant social work.

Widowhood for older women in Nigeria was an extremely difficult time (Durojaye, 2013; Iwobi, 2008). Durojaye (2013) highlighted that widowhood practices compromised women's rights to dignity and non-discrimination, among others, while Iwobi (2008) noted the 'extremely onerous obligations' (p. 37) they imposed: 'Nigerian widows are … marginalized and stigmatized, routinely discriminated against in a variety of ways, and frequently encounter varying degrees of economic hardship' (p. 38). Iwobi (2008) placed the situation of widows within the broader context of culture, patriarchy, and legal pluralism showing that 'the Nigerian cultural milieu is not only repressive towards women in general but also overtly antagonistic to widows' (Iwobi, 2006, p. 39). He delineated eight Ds of widowhood: (i) dethronement, (ii) defacement, (iii) defilement, (iv) disentanglement from post-mortem marital links, (v) denial rituals (that is, rituals specifically designed to establish that a widow was not complicit in her husband's death, (vi) diminution of personal liberty, (vii) deprivation of child custody, and (viii) dispossession.

Agbawodikeizu et al. (2018, 2019) noted that, in Igbo societies, though there were customary laws of inheritance, whereby the deceased's possessions and assets passed to male heirs, and communication surrounding burial plans, there remained a reticence about talk of death. Therefore, there was no end-of-life planning beyond these customary patrilineal inheritance and succession practices. This included burial plans given the importance of keeping the link between the living and the dead intact (Durojaye, 2013). The Igbo believed a proper burial warded off misfortune for the living, while among the Yoruba, it 'earned the organisers high social capital' (Azeez & & Salami, 2020, p. 26). Agbawodikeizu et al. (2018) saw end-of-life planning as a form human welfare, social protection, and empowerment, and an important focus of social work intervention, though found negative attitudes towards this practice in their study of Nsukku in Enugu State in the South-East.

Research showed that there was little understanding of dementia in Nigeria (Adebiyi et al., 2016; Ekoh et al., 2020b; Wahab & Ikebudu, 2014). Adebiyi et al. (2016) found this led to stigma surrounding dementia variously described as ageing disease, memory loss disease, disease of forgetfulness, disease of insanity, brain disorder, and dull brain. Nwakasi et al. (2019) noted the fatalistic cultural and religious beliefs leading to perceptions of dementia as indicative of proximity to, and communication with, ancestors. Given it spelt the end of life, there was little more one could do than pray. Beliefs about supernatural causes consolidated recourse to religious and traditional healing (Ogunniyi et al., 2005).

Social work role

Most social work writers highlighted social workers' role in providing psychosocial counselling, acknowledging social work's role in facilitating a good person-in-environment fit. This necessitated a focus on the individual and the social environment to determine the locus of, and solutions for, problems in coping. Animasahun and Chapman's (2017) narrative review indicated priority foci for social workers' psychosocial interventions to enhance older people's physical and mental wellbeing. They related to intervention to address the four primary factors affecting the psychosocial health of older Nigerians, namely, 'changes in family dynamics, increased demand for healthcare services, increased economic stress, and decreased functional independence' (p. 575).

From our discussion, we might conclude that *changes in family dynamics* have placed enormous pressures on families providing home-based care, creating problems of caregiver stress and elder abuse that also demand social workers' attention. Ibiezugbe's (2018) study found many older persons in poor health needing help with nutrition and physical care, especially bathing and dressing. Most received familial support (57.2%); 22.8% paid dependents to take care of them; 11.6% had caregivers; and 8.4% received informal support. There was a gendered dimension to care with caregivers predominately female (daughters or daughters-in-law). However, sociodemographic, and economic changes, including declining fertility, smaller families, rural-urban migration, and improved educational opportunities for girls were weakening these forms of social protection (Uwakwe et al., 2009). This had led to calls for institutional (Adegbite et al., 2020), community-based (Okoye, 2013), and palliative (Agbawodikeizu et al., 2018) care with social workers playing a pivotal role in service provision.

The *increased demand for healthcare services* highlighted the importance of social workers working in collaboration with other professionals caring for, and promoting the interests of, older people. Internationally, social workers played an important role in aged-care provision, along with community nurses and other allied health practitioners. Their community outreach, long-term care, and ongoing support complemented the primary healthcare focus on acute treatable disease and illness (Togonu-Bickersteeth & Akinyemi, 2014; Uwakwe et al., 2009). For hospital social workers, even brief (single session) and short-term casework enabled them to link older people to necessary formal healthcare and informal community-based resources. In the absence of geographically accessible health services, many older people relied on traditional healing, though traditional medicine played a diminishing role in contemporary Nigeria. Those with lower levels of education were more likely to consult traditional healers (Amaghionyeodiwe, 2008). Overall, older Nigerians tended to use a combination of traditional and Western medicine (Uwakwe et al., 2009). Where there were modern health services, due to inadequate training of health personnel, interventions were often unresponsive to the sociocultural needs and preferences of older people (Togonu-Bickersteeth & Akinyemi, 2014). Social workers were well-poised to address these with their understanding of culturally sensitive interventions.

The *increased economic stress* on families highlighted the need for adequate financial support (Ebimgbo et al., 2020). Ibiezugbe's (2018) social analysis of the living conditions of older persons (n=250) in five communities of the Edo Central Senatorial District in the South South geopolitical zone found many older persons living in poor social conditions in need of healthcare, due to financial stress. Most were not working or had low incomes. Less than a third received irregular pensions and 11.6% still ran businesses to stay afloat. In many instances, old people were forced to continue working.

To counter *decreased functional independence*, research showed that social support and community participation had a positive effect on older people's psychosocial functioning possibly more so than health factors (Animasahun & Chapman, 2017). Mojoyinola and Ayangunna (2012) believed the main goal of social work practice with older people was improvement in their quality of life by ensuring they had adequate social support and fulfilling social relationships. Social workers worked closely with the family as the main providers of care, encouraging social contact with children, relatives, friends, neighbours, and community groups to reduce isolation and loneliness. With the absence of psychological and environmental support services, engagement in meaningful social and cultural activities, such as village or community meetings, child-naming, marriage, and funerals ceremonies, were essential to older people's emotional and physical wellbeing (Ebimgbo et al., 2019, 2021). This included participation in policy and planning. Respecting older people's right to be treated with dignity, social workers promoted independence by upholding their right to self-determination and autonomy, that is, to make choices and decisions for themselves. Hence, older people's participation in policy, planning, and research was essential to take account of their needs and preferences in the context of sociocultural and religious norms and local socioeconomic realities (Uwakwe et al., 2009). Social workers played a valuable role in researching local people's needs and priorities and in working with older people's advocacy bodies to lobby for policy change, especially in human rights emergencies (Ugochukwu et al., 2020).

Conclusion

This chapter has shown how an absence of legislation to provide a framework and standards for the protection and promotion of the rights of people living with mental health conditions and older persons leads to problems in service provision to two highly vulnerable sectors of the population. It has shown the importance of a cultural understanding to understand barriers to treatment or the inhumane treatment of widows and childless women, for example. It has also shown that social work can play a crucial role and, as in other contexts of practice, highlights the need to educate policy makers and the general public on social workers' contribution to human wellbeing.

7 '5Ps' approach to human trafficking and the social work response

This chapter introduces the 5Ps approach to human trafficking: (i) Policy dominated by TPVA's 3Ps framework – prosecution, prevention, and protection; (ii) human trafficking as a political problem and complex sociocultural and economic issue that requires a strong commitment from the top down to prosecute traffickers and support trafficked people; (iii) postcolonial perspective that provides a critical perspective on legacies of colonialism; (iv) prostitution to highlight moralising responses and trafficking's disproportionate effect on women and children; and (v) provision of essential resources and services to support survivors. It highlights the importance of interventions at the micro, meso, and macro levels and the role of social work education to prepare social workers to provide multilevel interventions and join with other stakeholders to deal with the complex problem of human trafficking.

Nigeria has a severe mixed-migration challenge, due to prolonged internal displacement, migrant smuggling, unsettled returnees (former Nigerian migrants and refugees in other countries), internal refugees and asylum seekers, human trafficking, and the brain drain. The government created a single Ministry of Humanitarian Affairs, Disaster Management and Social Development in 2019 to ensure coordinated humanitarian assistance for these groups.

As regards migrants, refugees, and displaced people, Nigeria became a signatory to the Convention Governing Specific Aspects of Refugee Problems in Africa (OAU, 1969) in 1983, the International Convention on the Protection of the Rights of All Migrant Workers and Members of their Families (UN, 1990) in 2009, and the Convention for the Protection and Assistance of Internally Displaced Persons in Africa (Kampala Convention) (AU, 2009) in 2012, and introduced a National Policy on Internally Displaced Persons (IDPs) in 2021 (FRN, 2021) that, despite its single federal ministry, shifted responsibility for IDPs onto State governments (Abuja, 2021) now responsible for *inter alia* health (HIV and AIDS prevention) and medical care, education, food, shelter, and security in IDP camps (Akuto, 2017; Enwereji, 2008; Gimba, 2016).

Statistically, there were an estimated 1.7 million largely unsettled returnees, 74,000 in-country refugees and asylum seekers, and over 300,000 Nigerian refugees in neighbouring Niger, Chad, and Cameroon awaiting repatriation (Mamman-Daura, 2022). In addition, there were over three million IDPs, with

DOI: 10.4324/9781003382126-7

60% of the increase due to natural disasters and 40% due to conflict fueled by competition for land and Boko Haram insurgents (Gwadabe et al., 2018). The United Nations High Commissioner for Refugees (UNHCR) (2018) estimated that, in the northeastern region alone, there were 2,244,678 IDPs, including 211,516 Nigerian refugees in Cameroon, Chad, and Niger. Nwalieji and Oyebanjo (2019) reported that insurgency attacks by Islamists had displaced 85% of Nigeria's IDPs. Borno state was the epicentre of Nigeria's displacement crisis (European Asylum Support Office, 2018). Ongoing military operations forcibly displaced over 5,000 people in January 2018 as part of their attempt to dismantle Boko Haram in Borno State (UNHCR, 2018).

Territorial disputes between nomadic farmers and local communities and ethnoreligious issues have fuelled conflict in North Central (Adesina et al., 2020), Nigeria's fourth largest and third poorest geopolitical zone with an average poverty rate of 60.7% (NBS, 2019). In 2015, ongoing clashes between Fulani pastoralists and farmers, some of them Tiv, contributed to the internal displacement of nearly 50,000 people in North Central. Home to 14.5% of the population, the area is a convergence of several minority ethnic groups, most of whom are farmers. Though predominantly Christian, it has a sizeable Muslim population. In some cases, acts of violence attributed to inter-communal Tiv–Fulani conflict were, in fact, the work of Boko Haram, as it expanded its operations southward into the Middle Belt[1] of the north central region, where Abuja lies. The incumbent President, former military dictator Muhammadu Buhari, assumed office in 2015 on an election promise to deal with counterterrorism, but economic and political challenges have hampered the fight against Boko Haram (Mentone, 2018). Ojewale (2021a, 2021b) showed that, in the last decade, there had been 1,412 reported incidents of conflict and 7,399 deaths across the north central states.

The literature on human trafficking reflected an overreliance on reports and documents minimally informed by rigorous scientific research (Weitzer, 2014). The main producers of information were government ministries, international organisations, non-government agencies, and advocacy groups. They included the International Labour Organisation (ILO), International Organisation for Migration (IOM), Pathfinders Justice Initiative (PJI), United Nations Education, Scientific and Cultural Organisation (UNESCO), United Nations Office on Drugs and Crime (UNODC), and United States Department of State's (USDS) Trafficking Victims Protection Act (TVPA) and Trafficking in Persons (TIP) reports. In the '5Ps' approach to human trafficking discussed below, this is most evident in the policy domain. The 5Ps are as follows:

1   *Policy* dominated by TPVA's 3Ps framework – prosecution, prevention, and protection
2   *Political problem* and complex sociocultural and economic issue
3   *Postcolonial perspective* providing a critical perspective on legacies of colonialism
4   *Prostitution* to highlight moralising responses and effect on women
5   *Provision of essential resources and services* to support survivors

Policy - TPVA framework 3Ps – prosecution, prevention, and protection

The US constructed the dominant discourse of prosecution, prevention, and protection in its Trafficking Victims Protection Act (TVPA) (USDS, 2000). It relied on 'a single story (victim/criminal narrative) to address a complex problem' (Badejo, 2006, p. 9). This discourse presented trafficked persons as victims of sexual, rather than labour, exploitation based on morality tales of extreme sexual abuse rendered typical (Weitzer, 2014). For Capous (2007), this arose from TVPA's moral agenda to abolish prostitution, especially trafficking-related sexual exploitation globally. As the work of a US political coalition comprising conservative Christians, Republicans, Democrats, radical feminist organisations, human rights groups, and academics, among others, it reflected the political and religious beliefs of its main protagonists. According to Bromfield and Capous-Desyllas (2012), the main objective of this coalition was to avoid complex immigrations issues within the USA by preventing the entry of foreign nationals trafficked for prostitution purposes through fostering international cooperation to combat human trafficking. However, its stringent eligibility requirements, including mandatory victim cooperation with authorities, made victims' access to protection extremely difficult (Sadruddin et al., 2005). Its law-enforcement approach undermined humanitarian goals of assisting trafficked persons, thus few benefited from its protections, while its laws made them vulnerable to further abuse (Harré, 2022).

Adepitan (2020) noted that international policies generally downplayed global labour trafficking, possibly due to pressure from 'business groups in more powerful nations who continue to lobby against the inclusion of labor as a form of trafficking' (p. 10). These policies overlooked broader forced-labour and labour-migration issues and the framing of trafficking in terms of labour exploitation. This allowed powerful countries and global corporations to further their vested economic interests. Adepitan (2020) described these as 'persisting colonial legacies which still pervade contemporary global power and labor dynamics' (p. 46).

Prosecution

Harré (2022) noted that, from a transnational criminal law (TCL) perspective, international policies prioritised prosecution over victim protection and prevention requiring nation states to criminalise, prosecute, punish, and strengthen border controls. TCL was 'not a rights-protective system, but rather one that focuses on facilitating successful prosecutions of traffickers' (n.p.). Therefore, TCL prioritised foreign and domestic policy aims of nation states over the rights of individuals.

Ward and Fouladvand (2018) noted the difficulties involved in prosecuting human traffickers for a 'covert crime which presents complex evidential issues' (p. 139), not least the involvement of victims, whose 'cooperation plays an important role in a successful prosecution' (p. 139). However, there were numerous reasons why victims feared coming forward, not least the risk of secondary traumatisation through the legal process. Further, prosecution made victims responsible for prosecuting traffickers for a market-driven crime, accruing lucrative profits for traffickers and powerful companies employing trafficked people (Onyejekwe, 2005). Therefore, prosecution should be part of a wider 'responsibilisation strategy' that engaged a broad network of people responsible, including corporations employing trafficked labour, NGOs helping victims, and individual citizens with knowledge of its operations or who purchased sexual services from trafficked persons, in anti-trafficking efforts 'to help reduce criminal opportunities and enhance crime control' (Garland, 2002, p. 126). Responsibilisation also extended to law-enforcement agents, especially police, encouraging them to 'foster good relations with voluntary sector organisations working with victims with a view to those organisations encouraging their clients to provide intelligence to the police, and perhaps to become prosecution witnesses' (Ward & Fouladvand, 2018, p. 141).

Prevention

Prevention measures included stronger border control measures to prevent the movement of people through trafficking (Onyejekwe, 2005). Preventing the occurrence and reoccurrence or retrafficking of survivors required structural interventions to reduce poverty and gender inequality as primary problems and multilevel, collaborative interventions involving judicial, security, law enforcement, media, and service providers. Awareness and consciousness-raising campaigns sought to educate the public on the dangers of human trafficking and to reduce the social stigma and discrimination surrounding sex work and human trafficking. Capacity-building initiatives focused on skill acquisition and employment training to reduce vulnerability to human trafficking was another preventive measure (Dahal et al., 2015). However, there were several intractable problems that contributed to internal trafficking and displacement, including the poor conditions in IDP camps and baby factories that made women vulnerable to opportunistic traffickers (Obaji, 2020). Another was the Almajiri system that accounted for 81% of Nigeria's estimated 10.5 million out-of-school children (United Nations International Children's Emergency Fund (UNICEF), 2020). Once a system of moral education, AbdulQadir (n.d.) noted that, following the British invasion of the region, 'the Emirs lost control of their territories and accepted their new roles as mere traditional rulers [under indirect rule]' (n.p.). They also lost control of the Almajiri system that the British rendered ineffectual by abolishing state funding for religious schools. Pupils and their semi-literate teachers (Mallams), who resisted Western education, turned Almajiri into an inferior system of Islamic education. UNICEF (2020) noted that parents continued to send their children, mostly boys between the ages of 4 and 12 years, to Almajiri schools in distant locations to acquire a Koranic education. Many were from rural and poor families, who could not afford formal schooling. While parents believed they were fulfilling their obligation to provide a religious and moral education to their children free of charge, the teachers (Mallams) forced the children into begging to fund their education. State governments in northern Nigeria, however, banned the Almajiri system to reduce the spread of Covid and many children returned to their families and communities with the support of UNICEF. Change.org (n.d.) published a petition calling for the abolition of the Almajiri system as it made children begging on the streets vulnerable to unscrupulous operators, who recruited them into prostitution and other nefarious activities. Further, the conditions were so poor in many of the schools that children did not survive their harsh existence or ended up doing menial jobs on the streets as they lacked any formal work skills.

The common thread in trafficking, baby factories, and Almajiri schools is poverty. Thus, above all else, prevention means addressing the social and economic conditions that render people vulnerable to the lure of so-called income-earning opportunities that exploit them for profit.

Protection

Nigeria is a signatory to several international conventions relating to human trafficking: Convention against Torture and Other Cruel, Inhuman or Degrading Treatment or Punishment (UN, 1984); Optional Protocol to the Convention on the Rights of the Child on the sale of children child prostitution and child pornography (UN, 2000a); Convention for the Protection of All Persons from Enforced Disappearance (UN, 2010); and Convention against Transnational Organized Crime and Protocols to prevent trafficking in persons, especially women and children (UN, 2018). The government passed three policies that have a bearing on human trafficking in 2015. They are Trafficking in Persons (Prohibition), Enforcement, and Administration Act, as amended (FRN, 2015a); National Migration Policy (FRN, 2015b); and Violence Against Persons (Prohibition) Act (FRN, 2015c). The main laws protecting people from human trafficking in Nigeria is the Trafficking in Persons (TIP) Act, originally passed in 2003 and amended in 2005 and 2015 (FRN, 2015a). It criminalises human (sex and labour) trafficking and related abuses and stipulates penalties for trafficking infringements. Patterned on the Palermo Protocol (UN, 2000c) that recognised the voluntary nature of human trafficking and aimed to prevent, suppress, and punish trafficking in persons, especially women and children, the Nigerian TIP Act stipulates trafficked persons' entitlement to 'compensation, restitution, and recovery for economic, physical, and psychological damages' (Section 62 & 65, para. 1); 'access to adequate health and other social services'; protections against discriminatory treatment, barring discrimination on account of gender or sex or on the basis of the victim having worked in the sex industry (Section 61(a); and protection 'from intimidation, threats, and reprisals from traffickers and their associates' (Section 61, para. b & j).

Part II of the Act established a National Agency for the Prohibition of Trafficking in Persons (NAPTIP), Agency Transit Shelters for rescued trafficked persons, and a Victims of Trafficking Trust Fund to provide victim compensation. It forms part of Nigeria's international obligations as a signatory to the Convention on Transnational Organised Crime and its Protocol to Suppress, Prevent and Punish Trafficking in Persons, especially Women and Children (UN, 2000). The inter-ministerial committee on trafficking played a pivotal role in national policymaking, especially NAPTIP and the Federal Ministry of Humanitarian Affairs, Disaster Management and Social Development mainly responsible for trafficked and displaced people. In 2022, NAPTIP launched the five-year National Action Plan on Human Trafficking in Nigeria (2022–2026) developed with the assistance of the Swiss government and UNODC (FRN, 2022a). It revolves around five thematic areas: Protection and assistance; prevention; research and assessment, data management and statistics and monitoring and evaluation; prosecution law enforcement and access to justice; and partnership and coordination (UNODC, 2022).

Political problem

Human trafficking in Nigeria is a political problem that requires political solutions to combat exploitation at the highest level (Adedokun, 2016). These political solutions not only include direct measures to combat trafficking but also structural changes to stem unsafe migration and human trafficking, including extreme poverty, government corruption, and gender inequality. With its long history dating back to the precolonial slave trade, human trafficking is an area of humanitarian intervention in contemporary Nigeria, where cross-border and internal trafficking is escalating at an alarming rate. Nigeria is a major country of origin for human trafficking, with many Nigerians succumbing to cross-border trafficking annually, making this the third most common crime in Nigeria after drug trafficking and economic fraud (UNESCO, 2006). The USDS (2018) reported that 80% of victims of sexual exploitation in Europe were Nigerian. The Pathfinders Justice Initiative (PJI) (2022) reported that there were large numbers of Nigerian trafficked persons in 34 countries and four regions globally, though the exact number was unknown. It further reported that factors increasing unsafe migration and vulnerability to trafficking in Nigeria included extreme poverty (with Nigeria now the world's poverty capital), lack of economic opportunities, corruption, conflict and insecurity, climate change and resulting migration, and Western consumerism.

The United States Code (USC, 2022) is a consolidation and codification by subject matter of the general and permanent laws of the United States prepared by the Office of the Law Revision Counsel of the United States House of Representatives. USC 7106 contains minimum standards for the elimination of trafficking underlying the tiered system used for the US Department of State' (USDS) annual Trafficking in Persons (TIP) reports that ranked national governments into tiers based on their efforts to acknowledge and combat human trafficking within their jurisdictional areas as follows:

- Tier 1: Governments fully comply with the minimum TVPA standards.
- Tier 2: Governments do not comply fully with minimum TVPA standards, though are working to do so. Nigeria's is on the Tier 2 Watch List, due to a significant and or increasing number of victims of severe forms of trafficking and the government's failure to provide evidence of increasing efforts to combat severe forms of trafficking in persons from the previous year.
- Tier 3: Governments do not fully comply with minimum standards and are not making significant efforts to do so.

The USDS (2021) Trafficking in Persons report listed Nigeria as a Tier 2 country, since the government failed to 'meet the minimum standards for the elimination of trafficking' (p. 1). These standards included increased convictions and heavy terms of imprisonment for perpetrators, prosecutions of officials complicit in trafficking crimes, improved intra-governmental coordination on anti-trafficking operations, and the launch of nine new state taskforces in Rivers, Cross Rivers, Akwa Ibom, Ogun, Oyo, Enugu, Anambara, and Ebonyi. For the first time, the Federal Ministry of Defense acknowledged members of the military sexually exploited internally displaced persons (IDPs). However, 'corruption remained a significant concern in the judiciary and immigration services, and the Ministry of Defense did not finalize its handover protocol to refer child soldiers to care for the sixth consecutive year' (p. 1). Felbab-Brown (2018) reported that Nigerian security forces had, themselves, contributed to 'insecurity, dislocation, widespread human rights abuses, and radicalization' (n.p.). Further, the military had forced communities to vacate their villages and move into horrific conditions in IDP camps, where there have been many reports of abuse (Obaji, 2020). This has increased local communities' frustration with the security forces that could accelerate radicalisation of the most vulnerable. The government's failure to find a long-term solution to ongoing conflict and insecurity exacerbated the problem of human trafficking and forced displacement.

The Walk Free Foundation's Global Slavery Index ranked Nigeria 32nd of 162 countries with an estimated 1,386,000 people living in slavery (WFF, 2018). Geographic mobility, (unsafe) migration, and trafficking were so intertwined that over 600,000 Nigerians attempted to journey through the Sahara Desert into Europe in 2016 alone, 27,000 of whom died *en route*; 68% of the deceased were university graduates (Ahmed & Kebbi, 2017).

There was a lack of accurate statistics on transnational trafficking from Nigeria, due to the illicit, organised, and clandestine nature of this activity. However, there was some agreement that the problem was increasing. Adepitan (2020) noted that Edo state (particularly its capital Benin) in South South was the locus of Nigeria's trafficking problem, with over 94% of people trafficked internationally and 90% of women and children trafficked to Europe coming from this area. The IOM (2019) reported that, of the 119,000 migrants who arrived in Italy in 2017, 18,185 were

Nigerian. They included 5,425 women, of whom an estimated 80% were potential victims of trafficking and 94% were from Edo state. For this reason, the Edo State government appointed the stakeholder-representative Edo State Task Force Against Human Trafficking (ETAHT) in 2017 and passed the Edo State Trafficking in Persons Prohibition Bill in 2018. The Taskforce has had some success with PJI (2022) reporting that '2020 is the first in recent years that Edo State has not featured in the top five states for victims rescued by NAPTIP … due to efforts by local stakeholders' (n.d.).

Postcolonial construction of trafficking

The postcolonial perspective examines the relationship between colonial legacies and contemporary cultural and structural practices affecting human trafficking and its impact on the lives of Black people globally. It also offers a compelling lens for viewing trafficking experiences (Constance-Huggins et al., 2022). From his postcolonial perspective, Adepitan (2020) argued that 'neocolonial dynamics greatly influence the motivations for trafficking, while simultaneously enabling the practice on a global scale and establishing punitive measures primarily directed at economically and politically weaker participants' (p. 5). Trafficking protects and promotes powerful political and economic interests, while introducing measures like prosecution, prevention, and protection to catch the small fish in the global pond. These powerful interests prey on the lives of poor and vulnerable people exploiting their labour for profit. This 'underbelly of our global economic order thrives on shadow labor markets which, in many cases, amount to treating people as property, or worse' (Adepitan, 2020, p. 6). It exploits former colonies now comprising 'countries with the highest trafficking rates' (p. 14), areas already depleted of natural resources and now mined for human resources. Postcolonial human trafficking discourses highlight the race- and gender-based contours of human trafficking that disproportionately affects Black and indigenous people, and women of colour. They highlight intersecting structural factors at play in human trafficking as a racialised, gendered, social problem. They draw attention to its roots in slavery and colonial oppression and note its extension as modern-day slavery (Okeshola & Adenugba, 2018).

Noting the relationship between migration and trafficking, Adepitan (2020) believes cultural, political, and religious factors play a pivotal role in people's decisions to move to which Badejo (2016) adds distrust of the state to provide for them, hopelessness arising from their experiences of systematic class oppression, and inability to change things. The decision to migrate is a collective household rather than an individual decision, especially for families living in poverty (Adepitan, 2020; Badejo, 2016). Further, traditional beliefs and practices, such as child fostering, blurred the lines between child labour and child trafficking, as poor rural families routinely sent their children to extended family members living closer to education and employment opportunities (Badejo, 2016). Hence, Adepitan's (2020) plea for 'policy makers and other key players in the international scene to account for the meaning of victims of trafficking's lived experiences' (p. 4) within their normative sociocultural milieu, where the family unit and extended family network are influential factors (see also Badejo, 2016).

Postcolonial feminists aver the problematic construction of trafficking survivors as passive victims of circumstances, lacking voice and agency. They highlight the importance of victim engagement and voice and honouring their stories that bear testament to their courage, resilience, strength, and survival strategies in the face of persistent gender- and race-based exploitation (Chikadzi & Warria, 2022; Constance-Huggins et al., 2022; Hu, 2019; Nonomura, 2020; Warria et al., 2021).

Prostitution

Although a conservative estimate, the 2018 Global Slavery Index reported that there were about 40.9 million trafficked persons worldwide, with women and their daughters constituting about 71%. Many endured psychological trauma, physical torture, and societal stigma and discrimination (WWF, 2018). UNODC (2020) reported that human trafficking continued to affect women disproportionately; 50% of detected trafficked persons in 2018 were adult women and 20% were young girls. About a third were children, girls (19%) and boys (15%); only 20 per cent were adult men.

The TPVA's attempt to eliminate prostitution globally, apart from not having its desired effect, criminalises sex work and does nothing to address the structural causes leading to women's vulnerability to sexual exploitation. In Nigeria, Islamic and Christian teachings perceive prostitution as an immoral act and, in the North, the penal code, which follows Islamic laws, criminalises prostitution. Though not illegal in the South, law prohibits brothels and disallows people living on the earnings of prostitutes. However, degrees of tolerance differ widely, with the issue trivialised in many Edo State communities, where it is seen as an external problem and there is no public recognition of long-term internal trafficking for prostitution (UNESCO, 2006).

Moralising responses hampered anti-human trafficking public-awareness campaigns. Badejo (2016) noted that predominant state beliefs about people's voluntary participation in human trafficking threatened and undermined the success of prevention measures. It created a single 'deviant' social identity for 'voluntarily' trafficked persons and human traffickers and reproduced social, economic, and cultural inequalities because it discouraged citizen participation in the fight against human trafficking, while stigmatising trafficked persons. It also inadvertently promoted human trafficking as a possible source of wealth. Moralising responses focused attention on 'sex trafficking at the expense of other forms of human trafficking, thus marginalising other perspectives such as the much bigger problem of child trafficking … in Nigeria' (Badejo, 2016, p. 6). Most of the trafficked participants (n=13 men and women) in Badejo's (2016) small qualitative ethnographic study viewed human trafficking positively and did not see themselves as victims, because no-one had forced them into it. Badejo (2016) believed their positive mindset (false consciousness) concealed 'the realities of their subordination, exploitation, and domination at the hands of human traffickers' (p. 9). The fact that the trafficking of Nigerian women might begin with voluntary consent supported by family members, relatives, and community did not negate their right to protection if they subsequently suffered at the hands of their traffickers (in the spirit of the Palermo Protocol (UN, 2000c) (Okojie, 2009). Weitzer's (2014) finding, following her review of 100 academic articles, that few contained original data and most claims about trafficking had rarely arisen from rigorous scientific research, showed the need for micro-level studies on the lived experiences of trafficked people. He called for qualitative studies involving interviews with migrants and their facilitators in all forms of trafficking, that documented the sociocultural and ecological dynamics of migration and trafficking in various contexts.

Gender inequality, extreme poverty, conflict and insecurity, and climate change disproportionately affected women and children. In addition, the lack of educational and economic opportunities for women made them extremely vulnerable to labour trafficking, sexual exploitation, and people smuggling (Gesinde & Elegbeleye, 2011; Okeshola & Adenugba, 2018; UNESCO, 2006). Transnational trafficked persons were usually women, recruited from rural and urban locations, through an intermediary, for sexual exploitation in Europe, the Middle East, and elsewhere in Africa (Gesinde & Elegbeleye, 2011). Internal human trafficking included the sex trafficking of IDPs, and women exploited into forced surrogacy. The USDS (2021) reported on Nigeria's 'baby factories' that were widespread in the country. Often disguised as orphanages, maternity homes, or religious centres, traffickers in these criminal enterprises held women against their will, raped them, and forced them to carry and deliver a child, as discussed in Chapter 4.

Internal human trafficking also included the recruitment of child soldiers, children in domestic service, and forced to beg, and child sex tourism. Children working in agriculture, domestic work, and artisanal mining were highly vulnerable to trafficking (USDS, 2021). Shrouded in secrecy, internal traffickers recruited children from villages and remote locations, deceiving unsuspecting parents into letting them go on the promise of a better life elsewhere (Gesinde & Elegbeleye, 2011). The International Program on the Elimination of Child Labor (IPEC) (2002) estimated that about 3.2 million children of 8 million child labourers in Nigeria were victims of trafficking.

Provision: Services to human trafficking survivors

Human trafficking is a sociocultural issue that requires sociocultural solutions. Beyond 'judicial and procedural definitions' (Adepitan, 2020, p. 36) criminalising human trafficking, it requires social provision to address its highly debilitating and dehumanising effects for individuals caught in its net. Anti-trafficking initiatives advocate the criminalisation of traffickers, not those trafficked, and call for services to protect and support survivors, and provide – legal, medical, and psychosocial – support for their social integration. Social measures were needed to address the causes of human trafficking, including gender inequality, poverty, unemployment, social inequality, political instability, limited education opportunities, conflict-driven displacement, and family disintegration to stem the tide of unsafe migration to escape socioeconomic oppression in search of higher wages and better opportunities elsewhere (Badejo, 2016; Okeshola & Adenugba, 2018; Ross-Sheriff & Orme, 2015). As Adepitan (2020) noted, 'changes in economic and social policies and cultural and historical practices are needed to address structural factors that serve as root causes of migration and exploitation' (p. 36).

In Nigeria, the National Agency for the Prohibition of Trafficking in Persons (NAPTIP), situated in the Ministry of Humanitarian Affairs and Disaster Management, leads the federal government's efforts to combat trafficking. Others with responsibilities in supporting the country's criminal justice response to human trafficking included officials from the Nigerian Immigration Service, Nigerian Police Force, Labour Inspectorate, Economic and Financial Crimes Commission and Nigerian Financial Intelligence Unit, in coordination with prosecutors and the judiciary. However, the USDS (2021) reported that NAPTIP did not have resources to carry out its anti-trafficking operations across the country and the concentration of officers in state capitals hindered the identification and investigation of traffickers in many rural areas.

Non-government organisations played an important role in working with trafficked persons and survivors, and IDPs (Akuto, 2017; Otabor & Shodeinde, 2018). In Nigeria, for example, the anti-trafficking activities of the Women Trafficking and Child Labor Eradication Foundation (WOTCLEF) includes the prosecution of traffickers, protection of victims, and rehabilitation, retraining, and counseling of repatriated trafficked people (Dave-Odigie, 2008). However, noting the alarming rate of insecurity driven by kidnapping, banditry, and all forms of criminal activity on the rise in Kaduna State, HassanWuyo (2020) reported that some privileged Nigerians were defrauding international organisations in the name of NGOs and diverting funds and materials meant for IDPs.

Social work response

Amadasun (2022) claimed that social workers in non-government and government organisations were frontline responders to victims of human trafficking in Nigeria. With their person-in-environment perspective and guiding values and principles, social work services stretched beyond the psychological to the social in keeping with the Trafficking in Persons (Prohibition), Enforcement, and Administration Act (FRN, 2015a). His study of social workers (n=5) employed in NAPTIP found that the main interventions used were rehabilitation (psychological trauma-informed therapy), protection (accommodation or shelter provision), and prevention (capacity-building and reducing stigma). He noted the dominance of the casework method with social workers largely ignoring structural factors relating to human trafficking. Azorondu et al. (2021) believed social workers' cooperation with criminal justice would deter perpetrators from engaging in further human trafficking activities.

From their content analysis of secondary sources on the role of social workers with IDPs, Nwanna and Oparaoha (2018) noted that social workers were not visibly working with IDPs in Nigeria because the government did not recognise and support social work. Nevertheless, they noted multilevel roles and interventions from direct counselling work as specialist clinical practitioners to participating in policymaking processes and investigating the causes of displacement, to managing and evaluating projects for IDPs, social education, conflict mediation, and critical analyses of power dynamics and structural factors. Thus, they perceived wide-ranging roles for social workers at all levels of intervention.

Improving the social conditions of human trafficking survivors required holistic (ecological), long-term interventions that supported, promoted, protected, and upheld the rights and dignity of survivors (Barner at al., 2018; Miller-Perrin & Wurtele, 2017). For social work, this suggested a rights-based, social justice approach within a critical structural practice framework that provided insight into intersecting historical, individual, economic, political, and sociocultural factors, especially race and gender (Botha & Warria, 2020). Barner et al. (2018) advocated an ecological person-centred approach with interventions at the individual, family, local community, national policy, and global levels.

Several authors have noted the complicity of social workers in perpetuating structural power imbalances that constructed survivors of trafficking as passive victims of exploitation and injustice (Chikadzi & Warria, 2022; Constance-Huggins et al., 2022; Crampton, 2015; Hu, 2019; Nonomura, 2020; Waria, 2022). Without a critical structural response, social work interventions would leave discriminatory systems and stigmatising practices intact. Social workers stuck in the politics of rescue, for example, spoke for, and represented the interests of, victims rather than positioning them as experts on their exploitation and trafficking experiences, with agency to direct their own lives. The contemporary social work response in Nigeria fits this mould. It is mainly short-term casework, focused on survivors' immediate need for safety, emergency shelter, and protection to rescue and protect them from further risks from traffickers (Clawson & Dutch, 2007). Short-term victim protection does not necessarily lead to behavioural change (Warria, 2019, 2020). This requires structural interventions that enhance survivors' economic status, support gender equity, increase access to education and employment, and address gender-based violence and sexual exploitation. Though actively engaging survivors and honouring their trafficking stories is important, social workers must do much more to achieve lasting change. Barriers to effective service delivery in Nigeria include inadequate resources, a shortage of professionally qualified social workers, absence of specialist training programs, and lack of professionalisation with incompetent professionals and mediocre services, from mediocre practitioners (Amadasun, 2020).

Micro-level interventions

As noted, short-term individual and family casework is the main method of intervention that social workers in Nigeria use usually in the beginning stages of reintegration into mainstream society, arranging shelter and health and social care. There is a great push for trauma-informed therapy and therapeutic counseling, given the complex trauma and multiple traumatic events trafficked persons experience. There is some agreement that restoring optimal cognitive and psychosocial functioning and mental health requires trauma-informed assessment and therapy (Clawson et al., 2008; Hopper, 2017; Ross-Sheriff & Orme, 2015; Williamson et al., 2008). Hopper (2017) noted that trauma-informed assessment includes 'rapport-building and informed consent, safety assessment, needs assessment and goal-setting, history and vulnerability factors, trafficking narrative (including elements of force, fraud, and coercion) and trauma exposure, assessment of psychological symptoms, and strengths and coping' (p. 15).

Williamson et al. (2008) reported that mental health disorders in trafficked people were like those of survivors who had lived in an active war zone or experienced torture. Most experienced mood disorders, including depression, anxiety, and suicidal thoughts, dissociative disorders, and substance-related disorders (Ross-Sheriff & Orme, 2015; Williamson et al., 2008). Many had post-traumatic stress disorder (PTSD). These individualistic psychological responses required an anti-oppressive, intersectional framework that provided understanding of the structural trauma of racism, sexism, and gender-based violence characterising the experience of human trafficking survivors (Bryant-Davis & Tummala-Narra, 2017; Gerassi & Nichols, 2021).

Meso-level interventions

Meso-level interventions connect returned trafficked persons to resources, such as job training, healthcare, and education. These social responses emphasise the importance of social capital – social support networks, families and extended families, kith and kin, and community-based resources – that, given its large population, Nigeria has in abundance. However, the presence of natural helping (self-help) networks does not diminish the need for effective formal services and capacity-building programs providing training in the employment skills and capabilities necessary for social reintegration.

Macro-level interventions

Macro-level policy interventions seek to dismantle the social structures that increase the vulnerabilities of at-risk populations to trafficking. Failure to address structural factors leads to the re-occurrence of human trafficking, aggravates the predicament of trafficking victims, and undermines survivors' long-term recovery. Working in concert with other key stakeholders, social workers challenge unjust policies and structures that exacerbate the plight or undermine the recovery and reintegration of trafficking survivors (Okech et al., 2012). The government is majorly responsible for policy interventions at the national, state, and local levels. Again, working in concert with other key stakeholders, social workers could advocate that the government:

1 Implement the provisions of the law in the Trafficking in Persons (Prohibition), Enforcement, and Administration Act, as amended (FRN, 2015a), to the letter, especially through the provision of adequate resources to support survivors across the layers of rehabilitation, protection, and prevention of trafficking. In this regard, the government might review and expand the six-week window of in-shelter service to a 12-week minimum period.
2 Identify and suppress all forms of structural barriers militating against the reintegration of human trafficking survivors into mainstream society.
3 Engage the services of qualified professionals, such as social workers and psychologists, to ensure the successful reintegration of human trafficking survivors. In this regard, the government needs to expedite action toward the professionalisation of social workers to eliminate bottlenecks in service delivery.
4 Ensure and encourage the training and re-training of social service providers in statutory and non-government human service organisations to improve the quality of services offered (Amadasun, 2020).

Social work education

Postcolonial decolonisation scholars highlight the inadequacies of the kind of imported, Eurocentric models taught in many African schools of social work, noting that, lacking a critical framework, social work education tends to perpetuate disempowering discourses that rob victims of exploitation of agency and deny them a voice. One important legacy of imported social work is its individualistic casework focus that too often overlooks the structural causes of social problems and perpetuates blaming-the-victim approaches (Amadasun, 2022). Unless they take account of the victim-survivor's intersecting identities, short-term individualistic interventions run the risk of perpetuating shame, disconnection, and isolation (Warria, 2020, 2022).

Gerassi and Nichols (2020) believed instruction in social work needed to 'apply intersectional, anti-oppressive frameworks across micro, meso, and macro levels' (p. 20). Social work courses on micro-level responses to human trafficking needed to include content drawn from the direct experiences of victims and survivors, and their role in healing, recovery, and social integration. These experiences would reveal the nuanced nature of commercial sex work that might be empowering for some and oppressive for others, or a mix of these (Gerassi & Nichols, 2020). As Hume and Sidun (2017) observed, 'the common narrative of helpless victims misrepresents many women's actual experiences' (p. 9).

Long-term macro-level interventions require a focus on intersecting structural causes, such as economic and social inequalities and discriminatory gender and race relations. They require supportive legislation and systems to enforce it, including strong law-enforcement agencies and well-resourced social services. Thus, social workers require well-developed political-engagement skills to involve themselves in policy-making processes and agitate for resource provision along with an acute awareness of the diversity of trafficking experiences and the intersectional factors leading to this growing social problem informed by critical (anti-oppressive, postcolonial, race, and feminist) theories. Postcolonial theory highlights the colonial legacies of slavery and their links to human trafficking risks, while critical race theory emphasises the disproportionate representation of Black people in human trafficking statistics, and feminist theory notes the disproportionate representation of women and multiple intersecting oppressions they endure. These critical theories situate the root causes of human trafficking in structural deficiencies, inequalities, and injustices. Such understanding provides insights into the political interventions – policy advocacy, political lobbying, social action, and public-awareness campaigns – required to eliminate this persistent social problem. The targets of political action are influential figures in politics and institutions of power, such as religious leaders and traditional rulers, and local people susceptible to traffickers, as well as members of the public that sustain discriminatory, stigmatising attitudes that block resource allocation for trafficking survivors. Engagement and partnership with community, religious, and traditional leaders require social workers' visibility not only in communities but also in political and media platforms.

Conclusion

This chapter introduced the 5Ps approach to human trafficking: (i) Policy dominated by TPVA's 3Ps framework – prosecution, prevention, and protection; (ii) human trafficking as a political problem and complex sociocultural and economic issue that requires a strong commitment from the top down to prosecute traffickers and support trafficked people; (iii) postcolonial perspective that provides a critical perspective on legacies of colonialism; (iv) prostitution to highlight moralising responses and trafficking's disproportionate effect on women and children; and (v) provision of essential resources and services to support survivors. It highlighted the importance of interventions at the micro, meso, and macro levels and the role of social work education to prepare social workers to provide multilevel interventions and join with other stakeholders to deal with the complex problem of human trafficking.

Note

1 The 'middle belt' running across Nigeria has the highest concentration of minority ethnic groups. It comprises Taraba, Adamawa, Plateau, Nassarawa, Benue, and Kogi states, as well as Southern Zaria and Southern Kaduna. All these areas have witnessed intra-ethnic or inter-ethnic conflicts that have spread across different states (Tajudeen & Adebayo, 2013).

8 Nigerian social work and its quest for professional recognition

This chapter examines contemporary social work in Nigeria focusing on its quest for professional recognition. Following a review of processes through which professions gain recognition and legitimacy, it introduces an R-lexicon – regulation, relevance, recognition, representation, relational connections, rights, and research – pointing to key strategies to advance the Nigerian profession's interests. It ends with a brief overview of literature pertaining to social work practice showing the profession's minimal presence in several long-established contexts, such as corrections, juvenile justice, and child protection. With the goal of legitimation now achieved, the the chapter ends with a call to social workers to build bridges and establish strong networks to project a united front in the interests of the future development of the profession.

Establishing social work's professional credentials and achieving government sanction for its operations has been an important quest wherever social work is practised and is further along the line for countries where the profession has a long history (Teoh & Fuziah Shaffie, 2017). Most authors predate social work in Nigeria to indigenous support systems prior to the advent of European missionaries. As shown in Chapter 2, precolonial mission-based charity work began in the 19th century and became an important part of colonial welfare. These were precursors to *professional* social work in Nigeria, that is, social work practised by qualified professionals that gained momentum following the introduction of university-based social work education in 1976. Despite the development of social work education, as discussed in Chapter 9, the relatively young profession of social work in Nigeria has struggled to gain professional recognition even though the attainment of professional status has been a central issue of concern to social work educators, practitioners, and other critical stakeholders since the 1970s. From the outset, the profession's legitimacy rested on the extent to which it contributed to the 'continuous improvement and transformation in the quality of life of the people throughout the nation' (Federal Ministry of Social Development, 1977, p. 8). Colonial government administrators with a secondary school education or diploma and three- to six-months in-service training were Nigeria's first social workers (Jinadu, 1985; Mbah et al., 2017; Ojanuga, 1985). The small minority with a university education had trained overseas. Hence, the Guidelines for the Fourth National Development Plan

DOI: 10.4324/9781003382126-8

1981–1985 stressed the government's commitment to address the shortage of well-trained social workers on whom the success of social welfare depended (Federal Ministry of National Planning, 1981) but implementation failures of this and subsequent plans did little to alleviate the problem (Iheanacho, 2014), as discussed in Chapter 3. The push for social workers to engage in social development marked a watershed moment since it highlighted debates on social work's remit. Some social workers saw community development as incongruent with professionalisation and continued tensions between the casework and community development camps hampered professional unity and the search for legitimacy through the 1980s (Amadasun, 2021a). However, beginning in the 1990s, the indigenisation movement gained momentum, laying the groundwork for coalition building to strengthen social work's push for professionalisation. Several professional organisations emerged, but it was not until the turn of the century that the professionalisation movement intensified. However, hampering social work's efforts to advance professionalisation was the ongoing presence of large numbers of untrained, unqualified, public officials calling themselves social workers. Further, there were competing interests seeking to further social work's professional legitimacy. Our examination of Nigerian social work's professionalisation efforts highlighted the need for strategic direction for its professionalising objectives.

The discussion begins with an examination of social work's universal quest for a professional identity, highlighting criteria of professionalism and the processes by which professions gain social legitimacy. It then provides examples from other countries to show diverse processes of professionalisation that might guide Nigerian social work's ongoing quest for professional recognition. Thereafter, it examines Nigerian social work's path to professionalisation before introducing an analytical framework to highlight the interrelated processes by which it might establish its credentials and attain legitimation. These are registration and regulation, relevance, recognition, representation, relational connection, rights, and research. This R-lexicon highlights key strategic areas Nigerian social workers might address to advance their professional status.

Universal quest for a professional identity for social work

Criteria approach

The universal quest for a professional identity occurred wherever social work came to be practised beginning historically in England and the United States, where many employed by charitable institutions regarded their work as professional comparing it to law, medicine, and psychiatry (Gibbelman, 1999; Woodroofe, 1962). In 1915, US expert on professional education, Abraham Flexner, put professionalisation on social work's agenda, when, in his address to the *National Conference on Charities and Corrections* in Baltimore, he asked 'Is social work a profession?' He concluded that social work did not meet the hallmarks of a profession, which he described as an essentially intellectual operation with extensive individual responsibilities that derived its raw material from science and learning and applied this material to practical predetermined goals. Additionally, it had to have educationally communicable techniques and the ability to organise and monitor its altruistic activities. While he accepted social workers' altruistic motivations, he believed it lacked the responsibility and power of a true profession. Importantly, its aims were too wide and unspecific. Because of its broad scope, its practitioners lacked specialised skills and, despite its educational initiatives, social work lacked a systematic, scientific body of knowledge and theory to teach to aspiring professionals.

Flexner's (1915) assessment sparked a 'flurry of activity' (Du Bois & Miley, 1992, p. 35) in the United States, where the number of schools of social work expanded dramatically as the profession advocated training for all social workers. A professional accreditation body established standardised educational curricula in the belief that the singular, generic nature of social work skills, applicable in any setting, would enhance its professional standing.

Flexner's (1915) arguments rang true given that professionals laid 'claim to extraordinary knowledge in matters of great social importance … [that, in return, granted them] extraordinary rights and privileges' (Schön, 1983, p. 4). However, many years later, Gibbelman (1999) noted that social work's quest for a distinct professional identity was still 'hampered by the breadth of the profession, its relationship to the external socio-political environment and divisions within the profession itself' (p. 298) regarding the merits of professionalisation. While some viewed it as fundamental to effective service delivery, others saw it as a heritage of the medical model, with the similarly negative effects of distancing social workers from their clients and communities (Biklen, 1983; Hopp & Pinderhughes, 1987; Webb, 1984). This was consistent with African scholars' anecdotal observations that hurtful gerrymandering and 'perennial internal wrangling' (Amadasun, 2021a, p. 262) impeded agreement on a professional identity. This was exacerbated by persistent disagreements on the scope of the profession and the incessant split between micro (caseworkers) and macro (community workers) practice. The severest criticisms came from critical social workers who claimed social work's bid to gain a monopoly on dispensing social welfare came at the cost of sacrificing its reform impetus (Specht & Courtney, 1994). Gaining expertise to acquire professional power and privilege in the social domain could work against public interest and the profession's responsiveness to local people's needs (Biklen, 1983; Hamilton, 1976; Schön, 1983). Hence, drivers for professional recognition created several anomalies and paradoxes for social work given its concern with social change and accessibility to people who needed its services.

Social integration approach

While Flexner (1915) advanced a criteria approach to professionalisation, Hamilton (1976) stressed the social processes by which professions gained legitimacy, sanction, and social integration. She highlighted that the achievement of professional status depended on the occupational group's success in convincing society of the legitimacy of its claims. However, this was a twin-edged sword, as legitimacy hinged on the group's identification with ruling elites, conformity to social norms, and ability to convince those in power of its significant contribution to society. Professionalisation entailed establishing the occupational group's credentials as an integral part of the social fabric of society with the skills to support and strengthen its social norms and structures. The occupational group had to ensure that ruling elites remained persuaded of its positive value or, at least, its harmlessness, so they would not undermine its contribution and protect its domain from encroachment. Established authority granted the profession the autonomy to work in the domains to which it laid claim so long as it conformed to the standards and values of the *status quo*. What then arose was a situation in which the profession received sanction to operate within the confines imposed by politicians and other ruling elites. In the case of social work, in most Western countries, it brought the authority to provide welfare services and protect this domain from encroachment by other occupations. However, being part of the ruling hierarchy with a stake in keeping society as it was was an anomaly for an occupation that started out with a mission of social reform and change. Biklen (1983) believed this undesirable consequence of professionalisation created a paradox for social work with its avowed commitment to challenge injustice and promote change. He questioned whether professional recognition was worth this sacrifice.

The search for professional status involved a political process to occupy a position of power within society, drive out competition, and become the sole suppliers of particular services (Biklen, 1983; Hamilton, 1976). Such exclusivity imbued professions with a mystique supported by society's belief that only certain occupational groups had the knowledge and expertise to dispense certain services. Subsequent developments in the self-help movement questioned these claims to professional exclusivity and to the value of scientific knowledge and expertise over lived experience. The movement demonstrated people's dissatisfaction with professional services and formal helping systems (Biklen, 1983; Schön, 1983). It raised questions about professional accountability and effectiveness. To whom were social workers primarily accountable: the clients who used their services, the communities they served, the organisations that paid their salaries, the profession that set practice standards, or the government that sanctioned their existence? These perplexing questions related to the values and aims of social work and its roles and responsibilities in society that created multiple levels of accountability and sometimes-competing goals. Society expected professions to ensure adherence to social norms and the laws of the country. Professions received formal sanction when their values mirrored societal values. Social work's quest for social justice and work to change unjust norms and practices supported social legislation that afforded protection for vulnerable groups and sought to right wrongs through the justice system. Thus, being part of the social structure need not have a sinister face, especially where the profession and those in power shared a similar quest for social justice.

From this historical discussion, there are two ways to examine Nigeria's path to professional recognition. The first follows Flexner's (1915) criteria approach that depends on attaining standard markers of professionalism, such as professional education programs, professional associations and regulatory bodies, qualification standards, a code of ethics, and a scientific knowledge base. Social work in Nigeria has established university-based professional education programs and has made progress in establishing curriculum standards through its Benchmark Minimum Academic Standards (BMAS) guidelines for undergraduate bachelors and masters' courses in social work (National Universities Commission, 2017). It has also established professional associations and has a growing body of scholarly literature so has some achieved hallmarks of professionalisation.

It falls short, however, on the social integration approach (Hamilton, 1976). It has yet to receive public recognition and a state-sanctioned role in social service provision. Social work in Nigeria is not alone in its struggle for professional recognition. Social workers in many parts of the world have low status, work under extreme pressure, in poorly resourced services, with poor work conditions and low wages. In many countries, the quest for professional status has proved a long and drawn-out process. For example, Malaysia embarked on an approach of legal reform in 2010 proposing a Social Workers Act to bring education and practice in line with international standards through, among other things, the registration and licensing of social workers (Teoh & Fuziah Shaffie, 2017). China followed a centralised strategy of rapid training, regulation, and registration with control of the profession vested in the government Ministry of Civil Affairs (MOCA) through standardised national curricula and professional accreditation examinations, based on state-approved social work textbooks (Meng et al., 2019, 2021; Niu & Østbø Haugen, 2019). Its quantity-then-quality approach (Ma et al., 2015) aimed to train 1.45 million social workers by 2020 (State Council, 2016) but fell short of this goal. By 2018, there were 348 Bachelor of Social Work and 150 Master of Social Work programs at Chinese universities and colleges, and 430,000 certified social workers and assistant social workers, who had passed the accreditation examination (Ministry of Civil Affairs, 2019). South Africa, like China, has a government-mandated Council for Social Service Professions that includes individual professional councils for social work and child and youth care work (Gray, 2000; Gray & Lombard, 2022). It has also developed stringent accreditation standards and professional registration requirements yet remains an under-resourced, low-paid, low-status profession (Mazibuko & Gray, 2004; Sewpaul & Lombard, 2004).

The related processes of professionalisation and legislative sanction shown in these examples are important to social work's effectiveness in social service provision. Professional sanction comes with structures and processes that embed a system of professional organisation and regulatory codes of practice to ensure the maintenance of ethical standards. Mostly, professions regulate themselves through member-supported, voluntary professional associations. However, many countries have government or private regulatory bodies to set qualifications and standards for practice (DeAngelis & Monahan, 2012; Healy, 2013; McCurdy et al., 2020; Teoh & Shaffie, 2017).

Key strategic processes for professionalisation

Registration and regulation

Government registration and regulation are two key processes for raising social workers' professional standing, ensuring effective interventions, and protecting clients from harmful practice (DeAngelis & Monahan, 2012). A profession's status becomes secure once the government or a recognised professional body assumes regulatory responsibility for defining and monitoring its role and performance, including standards of professional knowledge and practice, and professional conduct. Registration ensures title protection; it provides legal proscriptions preventing unregistered practitioners from using the title social worker (Healy, 2013). Without registration and regulation, clients have little protection from harm arising from poor practice by qualified social workers or unqualified persons calling themselves social workers (McCurdy et al., 2020). Nigerian social work's attempts to achieve professional legitimacy, led to the legitimation of two regulatory bodies:

1   The Chartered Institute of Social Work Practitioners of Nigeria (C-ISOWN) (the Institute),when the government passed the Chartered Institute of Social Work Practitioners (Establishment) Act No. 25, August 2022 (FRN, 2022b).
2   National Council of Social Work (NCSW), when the President approved the NASoW-supported National Council for Social Work [Establishment] Act No. 40, December 2022.

In terms of Act 25 of 2022, membership of C-ISOWN (the Institute) included social workers and professionals in related fields, such as community development, adult education, sociology, psychology, and medical social welfare, provided that potential registrants possessed adequate interest in, and knowledge and understanding of, social work and related matters, with corporate membership for ministries, departments, agencies, or companies. Membership categories included fellow, full member, member, and associate member. The Institute was responsible for the registration and disciplinary conduct of practitioners, including criminal procedures, if necessary. It would also maintain a physical and online library comprising books and publications for the advancement of social work knowledge. The C-ISOWN legislation provided title protection, reserving use of the title 'Social worker' to professionals who had passed its Social Work Proficiency Certificate Examination (SWPCE) and who, following induction (taking an oath of Professional Membership), gained admission to the Institute's Register. According to this legislation:

'Social worker' means a person who is deemed to be a professional social worker, if registered and trained specifically in social work disciplines to:

a   build partnerships among other professionals working within the field of psychosocial intervention, caregivers, and families.
b   collaborate with the community, usually with the goal of creating supportive environments for clients or service users.
c   advocate for adequate service, treatment models and resources.
d   change social policy to address issues of poverty, employment, housing, and social justice.
e   supporting the development of preventive programs for the less privilege (pp. A814–A815).

Act 40 of 2022 charged the NCSW board with the general administration and management of social work, including the development of a professional code of ethics. The board would comprise representatives from professional social work associations, including NASoW, AMSWAN, NASWE, and ISOWN, the NGO and CSO sectors, and government ministries and departments for social investment, employment, labour, productivity, social development, and social welfare services. Its precursor, the Social Work Bill passed by the General Assembly in 2019, defined a social worker as 'a person trained and certified to practice' (in terms of the Social Work Act No. 25 of 2022):

> Helping people with interpersonal problems … offering help to families in dispute, juvenile delinquent(s), destitute [persons, people with disabilities, orphans, the sick, mentally retarded and disorderly persons, persons in conflict with the law and other vulnerable and disadvantaged groups (p. 5).

While C-ISOWN was a private enterprise, the NASoW-supported NCSW would be a quasi Federal Government body, with a government-appointed governing body regulating its activities (Badru, 2022). The Social Work Act No. 25 of 2022 would provide the legal framework for the regulation, legalisation, monitoring, and control of the activities of social workers in the country, while in terms of Act No. 40 of 2022, the National Council bore the major responsibility for promoting professional social work practice, in keeping with the profession's ethics and values, and determining professional standards relating to knowledge and skill requirements for social workers.

Relevance

Relevance rests on the idea that social work derives legitimacy from its fulfilment of socially accepted values, responsiveness to local people's interests and priorities, and role in implementing social policy and enhancing the use of social services. It necessarily involves culturally responsive practice compatible with Nigerian traditions, values, and norms and indigenous ways of assisting vulnerable people (Amadasun, 2021a; Anucha, 2008a, 2008b; Odiah, 1991; Ogundipe & Edewor, 2012). However, as already noted, it has proved extremely difficult to unseat colonial social welfare policies and structures and disembed inherently Eurocentric methods of helping unresponsive to local sociocultural mores and complexities. Beyond cultural responsiveness, to enhance their relevance, social workers need to engage with 'broader issues of sustainable human development and the social and political factors – patriarchy, corruption, political conflict, and gender, ethnic, and religious discrimination – that serve as barriers to human and social wellbeing' (Ugiagbe, 2017, p. 272).

Recognition

Recognition depends largely on social work's relevance and usefulness in society, which, in turn, determines the extent to which families and communities value and use social work services and government supports its activities. Such public recognition has eluded social work in Nigeria (Anucha, 2008a, 2008b). A necessary first step in getting Nigerians to use social work services is to create public awareness and understanding of social work. To do this, social work must promote a clear, unified message about what social workers do.

Factors affecting recognition

DEFINITION OF SOCIAL WORK

For the social work profession, recognition requires acceptance of its definition of social work as a professional activity conducted by social workers with a university qualification in social work. This is a global standard of social work education and a professional requirement for social work practice and now a legislative provision in Nigeria. This sets a precedent for large sections of the Nigerian services workforce, who were untrained and not professionally qualified, to meet legislative professional qualification requirements if they wished to use the title 'Social Worker'. In effect, this excluded large sections of the workforce, without access to tertiary education, from using this title (Badru, 2011). The legislation, nevertheless, brought greater regulation of the profession and an enforcement of codes of conduct and practice, bringing social work into line with international ethical standards. Prior to this legislation, anyone could 'practice or teach social work thereby making it impossible for real social workers to be taken seriously' (Onalu & Okoye, 2021, p. 581). There would, however, inevitably be a transition process in the multidisciplinary melting pot in which social workers plied their trade, where 'lived experience' was a valuable commodity. In a populous country, like Nigeria, a large percentage of the population, who had little or no access to tertiary education and were highly unlikely to achieve professional qualifications, nevertheless, made a valuable contribution to community development and service provision, many in a voluntary role. Class, gender, race, ethnicity, culture, religion, and privilege were all factors in access to professional education and promotional opportunities, where men had a distinct advantage over women. Thus, standards relating to the professional title might not address the dearth of trained social workers. China circumvented this problem by identifying three broad 'categories' of social work that had developed historically: (i) general social work performed mainly by community members and volunteers, (ii) administrative social work carried out by public officials, and (iii) professional social work involving social workers and assistant social workers certified by the Ministry of Civil Affairs (Wang, 2013a, 2013b). Nigeria's definition pertains only to the latter certified by C-ISOWN (FRN, 2022b). Section 34 of the Chartered Institute of Social Work Practitioners (Establishment) Act, 2022 (FRN, 2022b) defined 'social work' as:

> An applied or behavioral profession that simply promotes human rights, social justice, peace and conflict resolutions, engendering social change, problem solving and sustainable development in human relationships focusing on empowerment and liberation of people and enhancing the well-being of individuals, family, groups and communities, and utilising theories of human behavior and social systems (p. A814).

CLOSE TIES TO WELFARE

In most Western and colonial countries, social work evolved with close ties to social welfare and, in the case of Nigeria, to colonial administrations that greatly benefitted the middle class. However, Nigeria did not have a state-supported social welfare system (Anucha, 2008a). The central government designed the tripartite Federal Ministry of Social Development, Youth and Sports in 1972 to police and control voluntary welfare services and youth organisations, and national and international organisations (Ogundipe & Edewor, 2012). There were no state services for vulnerable people, including children, older people, and people with disabilities, hence Nigeria's reliance on voluntary, private, and faith-based non-government organisations (Garcia-Zamor, 2015). AIDS and HIV interventions and international poverty alleviation goals had brought huge injections in foreign aid for early childhood and school education and services for orphaned and vulnerable children, mostly through non-government organisations. In most cases, social workers worked in a multidisciplinary environment where they received variable degrees of recognition that kept them away from the frontline of service delivery.

LACK OF GOVERNMENT SANCTION AND CONFUSION ON SOCIAL WORK'S REMIT

The Nigerian government's unsupportive attitude towards social work and underfunding of social welfare services constituted a major obstacle for the profession (Akintayo, 2021; Idyorough, 2013; Onalu et al., 2020). The profession's lack of clarity on its scope, focus, functions, and roles worked against its legitimation (Amadasun, 2021a; Busari, 2019; Ogbonna, 2018). Part of the profession's confusion over its roles and responsibilities related to its broad ambit and internal wrangling over its micro (casework) and macro (community and social development) foci. The former carried the weight of colonial remedial predilections, and the latter reflected the thrust of non-government, private, voluntary organisations (Amadasun, 2021a). Social work education in Nigeria prepared practitioners mainly for casework practice dealing with personal problems and left them ill prepared for macro social problems and social development (Amadasun, 2019, 2020; Onalu et al., 2020; Ugiagbe, 2017). As shown in the social integration approach to professionalisation, professional recognition rested on social work's ability to carve out an exclusive professional service domain that, in turn, rested on the projection of a positive image of a profession united on its remit, roles, responsibilities, and goals. Amadasun's (2021a) study of public perceptions found a fair degree of understanding of what social workers did, though the profession needed to do more to enhance the public's awareness of its ideals, values, and contribution to Nigerian society. Establishing the public's trust in social workers was fundamental to the quest for professional recognition. The unprofessional and unethical conduct of 'social workers', who had not received professional training in social work, worked against this goal (Idyorough, 2013). Legislative provisions were only a first step in establishing professional recognition, however.

PROFESSIONAL DIVISION

There were several professional representative associations in Nigeria, including the Nigerian Association of Social Workers (NASoW), the Association of Medical Social Workers of Nigeria (AMSWON), and the Nigerian Association of Social Work Educators (NASWE) now the Association of Social Work Educators in Nigeria (ASWEN) (Mbah et al., 2017). The NASoW umbrella's support for a bill to establish a National Council of Social Work (NCSW) to oversee standards for professional education and practice and qualification requirements had been long in the making though events gained momentum in 2017, when it appealed to the National Assembly to accelerate the passage of the Social Work Bill (Guardian, 2021). Rather than direct government representation, NASoW's President made this appeal through the national media, in an interview with the News Agency of Nigeria in Lagos. Meanwhile, the competing Chartered Institute of Social Work Practitioners of Nigeria (C-ISOWN) that promoted different political interests and called for a Chartered Institute of Social Work Practitioners bill made direct representation to the government. Many expressed concerns about this threat to professional unity (Amadasun, 2021a, 2021b; Idyorough, 2013). In 2018, a further appeal to the country's President came from a group of professionally trained social workers across Nigeria called the Forum of Concerned Professional and Trained Social Workers in Nigeria (FCPTSWN) that expressed its solidarity with

NASoW, NASWE, AMSWON, and other professional representative bodies. Again, its representative lodged the appeal through the media calling on Nigerians to support the Social Work Bill, while criticising C-ISOWN's attempt to hijack the process and advance its position to control and regulate the profession of social work and its practitioners through a Chartered Institute of Social Work Practitioners bill. Competition of this nature generated by opposing political interests led to confusion and undermined social work's quest for recognition. FCPTSWN petitioned the President and key state functionaries to block C-ISOWN's competing bill introduced in the Federal House of Representatives. It called on relevant agencies to consider its petition and support the Social Work Bill the Nigerian Senate had passed in December 2017 but which the President had blocked in February 2018. Subsequent appeals and media statements were ignored, due partly to social work's lack of professional representation on essential decision-making structures and the politicking of competing interest groups. Finally, on August 29, 2022, the Senior Special Assistant to the President on National Assembly Matters (House of Representatives) issued the following statement:

> The Chartered Institute of Social Work Practitioners Act 2022 establishes the Institute of Social Work Practitioners charged with the responsibility for training and registration of persons aspiring to become Social Work Practitioners in Nigeria and determine the standards of knowledge and skill to be attained by persons seeking to become registered as chartered social work practitioners, and raise the standards as circumstances may permit, among others.
>
> (Sule, 2022, n.p.)

Then, on Tuesday, December 6, 2022, the President finally signed the National Council for Social Work [Establishment] Bill 2022 into law. This effectively legitimated two regulatory bodies, the NCSW and C-ISOWN, the former a quasi-government body and the latter a private enterprise.

Representation

Competing professional bodies representing the profession potentially weakened the profession's power to influence government decisions. The protracted process surrounding the Social Work Bill showed that social work's professional representative groups had to strengthen their power to influence the passage of key legislation. To have a unified voice on future developments, it was imperative that social work's professional bodies worked in unison with one another. To exercise their influence, social workers needed to have a seat at the decision-making table. This meant a social work presence on agency boards and committees, local community forums, and government advisory and decision-making structures. Through these structures, social workers needed to take a stand on professional standards for education and practice. They needed to take a strategic approach to ensure their political representation at various levels, seeking influential positions on government, organisational, and community decision-making structures.

Relational connection

Folgheraiter's (2004) theory of relational connection highlights the importance of the social networks to which social workers connect themselves. His relational approach sees social work as a social process concerned with identifying problems in coping, finding solutions, and creating the relational conditions necessary for change at various levels (Folgheraiter, 2004, 2007). Not only is this important in social workers' practice interventions that give them the visibility and presence in local communities so pivotal to recognition, but also to the structures on which they seek representation to further client interests. In short, social work's relevance, drive for recognition, and responsiveness to people's needs and interests depend largely on its relational connections with the clients and communities it serves. Visible community support is one of the factors that would enhance the likelihood of public sanction. Relationships are central to social work at every level of practice. They require presence and visibility. They require that people know where to find social workers. They require that social workers develop a sound reputation through respectful relationships with their clients and each other.

Ugiagbe and Eweka's (2014) analysis of systematic oppression among Nigeria's minorities highlighted the political, economic, and cultural pressures and leadership failures that made *coping* impossible for vulnerable groups, whose problems lay in social relationships and societal processes that led to systemic and institutional oppression. Sociocultural and ethnoreligious heritage sustained unjust practices and policies that enhanced the domination and exploitations of vulnerable members of Nigerian society with whom social workers worked. Privileged groups within the three major ethnic groups and religious bigots, among others, sustained the systemic oppression and social exclusion of women, older people, and ethnic minorities. To combat systematic oppression, social workers needed to establish inter-professional connections and engage with human rights activists and non-governmental organisations engaged in sustained advocacy for policy reform. They needed to engage in public education campaigns and make media statements aimed at changing damaging social perceptions of excluded groups. Social workers would enhance their visibility and presence in local communities by establishing and engaging in social networks of this nature. This was not only pivotal to professional recognition, but also to representing the interests of excluded groups.

Rights

Challenging systematic oppression required social workers with a sound knowledge and understanding of the profession's human rights and social justice foundations (Onalu & Okoye, 2021; Ugiagbe & Eweka, 2014). Chapter 2 listed the human rights charters to which Nigeria was a signatory, but as noted through various chapters, attendant domestic policies were absent or inadequate, and many were never enacted in law. Even when there were laws, these were not uniformly implemented across the 36 states, as shown by the discussion of the Child Rights Law in Chapter 4. Social work education has a key role to play in educating social workers on social policy and policy-making processes, as well as knowledge of the root causes of, and strategies and skills to address, injustice, inequalities, exploitation, and oppression (Onalu & Okoye, 2021). The roots of injustice lay in the patriarchal nature of Nigerian society, where traditional, cultural, and religious beliefs supported the subjugation and marginalisation of women and minority groups. Addressing myriad injustices lay in anti-oppressive rights-based practice, advocacy, and social action (Atumah et al., 2019; Onalu & Okoye, 2021; Ugiagbe & Eweka, 2014). Social workers challenged social injustices and rights violations *inter alia* through their engagement in policy processes, conscientisation, public education, and legal redress, working in concert with key stakeholders, networks, and interest groups.

Research and theory

Social work education and practice in Nigeria has yet to harness local literature on related issues outside the conventional social work domain of social welfare, especially relating to national development and sociological analyses of social problems. Further, there is a growing local literature providing cultural analyses to inform culturally appropriate social work practice, as shown throughout this book. Local research, or research on Nigerian issues and problems, offers a rich source of knowledge for those seeking culturally relevant approaches that would enhance people's responsiveness to social work services. An important aspect of a profession is its grounding in a systematic, scientific body of knowledge and theory to teach aspiring professionals and guide qualified practitioners. Sound research and scholarly publications on social work's role and contribution in Nigerian society would greatly enhance social work's professional standing. Research is also essential to effective practice. Basing social work interventions on sound evidence furthers trust in social work's effectiveness and usefulness in society. Theories of human behaviour and society offer diverse explanations of the causes of human and social problems and provide a perspective on what to do to enhance human coping and change oppressive systems and practices. The following discussion highlights local literature on contexts of social work practice in Nigeria and theories in use to guide practice.

Contemporary social work practice

Over the years, criticisms of social work centred on its overuse of the remedial casework model and neglect of structural issues. Western psychosocial models of generalist practice with their person-in-environment perspective continue to dominate, especially in clinical practice settings, along with strengths-based approaches drawing on the strengths and resilience of individuals, families, groups, and communities and the theory of social capital (Amadasun, 2020a Ugiagbe & Okaka, 2014). Other models include:

- Anti-oppressive practice to challenge discriminatory social policies and practices (Amadasun & Omorogiuwa, 2020; Ugiagbe & Eweka, 2014).
- Feminist approaches to challenge the systemic exclusion of women (Uchendu et al., 2019).
- Rights-based practice to challenge social injustice and advance the rights of vulnerable groups (Amadasun, 2020b; Atumah et al., 2019; Onalu & Okoye, 2021).
- Culturally relevant interventions to enhance practice relevance by drawing on, and reinforcing, indigenous values of mutual coexistence, collective responsibility, and respect for diversity (Okoye & Eromosele, 2013; Udeani, 2019; Ugiagbe, 2015).

Nwatu et al. (2020) claimed that social workers had paid little to no attention to the role of spirituality and religion in practice, especially with regard to sorcery and witchcraft, which led to the stigmatisation and ostracisation of Nigerians living with disabilities, AIDS and HIV, and mental illness, among other issues. They described this practice within Edo culture, where people attributed the 'origins of strange diseases, sudden deaths, accidents, childlessness, impotence, and other misfortunes to witchcraft' (Nwatu et al., 2020, p. 515). They perceived a role for social workers in raising awareness of, and educating people about, the negative impacts of violence against those falsely accused of witchcraft to change harmful erroneous supernatural beliefs. Other social work studies on witchcraft included Archibong et al.'s (2017) investigation on its impact on pregnant women in Calabar, South Cross River State's belief of supernatural causes of illness found they had a strong impact on their health-seeking behaviour and led to high rates of morbidity and mortality in infants and mothers. Eboiyehi (2017) reported that the persecution of older persons accused of witchcraft continued unabated in Nigeria, with suspected elderly witches 'often seen walking around … destitute [and] without any permanent home' (p. 27). However, social work scholars have addressed ethnocultural considerations more generally, such as issues relating to traditional medicine and indigenous healing practices (Abdullahi, 2011).

There is a lack of social work presence in several key areas, once the domain of colonial social welfare, including adult corrections, juvenile justice, and child protection (Atilola et al., 2017, 2019; Holmes & Akinrimisi, 2012; Osayi, 2015; Sa'ad, 2008; Yekini & Salisu, 2013). As regards adult probation and corrections, Osayi (2015) claimed there were no social workers employed in this sector. The recently created Federal Ministry of Humanitarian Affairs, Disaster Management and Social Development and Ministry of Women Affairs and Social Development both have social work portfolios. The former situates social workers' role in humanitarian interventions, such as emergency responses to disasters; humanitarian efforts to combat human trafficking; assistance to migrants, refuges, displaced people, and victims of torture and violence; and emergency child protections responses. The latter cements social work's role in furthering women's interests and contributing to social development. Temilola's (2020) study of social workers' (n=24) employed in the Ministry of Women's Affairs found their domestic violence interventions involved counselling, referral, and, to a lesser degree, alternative dispute resolution. They also conducted annual sensitisation programs to enhance community awareness of domestic violence. However, due to the absence of government service provision, social workers were most likely to encounter and work with human trafficking victims, migrants, refuges, and displaced people, and victims of torture and violence in non-government and faith-based organisations.

Though several social work scholars have a background in gerontological social work, there was very little literature on social workers working in aged care, beyond encountering older people in health settings. Okoye (2019) noted that government health facilities employed social workers, as did a few state-government tertiary health services, while Ogbonna (2017) noted that social welfare services reached 'less than 5% of vulnerable people in government hospitals' (p. 101).

As shown in Chapter 5, Amadasun (2020a) claimed that, although social workers had been at the forefront of delivering social services to people with disabilities in Nigeria over the years, there was very little literature or research on the nature and context of this work. His study of social workers (n=7) in a not-for-profit non-government organisation found that social work rehabilitation services involved counselling and the organisation of recreational activities, while noting the abandonment of education and empowerment programs to improve the lives of people with disabilities.

There was some mention of developmental and rural social work to alleviate poverty, promote socioeconomic development and regional integration, and reduce spatial inequalities (Amadasun, 2019; Ugiagbe, 2017; Ugiagbe & Vincent-Osaghae, 2014). Yet none of the articles the authors' reviewed moved beyond mention of various models in passing or hortatory invocations that 'social work could or should play an important role in … '. There was little concrete description or analysis of social work practice applying these models in local contexts or research on their effectiveness. The ongoing Western influence suggests most social workers work in cosmopolitan areas in clinical contexts, where they use casework or, more specifically, psychosocial interventions and, to a lesser extent, group and community work. Overall, descriptions of contemporary social work practice drew heavily on international literature showing the continued influence of Western social work theory and practice in Nigeria (Amadasun, 2020a; Atumah et al., 2019; Chukwu et al., 2017; Ebue et al., 2017; Mojoyinola, 2006; Okoye, 2009, 2015; Osayi, 2015; Udeani, 2019; Ugiagbe, 2015).

Conclusion

The brief overview of literature pertaining to social work practice shows social work's minimal presence in several long-established contexts, such as corrections, juvenile justice, and child protection. This chapter discussed key processes by which professions generally gained legitimation and, through the R-lexicon, pointed to key strategic processes to advance the profession's interests through:

1   Structures for *registration and regulation* to legitimate social work and ensure the maintenance of ethical practice standards, as these two key processes would ensure effective interventions and protect clients from harmful practice, thus raising social workers' professional standing.
2   Increased local content in the social work curriculum to enhance the profession's *relevance* and culturally responsive practice. Social workers could do this by engaging with broader national development issues and considering culturally appropriate ways of addressing social and political factors that hamper human wellbeing and social development.
3   Unified statements on the scope and domain of social work, its roles and responsibilities in Nigerian society and contribution to social welfare to increase professional *recognition* and attain public sanction. Social workers need to ensure that families and communities, and government officials, that value and use their services raise awareness of the important role social work plays in Nigerian society
4   A strategic approach to harness social workers' political leverage at various levels and gain influential positions on government, organisational, and community decision-making structures to increase professional *representation*.
5   Key strategic networks to enhance *relational connections*, such as inter-professional service platforms, advocacy fora, and government advisory bodies. Their presence and visibility on these fora offer social workers the opportunity to raise awareness of their role and location in social systems and develop a sound reputation through respectful relationships with others.
6   Promoting human *rights* and challenging systematic oppression by equipping social workers with knowledge of the root causes of, and strategies and skills to address, social injustices and inequalities. Social workers do this through their engagement in policy processes, conscientisation, public education, and legal redress, working in concert with key stakeholders, networks, and client interest groups.
7   *Research* to provide evidence of social work's effectiveness, enhance trust in its usefulness in Nigerian society, and provide culturally appropriate theories of how to proceed towards greater human rights observance and taking social justice seriously.

The chapter argued that these measures would go some way to address the deep-rooted political and sociocultural barriers impeding social work's push for professional recognition, with legislation an important first step. It discerned the importance of social networks and concerted action of key stakeholders to help the profession navigate the complex and tumultuous politicking hampering its advancement. A lack of clarity on the profession's remit, roles, and responsibilities ostensibly thwarted its progress. This hearkened back to Flexner's criticism that social work's wide and unspecific aims watered down its value and weakened its power. With the goal of legitimation now achieved, the divisive processes surrounding the passage of the Social Work Acts No. 25 and 40 of 2022 pointed to the need for social work's professional bodies to build bridges and establish strong networks to project a united front in the interests of the future development of the profession. The following chapter shows social work education's efforts to enhance professional relevance and recognition.

9 Enhancing the relevance of social work education

The chapter discusses social work education and the work of Nigeria's universities to create curricula with indigenous content relevant to Nigerian society. It provides suggestions to enhance the relevance of social work education, including agreement on the profession's remit, educational standards, systematic curriculum revision, cultural relevance, a developmental perspective, fieldwork, and digital connectivity. It highlights the National Universities Commission (NUC) role in course accreditation and curriculum review and challenges for social work educators, not least the provision of concrete practice examples for use in teaching. This chapter argues that relevance requires curriculum revision and renewal, and the integration of a developmental perspective. It suggests that, where possible, greater use of online digital resources, for communication, networking, and online learning, would greatly enhance processes to achieve greater relevance in social work education.

Not only is locally relevant social work education essential to Nigerian social work's struggle for professional recognition and public legitimacy, but it is also pivotal to efficient and effective service delivery and the profession's responsiveness to myriad social issues warranting skilled intervention. Put another way, social workers' responsiveness and effectiveness depends on the quality and relevance of the education they receive at the start and throughout their professional careers. Given the pivotal role of social work education in preparing Nigeria's social workers for practice, it could be a major force in enhancing the profession's cultural responsiveness across Nigeria's ethnoreligiously and socio-economically diverse sub-regions. This chapter examines social work education, its relatively recent origins, and issues in contemporary Nigerian society highlighting the ongoing need for sociocultural relevance in the interests of professional recognition. It proposes that social work educators and administrators have a crucial role to play in enhancing the profession's relevance and suggests a way forward.

As noted in Chapter 1, issues of relevance were first raised further north, by the UN Regional Adviser on Social Welfare, Professor Abdul Muneim Shawky, from Egypt, in his seminal work that sparked the indigenisation movement in Africa (Shawky, 1972). Ragab (2017) described Shawky as 'unique among his

DOI: 10.4324/9781003382126-9

generation of pioneers in Egyptian social work education, all of whom were well-respected scholars who had graduated from renowned US universities' (p. 33). He recounted that Professor Shawky inspired a strong spirit of confidence in young academics, who questioned imported social work models that 'many thought had indisputable validity' (Ragab, 2017, p. 33). Thus, Africa's movement on indigenisation began.

African indigenisation scholars have long called for a critical interrogation of imported theories and models, questioning their fit with local sociocultural realities (Gray, 2017; Gray et al., 2008, 2013). Gray et al. (2014) outlined the difficulties the Association for Social Work Education in Africa (ASWEA) experienced in its attempts to indigenise social work education in Africa between 1971 and 1989. Nigerian scholars have highlighted that the lack of indigenous content in the social work curriculum raised questions about social work's compatibility with embedded traditional beliefs and practices, and its resonance with Nigerian families and communities (Odiah, 1991; Ugiagbe, 2015, 2017). However, it has proved extremely difficult to supplant Western curriculum content, despite ongoing attempts at indigenisation to enhance its relevance (Levy et al., 2022; Okoye, 2014; Ugiagbe, 2015, 2017; Ugiagbe & Ugiagbe, 2015). Ekoh and Agbawodikeizu (2022) found that social work educators' indigenisation efforts had failed because of irreconcilable differences between professional values and principles and local cultural and religious beliefs. As Ugiagbe (2017) observed, 'international frameworks have proved remarkably resilient and impervious to cultural transformation' (p. 272) and continue to dominate across Nigeria's diverse sociocultural contexts. He called for a move to a decolonising approach that engaged with local cultures and traditions and harnessed local cultural practices to positive ends. This chapter argues that social work education should be at the forefront of this change.

Social work education in Nigeria

As noted in Chapter 2, formal social work education in Nigeria is a relatively recent phenomenon beginning in 1976 at the University of Nigeria, Nsukka (UNN). Its aim at the time, as applied to many public education programs, was to train middle-level managers to run social welfare departments (Mbah et al., 2017). Following UNN, the University of Benin (UNIBEN) established a social work unit in the Department of Sociology and Anthropology in 1979. The quality of these education programs varied greatly and had a sociological emphasis, since most faculty members were sociologists (Ogundipe & Ediwor, 2012). For example, the Nsukka undergraduate social work curriculum included an introduction to sociology and anthropology, ethnocultural relations, demography, social deviance, social statistics, and social research methods. There was a heavy emphasis on social problems, deviance, and criminology to prepare social workers for work in juvenile justice and the correctional field. Given the casework focus, there were also courses on marriage and family, including family planning. Okoye (2013) noted that there was little understanding of the nature of social work and many students found it easier to say that they were studying sociology in the early days. Further, many of the pioneering academics had received their professional social work education abroad, though, generally, it was difficult to find qualified teaching staff, non-Western literature, and local case examples.

As education and knowledge dissemination became a highly lucrative and competitive field in neoliberal economic systems like Nigeria, without regulation, the number of institutions, schools, and programs offering social work grew exponentially making it difficult to find accurate information. Canavera et al. (2020) provided the first comprehensive study showing the diverse range, level, and quality of social work training provided under public and private auspices. They concluded that, while universities and polytechnics provided a range of social work, administration, welfare, and development programs, the lack of consistency and clarity in social workers' job descriptions and legal mandates posed a challenge for social work education and ongoing professional development in Nigeria. They also found that outside of established institutions, international agencies tended to provide *ad hoc*, short-term, issue-based training through NGOs and CBOs that focused on their priorities. They included *inter alia* children's rights, gender-based violence, identifying and caring for orphans and vulnerable children, child trafficking, HIV and AIDS, child protection, and child labour. Aimed at preparing workers, often volunteers, to carry out 'specific tasks on behalf of international NGOs and [the] UN and government agencies' (Canavera et al., 2020, p. 89), these training programs rarely included basic social work skills, principles, and approaches or addressed local realities. Hence, Canavera et al. (2020) found 'few examples of culturally adapted training materials for workers at all levels' (p. 89). They concluded that 'abbreviated training of this nature results in a piecemeal approach to education, precluding holistic understanding of key issues and solutions' (p. 90). Thus, when describing their daily work, they found Nigerian social workers could not provide examples of training or coursework that helped in their daily decision-making, despite the National Universities Commission's (NUC) (2007) mandate for five-yearly curriculum reviews to accommodate broader changes. Idyorough (2013) saw the NUC's initiative to develop benchmark minimum academic standards for undergraduate social work as an important development. It bolstered the National Board for Technical Education's (NBTE) initiatives to develop a standardised curriculum for the national diploma in social administration, as well as specialisations in social welfare, community development, youth development, and home management in the higher diploma. These developments were ongoing. Following a two-day Stakeholders' Workshop organised by the Twinning for Health Support Initiative, a non-government organisation, working in collaboration with the NUC, several Nigerian universities, and the Federal Ministry of Women Affairs and Social Development, the NUC (2017) reviewed the minimum standards for undergraduate and postgraduate social work programs. Representatives for social work came from three Northern – Federal University of Lafia (ULAFIA), University of Jos (UJ), and University of Ilorin (UNILORIN) – and two Southern – UNN and University of Calibar (UC) – universities. Consequently, five-yearly accreditation reviews needed to demonstrate adherence to the standards for, and progress in, indigenising the curriculum (Onalu & Okoye, 2021).

We found it difficult to find accurate information on social work education providers. Table 9.1 shows the auspices and location of those we identified. Most (n=10) were in the Northern regions. Five were in the Southern regions, with four private programs in the wealthy South West. We did not find any universities offering social work in the impoverished and conflict-ridden North East.

An examination of NUC's (2017) curriculum guidelines for undergraduate degrees in social work, shown in Table 9.2, revealed a packed curriculum with relatively little content focused directly on socioculturally responsive interventions until the fourth year, though there was plenty of content contributing to knowledge to inform this. Each two-unit course involved two-hour weekly lectures over a 14-week semester. The description of the course on the history of social work revealed grounding in social work's roots in Britain and the USA and an emphasis on the Poor Laws and Charity Organisation Society (COS) rather than traditional indigenous ways of helping. The course traced social work's colonial origins and introduced fields of practice and issues pertaining to the social work profession and social welfare services (government and voluntary) in contemporary Nigeria. The social work theories and models covered included problem solving, psychosocial, functional, behaviour therapy, crisis intervention, and the four systems (presumably the ecosystems perspective). The areas covered in the values and ethics course were individualisation, acceptance, controlled emotional involvement, non-judgmental attitude, client-self-determination, confidentiality, interviewing processes, intervention models, directive and non-directive approaches, needs assessment, participation, collective responsibility, communication and recording, hinting at a strong casework focus. There remained a heavy clinical psychodynamic focus through courses on psychology for social work. Community needs assessment and development focused on the relationship between adult education and development. Two courses focused on Nigeria, its people's and cultures and structures and the course on group dynamics and intergroup relations covered core material for culturally relevant practice, relating to cultures, ethnicities, ideologies, and religions in a plural Nigeria. Also most relevant was the level 4 course on cross-cultural social work and cultural diversity using comparative examples from Western and non-Western cultures. Various courses covered contexts of practice, though many were electives. There was a broad array of courses with care taken not to omit anything that might be important. The key issue for a culturally relevant curriculum is the extent to which course content draws on local literature and case examples and prepares students for practice responsive to local realities.

Table 9.1 Institutions offering social work education and related programs

Institution	Auspices	Region	Programs and courses
University of Benin (UNIBEN), Department of Social Work	Public	South South	Part- and full-time undergraduate BSc (SW) and postgraduate MSc (SW) https://uniben.edu.ng/social-work/?nwp_faculty=88
University of Calabar (UC), Department of Social Work			Four-year full-time undergraduate BSc (SW) and MSc (Social Work) http://www.unical.edu.ng/department/department-of-social-work
University of Port Harcourt (UNIPORT), Department of Sociology			Four-year BSc (SW) and one-year MSc (SW) https://news.iu.edu/live/news/27671-iu-helping-establish-first-social-work-program-in
University of Ilorin (UNILORIN), Department of Social Work	Public	North Central	Full-time BSc (SW) and MSc (SW) http://socialsciences.unilorin.edu.ng/social-work
University of Jos (UJ)			Bachelors, masters, and PhD degrees in social work
Federal University, Lafia (FULAFIA), Department of Sociology			Four-year BSc (SW) https://fulafia.edu.ng/departments.php?page=sow
Nigeria Police Academy, Wudil (NPA/POLAC)	Public	North West	Coursework on child-friendly policing integrated into the curriculum
Kaduna Polytechnic (KP), Department of Social Development			Offers 13 programs, including a Diploma in Medical Social Work https://www.kadunapoly.edu.ng/departments-page.php?token=6921476=d=d9083l067&tokeni=40&token=69214176=d=d9083l067
Afe Babalola University, College of Social and Management Sciences, Department of Media, Communication and Social Studies	Private	South West	Four-year Bachelor of Sociology and Social Work
Obafemi Awolowo University, Ife Ife			Postgraduate Diploma in Social Work and Social Development

Institution	Type	Region	Programme
Redeemer's University, Nigeria (RUN), Department of Behavioural Studies			Postgraduate Diploma in Social Work https://run.edu.ng/post-graduate-programmes/
Babcock University (BU), Ilishan-Remo, Department of Social Work and Human Services			Four-year BSc (SW) https://www.babcock.edu.ng/school/VASS/dept/social-work
Lead City University (LCU), Ibadan	Public		BSc (SW) https://lcu.edu.ng/index.php/template/typography/overview
University of Lagos (UNILAG), Department of Social Work and Community Development	Public		Four-year BSc (SW) (through entrance exam), Postgraduate Diploma (PGD), Master of Science (MSc) and Doctor of Philosophy (PhD) degrees in social work https://staffprofile.unilag.edu.ng/?person_rareas=social-work
University of Ibadan (UI), Department of Social Work			Part- and full-time undergraduate BSc (SW) and MSc (SW) https://www.ui.edu.ng/socwor
University of Nigeria, Nsukka (UNN), Department of Social Work	Public	South East	Four-year Bachelor of Social Work and Community Development, MSc (by research), and PhD (Social Work) https://www.unn.edu.ng/department-of-social-work/#
Ebonyi State University (EBSU), Abakiliki, Department of Social Work			BSc (SW) https://ebsu.edu.ng/facultyscience/index.html#
Federal College of Dental Technology and Therapy, Enugu (FEDCODTTEN)			Five-year BTech Public Health Social Work and Certificate Course in Auxiliary Social Work, commencing in 2023

Table 9.2 BMAS guidelines for undergraduate courses

BMAS Curriculum guidelines for undergraduate courses (2 units per course except where otherwise specified) (n=148 units)

	Year 1: Semester 1 (22 units)	Year 2: Semester 1 (18 units)	Year 3: Semester 1 (17 units)	Year 4: Semester 1 (19 units)
Core	Communication in English	Peace and Conflict Management	Field Work Practicum I – 3 units	Project Seminar
	Use of Library, Study Skills and Information and Communication Technology (ICT)	History of Social Work	Entrepreneurship Development II	Field Work Practicum II – 3 units
	Nigerian Peoples and Culture	Social Work Theories	Social Work Research Methods I	Social Work Intervention with Individual and Families
	Introduction to Computer	Social Statistics I	Community Development	Conflict Analysis and Management
	Introduction to Social Work and Welfare	Social Work Principles, Ethics and Values	Child and Maternal Welfare Services	Social Group Work
	Introduction to Indigenous Social Welfare	Social Psychology		Child Development
		Substance/Drug Abuse		Gerontology and Geriatric Social Work
Required	Introduction to Sociology I		Sociology of Crime and Delinquency	
Elective (x 2)	Introduction to Anthropology Introduction to Psychology I Introduction to Business	Moral Philosophy and Discipline	Women and Social Policy	Social Work with Women
	Economic Theory/Principles I	Principles and Techniques of Management	Housing and Urban Environment	Social Work with Disaster Victims

	Year 1: Semester 2 (18 units)	Year 2: Semester 2 (18 units)	Year 3: Semester 2 (18 units)	Year 4: Semester 2 (18 units)
	Introduction to Law I Introduction to Political Science I Religion and Human Values	History of Social Thought Nigerian Social Structure	Law and Welfare Rights The Political Economy of Social Welfare Social Work and Environmental Protection Contemporary Sociological Theories Sociology of Education	Social Work with Minorities Social Work in Rural Environment Social Work with Children and Youth
Core	Use of English II History and Philosophy of Science Logic, Philosophy, and Human Existence Field Visits in Areas of Social Work Practice Civic Education and Nation Building	Entrepreneurship Development I Community Needs Assessment and Development/Organisation Psychology for Social Work Academic Writing Communication Skills in Social Work Death, Loss, Grief, and Rehabilitation Social Statistics II	Social Problems and Social Work Social Work Research Methods II Reproductive Health and Population Studies Group Dynamics and Intergroup Relations	Research Project – 4 units Comparative/Cross Cultural Social Work Social Work and Rehabilitation School Social Work Medical and Clinical Social Work Forensic Social Work
Required	Introduction to Sociology II Introduction to Psychology II		Human Sexuality and Social Work Social Security Services and Insurance Social Policy, Legislation and Administration	

(Continued)

Table 9.2 (Continued)

BMAS Curriculum guidelines for undergraduate courses (2 units per course except where otherwise specified) (n=148 units)			
Electives (x 2)	Social Deviance and Social organisation	Food and Nutrition in Nigeria	Social Work and Mental Health	Social Work and the Law
	Introduction to African Societies	Industrial/Organisational Social Welfare	Sports and Recreational Services	Social Work and Migration
	Introduction to Business	Sociology of the Family	Social Work and Diseases	Social Work and Terrorism
	Economic Theory/Principles I	Gender in Society	Spirituality and Social Work	Social Work Intervention in Domestic Violence
	Introduction to Law II	Sociology of Law	Social Inequality	Criminal Justice System
	Introduction to Political Science II		Sociology of Health and Illness Behaviour	
	Religion and Human Values		Sociology of Industry	

Suggestions to enhance the relevance of social work education

There is some agreement that relevant social work education would:

- Train practitioners to contribute to development and poverty alleviation by engaging in developmental activities that enhanced people's welfare and contributed to economic development. This necessitated training in empowering macro-level community development focused on self-help and co-operative initiatives to enhance people' income-generation potential (Anucha, 2008a, 2008b; Odiah, 1991; Osawe, 2018; Ugiagbe, 2015).
- Draw on and integrate local indigenous or traditional knowledge into the social work curriculum (Ekoh & Agbawodikeizu, 2022; Gray & Amadasun, 2022; Levy et al., 2022; Nnama-Okechukwu & McLaughlin, 2022; Nnama-Okechukwu et al., 2022; Olaleye, 2013).

Social work academics have an important role to play in enhancing the relevance of the social work curriculum. This final section suggests several areas for attention towards this objective.

Agreement on social work's remit

Canavera et al. (2019) concluded that the proliferation of diverse training programs and lack of role clarity undermined 'the profession's development and its inclusion in national development planning and implementation. The lack of clear objectives for the social work profession has profound implications for social work training' (p. 90). To achieve clarity in social workers' job descriptions and legal mandates, social work educators would need to work closely with practitioners and policy makers through their professional bodies. Such engagement was essential given criticisms that educational content was out of step with practice realities, due to its continued reliance on international literature and attempts to meet global education standards. Most scholars and websites cite the IFSW/IASSW's international definition of social work. Osawe (2018) saw this as yet another oppressive imposition reminiscent of colonialism, arguing that implementing an international definition, grounded in human rights and social justice, was particularly difficult given the scale of Nigeria's social problems and deep-seated ethnoreligious value differences. Graham (1999) highlighted that Afrocentric perspectives challenged the profession's core principles of equality, social justice, and self-determination. Ekoh and Agbawodikeizu (2022) highlighted this noting contentious areas surrounding social work engagement with sexual minorities – lesbian, gay, bisexual, transgender, and intersex (LGBTI) people, given ethnoreligious beliefs on gender and the Same-Sex Marriage (Prohibition) Bill of 2013 (George & Ekoh, 2020; FRN, 2013e). Similarly affected were issues surrounding abortion and gender equality.

Because of the diversity of contexts, where social workers practice, standardised definitions tend to be extremely broad and lack specificity on social work's role (Gray, 2016; Gray & Webb, 2014). A Nigerian definition of social work would need to include traditional support systems, community development practitioners, and public officials without professional training who carried out responsibilities included under social work's umbrella. The aim, however, would be to make training accessible to these groups of practitioners in as far as is possible. Nigeria might follow South Africa's example of developing minimum standards for various levels of education and training (Lombard et al., 2003).

Agreement on educational standards

Many countries in the Global North and South have an accreditation body that sets standards for social work education to suit their national context. Minimally, they set prerequisites for entry into social work and accredit educational providers that meet education standards. In countries like the USA and Australia, professional bodies accredit and monitor the quality of social work programs to ensure they meet qualification requirements, usually a four-year undergraduate BSW as a starting point. Onalu and Okoye (2020) highlighted the importance of government recognition and regulation in Nigeria. Until very recently, there was no regulation of social work education other than the NUC's (2017) curriculum guidelines, which provided a good starting point from which to proceed on ensuring culturally relevant courses that included local literature. This changed with the recent Chartered Institute of Social Work Practitioners Act 2022 and Chartered Institute of Social Work Practitioners charged with regulating education and practice. However, the omission of the Association of Social Work Educators in Nigeria (ASWEN) and other professional groups, especially NASoW, in the legislative process suggests a rocky road to agreement on educational standards.

Standards for social work educators

Badru (2011) claimed some social work educators in Nigeria, especially in the northern region of the country, did not have a professional social work education, while Onalu and Okoye (2021) observed that anyone in Nigeria could teach social work. For Badru (2011), a master's degree should be the minimal requirement for social work educators. He believed that 'unlettered' social work educators should have access to affordable postgraduate study within Nigeria, arguing that the effective delivery of social welfare services called for sound social work education, training, and continuous and continued education and retraining, for practitioners and educators alike. He drew attention to Ejikeme's (2010) observation that many social work clients were educated; hence, social workers should have the requisite professional education and knowledge to provide appropriate assistance. To improve access to professional social work education, the national association of social work educators should increase its efforts to raise public awareness of what social work was all about and let the government and the Nigerian people know the importance of social work and where and how to access professional social work services. Secondly, there was a need to improve indigenous social work literature and knowledge with subsidised printing and publishing for local books on social work. The materials should relate to contemporary issues, such as human rights violations, gender discrimination, natural disasters – earthquakes, landslides, climate change, floods, droughts – to save human and animal lives, reduce damage to property during disasters, provide disaster relief, support, rehabilitation, reintegration, and disaster management. Thirdly, the national association should ensure that professional social workers worked directly with families and were available when needed. He argued for a re-engineering and rebranding of professional work education, as the present state of social work education in Nigeria was unacceptable. The goal would be for every practising social worker in Nigeria to have a professional education beyond the first-degree level and for all social work educators in universities and institutes training social workers to have the minimum of a master's degree along with a basic degree in social work. He saw the need for a council of social work education to shape a better social work profession with social work education responsive to the sociocultural terrain.

Systematic curriculum revision

Canavera et al. (2020) reported that their 'field visits to social work libraries in Nigerian training institutes revealed an abundance of social work textbooks from North America and Europe' (p. 89), though professionals 'continually expressed the need for locally developed principles and training materials to address the unique needs of their respective countries' (p. 89). They wanted specialised training to 'equip them to deal with local realities' (p. 89). One of their recommendations was that policy makers and education providers had to address the gap between educational curricula and local realities and introduce some consistency to the proliferating education programs through 'systematic, sustained curriculum reform' (p. 90). Chukwu et al. (2022) believed the process began with building an empirical foundation – a local knowledge base – for Nigerian social work through research and publication. They thought that including practitioners, service users, community representatives, and early-career academics in curriculum review processes was another way to embed local knowledge in social work education. Curriculum review and revision required a strategic long-term plan systematically implemented across educational institutions offering social work degrees and courses. Its aim would be to reach agreement on curriculum and course content responsive to local sociocultural, ethnoreligious, political, and economic realities. This would include the embrace of a decolonising developmental perspective and realistic integration of the generalist model incorporating micro-level casework and group-work and macro-level developmental interventions. Given the enormous regional disparities, the curriculum review should take account of context-based variations and be responsive to these. The growing literature on Islamic social work might be helpful for social work educators in northern Nigerian schools of social work (Al-Krenawi & Graham, 2000; Ashencaen Crabtree & Baba, 2001; Ashencaen Crabtree et al., 2008; Barise, 2005; Lovat, 2010; Ragab, 2016, 2017; Schmid & Sheikhzadegan, 2022).

Indigenous and culturally relevant curriculum content

Thirty years ago, Odiah (1991) highlighted the absence of indigenous, culturally relevant content in the social work curriculum, and this seems the case even today. Ekoh and Agbawodikeizu (2022) believed indigenisation might be unattainable given the ethical dilemmas arising from oppressive and discriminatory cultural and ethnoreligious beliefs conflicting with social work principles and values, such as preference for male children, inheritance rights, widowhood practices, early marriage, and limited educational opportunities for girls. Thus, the inclusion of indigenous and culturally relevant curriculum content could lead to contentious debates given Nigeria's ethnoreligious diversity. Nevertheless, Agbawodikeizu et al., 2022) noted that teaching religion and spirituality had long been a part of the Nigerian social work curriculum, however, as part of elective courses rather than a discrete social work course (except at Ebonyi State University of Science and Technology), even though this formed part of the NUC's (2017) curriculum guidelines. Their small study of 12 social work educators did not find any complexities surrounding the teaching of religion and spirituality, which was generally seen to bolster strengths-based practice. Writers who emphasise the inclusion of indigenous and culturally relevant content in the curriculum see this as essential to social work's relevance to, and resonance with, local Nigerian communities (Anucha, 2008a, 2008b; Gray & Amadasun, 2022; Levy et al., 2022; Nnama-Okechukwu & McLaughlin, 2022; Nnama-Okechukwu et al., 2022; Odiah, 1991; Olaleye, 2013).

Relevance of a developmental perspective

Amadasun's (2019) study of social work students in one major university in southern Nigeria found limited evidence of a developmental perspective in social work education courses, though several Nigerian scholars had called for an increased focus on poverty alleviation and development (Anucha, 2008a, 2008b; Onalu & Okoye, 2021; Ugiagbe, 2017). This suggested the need for a developmental perspective focused on poverty alleviation and societal relations that exacerbated inequality and marginalised groups of people rendering them vulnerable to institutional abuse, oppression, stigmatisation, exploitation, and discrimination (Anucha, 2008a, 2008b; Onalu & Okoye, 2021; Ugiagbe, 2017). It highlighted the social rather than the individual causes of poverty and the impossibility of eliminating economic inequality on a case-by-case basis. Poverty was a social not an individual problem. It affected households, communities, and vulnerable groups of people, denying them access to social resources like education and welfare support. The goals of developmental social work were the promotion of social and economic equality, upholding the dignity and worth of peoples, ensuring environmental and community sustainability, and strengthening recognition of the importance of human relations (Lombard, 2015). Developmental interventions required social workers to work towards the inclusion of people in matters affecting their daily lives that resulted from social injustices and the violation of their human rights (Onalu & Okoye, 2021). To enhance its relevance, Onalu and Okoye (2021) believed the social work curriculum should teach students about, and how to respond to, local issues and social problems. It should 'equip students with the necessary knowledge and motivation to identify the root causes of injustice, inequalities, and oppression and provide a means of addressing them in Nigeria' (Onalu & Okoye, 2021, p. 581). Social injustices included gender-based discrimination, seen in widowhood practices, girl-child marriage, female genital cutting, child witchcraft accusation, denial of inheritance to female children, and discriminatory practices against older adults, disabled people, and albinos. Other contemporary issues included HIV and AIDS, and vulnerable and orphaned children. Thus, to incorporate a developmental perspective required curriculum content on social problems like these viewed through a social justice and human rights lens. Social work was partisan in this respect and needed more than objective sociological analyses of social problems to find ways to alleviate poverty and associated social injustices.

Addressing issues with fieldwork practice

Like most social work institutions in the West, Nigerian social work education had embraced a generalist model with fieldwork a central requirement (Amadasun, 2020). Though supervised fieldwork placements in social agencies had formed a core part of Nigerian social work education from the outset, the availability of placements and qualified field supervisors presented an ongoing challenge to student learning, especially as these programs proliferated (Mere, 1981). Many social work academics lacked professional training (Badru, 2011; Okoye, 2013). This resulted in minimal supervision of students on field placements and 'situations where students have had to teach the staff their job' (Okoye, 2013, p. 171). Sometimes, this led to fieldwork agencies rejecting students for placements. Several studies of fieldwork education in Africa have reported consistent findings of increased competition between academic institutions for, and an acute shortage of, relevant placements and professionally trained social work supervisors noting consequent issues for student learning and professional role modelling (Chitereka, 2009; Dhemba, 2012; Dziro, 2013; Gray et al., 2018; Hochfeld et al., 2009).

Given the problems relating to social work supervision in social agencies, educators have to reach agreement on realistic expectations for fieldwork through curriculum reform. This issue was not unique to Nigeria. The proliferation of social work education programs worldwide had raised issues surrounding the availability of fieldwork placements. One option might be an expansion of fieldwork opportunities beyond formal social agencies to non-government and community-based organisations, or university-driven community projects, with an independent university-appointed supervisor with practice experience working with unqualified agency supervisors and community agents (Gray & Simpson, 1998; Travis et al., 1999).

Enhancing digital connectivity

The COVID pandemic highlighted the importance of social work education's digital connectivity, especially its capacity to move to online learning. Digital connectivity enables educators and students to gain access to information and network with colleagues and peers around the world. Social work schools in Nigeria have been unable to make the transition to online learning, due, *inter alia*, to a lack of access, online resources, and digital literacy, despite the fact that Nigeria is one of the leaders of Africa's technology innovation and 'pillars of innovation and high-tech entrepreneurship' (Osiakwan, 2017, p. 56). Practitioners, too, had minimal involvement 'in the fight against COVID-19 in Nigeria' (Agwu & Okoye, 2021, p. 763). Agwu and Okoye (2021) interviewed six mainstream health workers and six medical social workers and found the health workers had only vague knowledge of the social work profession, while managers had asked the social workers to stay at home or continue with their usual routines that excluded COVID-19-related responsibilities. Onalu et al. (2020) reported similarly that a 'few social workers on the ground had little or nothing to do in terms of intervention' (p. 1038). Equally absent during the pandemic was social work education, due to the lack of access to online learning, despite young people's increasing digital connectivity and literacy. Osiakwan (2017) noted that there was 'a critical mass of youthful people creatively leveraging the mobile web platform to create solutions for businesses and solve social problems, some of which may become global role models' (p. 60). Yet, educational institutions have yet to capitalise on this. There are many factors involved, such as the high costs universities must meet to access online learning resources and web-based online learning platforms. As well as benefits, the digital revolution introduced a new range of issues into social work education, such as the need for access to, and literacy in using, online resources. Hence, Ebere (2016) found moderate use of digital technology in his study of social work education at the University of Nigeria, Nsukka (UNN), despite the availability of digital media. Among other factors, electrification issues and a lack of computer skills affected the 'effective use of ICT in social work practice and teaching' (p. 2). Idyorough (2013) noted social workers lacked training in the use of computers. However, most schools of social work and the university system did not have access to online resources. For example, apart from libraries in some of the major institutions, faculty and departmental libraries do not have wireless connectivity and other basic internet tools. Despite talks about the use of online education during the pandemic, few schools – mostly private universities – were able to accomplish this, since those in the public domain came to a halt largely because of educators' industrial action. Hence, the COVID-19 pandemic exposed digitalisation gaps in Nigeria's education system generally and heightened the importance of social work's digital connectivity (Azubuike et al., 2020). However, greater use of digital media would enhance processes surrounding curriculum revision and renewal towards greater relevance.

Conclusion

Social work programs across Nigeria's universities are working to create curricula with indigenous content that is relevant to Nigerian society. The NUC that accredits and supports courses and curricula requires a program review every five years that reports on progress in indigenising university curricula. There are several challenges for social work educators, not least instituting a unified strategic process of curriculum review and achieving agreement on course composition and content that takes account of regional diversities and the continued dominance of sociology in many universities. While there is a burgeoning literature on African and Nigerian social work, there are not enough concrete practice examples for use in teaching. Such locally relevant social work education and training is essential to professional recognition and efficient and effective service delivery. This chapter argued that relevance required curriculum revision and renewal, and an integration of a developmental perspective. However, agreement on a definition of social work – its scope, roles, and responsibilities – along with agreement on educational standards – prerequisites, entry requirements, and levels – needed to precede curriculum review. The chapter suggested that, where possible, greater use of online digital resources, for communication, networking, and online learning, would greatly enhance processes to achieve greater relevance in social work education.

10 Conclusion

This brief concluding chapter suggests that Nigeria offers a global audience a glimpse of what's possible when people work together towards a common goal. It highlights the miracle of social work's development, growth, and survival in a country with a dismal record of policy implementation, minimal public service provision, and even less support for social workers, an army of which is needed to tackle deepening poverty and social problems. It suggests that this book offers international readers insight into Nigeria's developmental issues and social problems and a local audience – social science and human service researchers, educators, practitioners, students, and policymakers – a postcolonial understanding to inform future policy, service, and practice development.

By not following the example of countries elsewhere in Africa and the Western world, Nigeria has not supported social workers and has a weak system of social welfare provision. It needs an army of social workers to address the wide-scale problems discussed in previous chapters. Social workers should be at the forefront of human, emergency humanitarian, child protection, aged and disability care, and community service provision, as they have the relational skills to engage with people and a value system that places human interests at the centre of helping. The government should know that social workers are committed to human rights and social justice. They work with the most vulnerable groups in society, engaging them at the personal micro-level, meso group and organisational levels, and the macro community and policy levels. They have a valuable role to play in mass education and awareness-raising campaigns and at the policy level in informing policymakers of people's day-to-day struggles and experiences. They strive for cultural relevance and tailor their interventions to respond to local problems and issues. They have an understanding of the critical role of family and kin networks in people's lives, as well as the role religion and spirituality play in helping individuals cope with life's adversities. They also understand the importance of community networks and social support structures, working with community leaders to engage people in local programs and services.

Why the President refused to approve a bill to legitimate social work that had been in the making for 42 years beggars belief. Between 1975 and 2017,

DOI: 10.4324/9781003382126-10

the social work professionalisation bill failed in successive legislative assemblies, due to the ignorance of successive governments on the valuable social role professional social workers played globally in contributing to individual and collective wellbeing, especially in family and child welfare. Its multicultural models made it responsive to issues of parenting and child raising all over the world (Akintayo, 2021). With the advent of its Global Agenda (2010–2020), social workers were moving increasingly towards social development and poverty-related issues, including government inertia, climate change, violence, conflict, discrimination, and the unequal treatment of women. The second Global Agenda (2020–2030) focused attention on the importance of human relationships and building relational connections through the philosophy of ubuntu, discussed in Chapter 2, to strengthen social solidarity. This surely was the glue Nigerian society needed to bring its diverse ethnic groups together in building connectedness to put an end to long-standing enmities and conflicts.

While postcolonial scholars have helped build a strong understanding of the impact of colonial legacies, a more optimistic social work perspective tells us there is something we can do. It says we need to tackle problems from top to bottom, through direct interventions with individuals and families, and indirect structural interventions through system and policy change. Time will tell whether recent legislative changes will lead to greater support for, and recognition of, the thousands of social workers in the country with professional social work qualifications implementing their interventions and practising their skills. The President could consolidate his support by attracting Nigerian social workers working abroad to return to Nigeria and apply their international experience to domestic issues and problems at all levels. Other supportive measures might include the creation of policy and management roles for experienced social workers and the funding of positions in state and local government to bolster direct services in government departments, and a mass education campaign endorsing social work's position in Nigerian society.

In this book, we have highlighted the potential of the profession and the value of its ideals rooted in universal rights, social justice, and a belief in the dignity and worth of human beings, deserving of respect, empathy, acceptance, tolerance, and inclusion. With myriad social development challenges threatening Nigeria's social cohesion and national identity, the country needs professionals who are responsive to broader social issues and committed to human rights and social justice. We hope there will be further opportunities for social workers to work with Nigeria's most vulnerable populations, trafficked and displaced people, women and children, people with disabilities, young people in trouble with the law, many of whom have serious and neglected complex mental health issues, and older people so they can live dignified lives with family and government supported. We have highlighted the numerous policies that support social work intervention and their implementation challenges. Social workers play an important role in policy implementation through their daily engagement with *inter alia* clients, co-workers, and government officials. Above all, social workers believe in common human needs and in uniting, rather than dividing, people. This book offers a global audience insight into Nigeria's developmental issues and problems and a local audience – social science and human service researchers, educators, practitioners, students, and policymakers – a glimpse of what's possible when people work together towards a common goal.

References

Abari, C. A., & Audu, D. T. (2013). A study of street children in Kaduna Metropolis, Nigeria. *IOSR Journal of Humanities and Social Science (IOSR-JHSS)*, *15*(1), 44–49.

Abdullahi, A. A. (2011). Trends and challenges of traditional medicine in Africa. *African Journal of Traditional, Complementary and Alternative Medicine*, 8(S), 115–123.

Abdulmalik, J., Kola, L., & Gureje, O. (2016). Mental health system governance in Nigeria: Challenges, opportunities and strategies for improvement. *Global Mental Health*, *3*(e9), 1–11. 10.1017/gmh.2016.2

AbdulQadir, I. A. (n.d.). *The Almajiri system of education in Nigeria today*. Retrieved from http://www.gamji.com/article5000/news5956.htm

Abdulraheem-Mustapha, M. A. (2016). Child justice administration in the Nigerian Child Rights Act: Lessons from South Africa. *African Human Rights Law Journal*, *16*, 435–457. 10.17159/1996-2096/2016/v16n2a6

Adah, A. A., & Abasilim, U. D. (2015). Development and its challenges in Nigeria: A theoretical discourse. *Mediterranean Journal of Social Sciences*, *6*(6) S2, 275–281. 10. 5901/mjss.2015.v6n6s2p275

Adebiyi, A. O., Fagbola, M. A., Olakehinde, O., & Oguniyi, A. (2016). Enacted and implied stigma for dementia in a community in south-west Nigeria. *Psychogeriatrics*, *16*, 268–273. https://pubmed.ncbi.nlm.nih.gov/26551624/

Adegbite, O. S., Ezeokoli, R. N., Anozie-Obi, S., Aina, F. O., & Oyedokun, S. O. (2020). Institutional support and the wellbeing of institutionalised senior citizens in selected assisted living facilities in Lagos State, Nigeria. *Babcock Journal of Education*, *6*(1), 39–49.

Adedeji, A., & Senghor, J. C. (1989). *Towards a dynamic African economy: Selected speeches and lectures 1975-1986*. London: Routledge.

Adedokun, M. O. (2016). Curbing the menace of human trafficking in Nigerian communities. *International Journal of Research in Education Methodology*, *7*(4), 1295–1301. 10.24297/ijrem.v7i4.4353

Adegbami, A., & Adeoye, J. O. (2021). Violent conflict and national development in Nigeria. *Hatfield Graduate Journal of Public Affairs*, *5*(1), 1–22. 10.15760/hgjpa.2021.5.1.9

Adeleke, R. O., Adebowale, T. O., & Oyinlola, O. (2017). Profile of elderly patients presented with psychosocial problems in Ibadan. *MOJ Gerontology & Geriatrics*, *1*(1), 26–36. 10.15406/mojgg.2017.01.00006

Adepitan, O. (2020). *Decolonizing human trafficking: A case study of human trafficking in Edo State Nigeria*. Masters Thesis. University of South Florida. Retrieved from https://digitalcommons.usf.edu/cgi/viewcontent.cgi?article=9346&context=etd

Aderinto, S. (Ed.). (2015). *Children and childhood in colonial Nigerian histories*. New York: Palgrave Macmillan.

Aderinto, S. (2018). Empire Day in Africa: Patriotic colonial childhood, imperial spectacle and nationalism in Nigeria, 1905-60. *Journal of Imperial and Commonwealth History*, 46(4), 731–757. 10.1080/03086534.2018.1452538

Adesina, M. A., Adesanya, T., & Olufadewa, I. (2020). Mental health and conflict in Nigeria: An overview. *European Journal of Environment and Public Health*, 4(1), 1–4. 10.29333/ejeph/7806

Adeyemi, O. S., & Oluwaseun, O. (2013). Economic factors as correlates of streetism among urban children in Ibadan Metropolis, Nigeria. *Developing Country Studies*, 2(9), 87–93.

Adie, E. U., & Shamagana, Y. N. (2018). Towards improved inclusion of women and girls with disabilities in the development agenda in Nigeria. *International Journal of Integrative Humanism*, 10(1), 1–16.

Afolayan, G. E. (2015). Contemporary representations of disability and interpersonal relationships of disabled women in south-western Nigeria. *Agenda*, 29(2), 54–65. 10. 1080/10130950.2015.1061780

African Commission on Human and Peoples' Rights. (1981). *African Charter on Human and Peoples' Rights (Banjul Charter)*. Retrieved from https://www.achpr.org/legalinstruments/detail?id=49

African Union (AU). (1990). *African Charter on the Rights and Welfare of the Child*. Retrieved from https://www.achpr.org/public/Document/file/English/achpr_instr_charterchild_eng.pdf

African Union (AU). (2003). *Protocol to the African Charter on Human and Peoples' Rights on the Rights of Women in Africa*. Retrieved from https://au.int/en/treaties/protocol-african-charter-human-and-peoples-rights-rights-women-africa

African Union (AU). (2009). *Convention for the Protection and Assistance of Internally Displaced Persons in Africa (Kampala Convention)*. Retrieved from https://au.int/en/treaties/african-union-convention-protection-and-assistance-internally-displaced-persons-africa

African Union (AU). (2022). *Agenda 2063: The Africa we want*. Retrieved from https://au.int/en/agenda2063/overview#:~:text=Agenda%202063%20encapsulates%20not%20only,rapid%20transformation%20of%20the%20continent.

African Union (AU) & HelpAge International. (2021). *AU Draft Policy Framework and Action Plan on Ageing*. Nairobi, Kenya: HelpAge International Africa Regional Development Centre. Retrieved from https://www.un.org/esa/socdev/ageing/documents/implementation/AUFrameworkBook.pdf

Agbo, M. C. (2019). Child rape in Nigeria, implications on the education of the child. *Children and Teenagers*, 2(1), 13–31. 10.22158/ct.v2n1p13

Agbawodikeizu, P. O., Agwu, P. C., Okoye, U. O., & Oyeoku, E. K. (2018). Perception and attitudes to end of life planning and implications for social work practice in Enugu State, Nigeria. *International Social Work*, 62(2), 892–904. 10.1177/0020872818755862

Agbawodikeizu, P., Agwu, P., Okoye, U., & Igwe, I. (2019). Controversies in preparing for end-of-life in Nsukka town of Nigeria and suggestions for Nigerian based social work practice. *Social Work & Social Sciences Review*, 20(2), 95–112. 10.1921/swssr.v2 0i2.1140

Agbawodikeizu, P. U., Levy, S., Ekoh, P. C., Chukwu, N. E., & Okoye, U. O. (2022). Religion and spirituality as a core module in social work education in Nigeria: Perspectives of social work educators. *Journal of Religion & Spirituality in Social Work: Social Thought*, 1–18. 10.1080/15426432.2022.2089316

Agunbiade, M. (2016). *Socio-cultural constructions of sexuality and help-seeking behaviour among elderly Yoruba people in urban Ibadan, Southwest Nigeria*. Johannesburg: Doctoral Thesis submitted to the Faculty of Humanities, University of the Witwatersrand.

Agwu, P., & Okoye, U. (2021). Social work and COVID-19: A gap in Nigeria's intervention. *International Social Work, 64*(5), 761–770. 10.1177/0020872820980799

Ahmed, I., & Kebbi, B. (2017). '602,000 Nigerians Migrated to Europe in 2016, Says UN Ex-envoy'. *The Guardian Nigeria News - Nigeria and World News*. Retrieved from https://guardian.ng/news/602000-nigerians-migrated-to-europe-in-2016-says-un-ex-envoy/

Ajala, A. S. (2006). The changing perception of ageing in Yoruba culture and its implications on the health of the elderly. *Anthropologist, 8*(3), 181–188.

Ajala, E. M. (2010). Economic status, family size and educational status of the child as determinants of child labour in Ondo State, Nigeria. *African Journal of Educational Research, 14*(1&2), 116–125.

Akinbowale, O. E. (2018). National development plan, human capital investment and economic growth in Nigeria: A survey of literature. *International Journal of Academic Management Science Research (IJAMSR), 2*(5), 27–32.

Akintayo, T. (2021). Options for Africa's child welfare systems from Nigeria's unsustainable multicultural models. *Sustainability, 13*, 1118. 10.3390/su13031118

Akuto, G. W. (2017). Challenges of internally displaced persons (IDPs) in Nigeria: Implications for counselling and the role of key stakeholders. *International Journal of Innovative Psychology & Social Development, 5*(2), 21–27.

Al-Krenawi, A., & Graham, J. (2000). Islamic theology and prayer: Relevance for social work practice. *International Social Work, 43*(3) 289–304. 10.1177/002087280004300303

Alapiki, H. (2009). *Politics and governance in Nigeria*. Owerri, Nigeria: Corporate Impressions.

Aluko, O. A., & Mbada, K. (2020). Rural poverty among women in Nigeria. *Journal of Sustainable Development in Africa, 22*(3), 82–95.

Amadasun, S. (2019). Mainstreaming a developmental approach to social work education and practice in Africa? Perspectives of Nigerian BSW students. *Social Work and Education, 6*(2), 196–207. 10.25128/2520-6230.19.2.8.

Amadasun, S. (2020a). Social work services for persons with disabilities in Nigeria: A qualitative inquiry. *International Journal of Social Sciences Perspectives, 6*(2), 59–67.

Amadasun, S. (2020b). Applying a rights-based approach to social work practice in Africa: Students' perspectives. *International Journal of Social Sciences Perspectives, 7*(1), 1–9.

Amadasun, S. (2020c). *Social work for social development in Africa*. Ibadan: September Publishing House.

Amadasun, S. (2021a). Social work in Nigeria: A timeline account. Retrieved from https://advance.sagepub.com/articles/preprint/SOCIAL_WORK_IN_NIGERIA_A_TIMELINE_ACCOUNT_docx/14129972

Amadasun, S. (2021b). Public perceptions of social work in Nigeria: Does the profession has what it takes to address Nigeria's social problems? *British Journal of Social Work, 51*: 259–278.

Amadasun, S. (2022). Social work interventions for human trafficking victims' in Nigeria. *International Social Work, 65*(2), 343–355. 10.1177/0020872819901163

Amadasun, S., & Gray, M. (2022). Enhancing the relevance of social work education in Nigeria. *British Journal of Social Work (2022)*, 00, 1–18. 10.1093/bjsw/bcac144

Amadasun, S., & Omorogiuwa, T. B. E. (2020). Applying anti-oppressive approach to social work practice in Africa: Reflections of Nigerian BSW students. *Journal of Humanities and Applied Social Sciences, 2*(3), 197–213. 10.1108/JHASS-12-2019-0082

Amaghionyeodiwe, L. A. (2008). Determinants of the choice of health care provider in Nigeria. *Health Care Management Science, 11*, 215–227.

American Historical Association. (2022). *The corrupting influences of the West (text by Nwafor Orizu)*. Retrieved from https://www.historians.org/teaching-and-learning/teaching-resources-for-historians/teaching-and-learning-in-the-digital-age/through-the-lens-of-history-biafra-nigeria-the-west-and-the-world/the-colonial-and-pre-colonial-eras-in-nigeria/the-corrupting-influences-of-the-west

Anah, C. (2014). Who benefits? The political economy of national development plans in Nigeria. *Journal of Alternative Perspectives in the Social Sciences, 6*(1), 100–115.

Anazonwu, N. P. (2019). Socio-cultural factors associated with perception of child abuse among women in Nsukka LGA: Implications for social work practice in Nigeria. *Journal of Social Work in Developing Societies, 1*(3), 59–74.

Ani, M., & Adams, S. (2020, May 5). Updated: Sokoto, Taraba, Jigawa record highest poverty rates as Nigeria's poor now 82.9m … Analysts call for larger sample size to reflect economic realities. *Business Day*. Retrieved from https://businessday.ng/exclusives/article/updated-sokoto-taraba-jigawa-record-highest-poverty-rates-as-nigerias-poor-now-82-9m/

Animasahun, V. J., & Chapman, H. J. (2017). Psychosocial health challenges of the elderly in Nigeria: A narrative review. *African Health Science, 17*(2), 575–583. 10.4314/ahs.v17i2.35

Anucha, A. (2008a). Envisioning African social work education. In S. N. Dlamini (Ed.), *New directions in African education: Challenges and possibilities* (pp. 147–170). Africa, missing voices series 4. Calgary, Alberta: University of Calgary Press.

Anucha, U. (2008b). Exploring a new direction for social work education and training in Nigeria. *Social Work Education, 27*(3), 229–242.

Araromi, M. A. (2015). Protecting the rights of old people in Nigeria: Towards a legal reform. *Journal of Law, Policy and Globalization, 40*, 131–143. Retrieved from https://core.ac.uk/download/pdf/234650285.pdf

Archibong, E. P., Enang, E., & Bassey, G. E. (2017). Witchcraft beliefs in diseases causation and health-seeking behaviour in pregnancy of women in Calabar South – Nigeria. *IOSR Journal of Humanities and Social Science (IOSR-JHSS), 22*(6), 24–28.

Arimoro, A. E. (2019). Are they not Nigerians? The obligation of the state to end discriminatory practices against persons with disabilities. *International Journal of Discrimination and the Law, 19*(2), 89–109. 10.1177/1358229119846764

Aruna, J. O. (2018). Trends in child sexual molestation, rape and incest: A view from South West Nigeria. *Humanities and Social Sciences Letters, 6*(4), 137–148. 10.18488/journal.73.2018.64.137.148

Ashencaen Crabtree, S., & Baba, I. (2001). Islamic perspectives in social work education. *Social Work Education, 20*(4), 469–481. 10.1080/02615470120057479

Ashencaen Crabtree, S., Husain, F., & Spalek, B. (2008). *Islam and social work: Debating values, transforming practice*. Bristol, UK: The Policy Press.

Association of Psychiatrists in Nigeria. (2020). *We are psychiatrists in Nigeria committed to holistic care for persons with mental illness and the promotion of positive mental health*. Retrieved from https://www.apn.org.ng/#home

Atilola O., Ola B., Abiri G., et al. (2017). Status of mental-health services for adolescents with psychiatric morbidity in youth correctional institutions in Lagos. *Journal of Child & Adolescent Mental Health, 29*(1), 63–83.

Atilola, O., Abiri, G., & Ola, B. (2019). The Nigerian juvenile justice system: From warehouse to uncertain quest for appropriate youth mental health service model. *British Journal of Psychology International, 16*(1), 19–21.

Atumah, O. N., Agwu, P. C., & Okoye, U. O. (2019). The place of social work in preserving human rights in context of changing gender roles in Nigeria. *International Journal of Research and Innovation in Social Science, 3*(4), 1–5.

Australian Human Rights Commission. (2014). *Equality before the Law.* Retrieved from https://www.humanrights.gov.au/publications/equal-law

Avidime, S., Ameh, N., Adesiyun, A. G., Ozed-Williams, C., Isaac, N., Aliyu, Y., Sullyman, K., Idris, H., & Ojabo, A. (2013). Knowledge and attitude towards child adoption among women in Zaria, northern Nigeria. *Nigerian Medical Journal, 54*, 261–264.

Ayatse, F. H., & Akuva, I. I. (2013). The origin and development of ethnic politics and its impacts on post colonial governance in Nigeria. *European Scientific Journal, 9*(17), 178–189.

Ayegboyin, M., & Salami, K. K. (2019). Social dimensions of musculoskeletal pain experiences among the elderly in southwestern Nigeria. *Health, 11*(7), 953–970. 10.4236/health.2019.117077

Ayimoro, O. (2020). An appraisal of rights-based approach to achieving gender equality and empowerment of women and girls in Nigeria. *KIU (Kampala International University) Journal of Social Sciences, 6*(2), 381–389.

Ayobade, A., & Agugua, A. (2020). Social work implications of de-industrialization and entrepreneurs dynamism in Ikeja Lagos State. *Journal of Positive Psychology and Counselling, 4*, 92–106. https://www.ppacjournals.org/download.php?filename=JPPCVOL4,2020.Ayobade, Agugua.92-106.pdf

Ayodele, O. S., Obafemi, F. N., & Ebong, F. S. (2013). Challenges facing the achievement of the Nigeria vision 20:2020. *Global Advanced Research Journal of Social Science (GARJSS) 2*(7), 143–157.

Ayodele, K. O., Olaleye, Y. L., & Adebusuyi, R. J. (2018). Integrative multi-disciplinary teams intervention on community social work programmes in Nigeria. *Jos Journal of Social Issues, 11*(1), 86–95.

Azeez, A., & Salami, K. K. (2020). Giving back to the elderly: Cross-cultural construction of befitting burial for the dead in Nigeria. *Journal of Population Ageing, 13*, 25–39. 10.1007/s12062-018-9231-9

Azi, S. A., & Abubakar, I. S. (2016). The effect of child abuse on the academic performance of school children: Implication on the Nigerian economy. *Asia Pacific Journal of Education, Arts and Sciences, 3*(3), 23–27.

Azorondu, A. A., Adegbite, O. S., Adeyeye, B. E., & Ajike, J. O. (2021). Combatting human trafficking in Nigeria: Exploring social workers' intervention strategies. *IFE PsychologIA: An International Journal, 29*(2), 89–99.

Azubuike, O. B., Adegboye, O., & Quadri, H. (2021). Who gets to learn in a pandemic? Exploring the digital divide in remote learning during the COVID-19 pandemic in Nigeria. *International Journal of Educational Research Open, 2*, 1–10. 10.1016/j.ijedro.2020.100022

Badejo, F. A. (2016). *Understanding human trafficking as a social issue in Nigeria: A multi-stream formative social marketing approach.* PhD Thesis. Griffith Business School. Griffith University, Queensland, Australia. Retrieved from http://hdl.handle.net/10072/365561

Badru, F. A. (2011). Towards enhancing access of professional social work education in Nigeria. *Journal of Nigerian Social Work Educators, 1*(1), 101–116. https://ir.unilag.edu.ng/handle/123456789/10530

Badru, A. (2022, Dec 12). Buhari, NASS hailed over assent to National Council for Social Work bill. Vanguard. Retrieved from https://www.vanguardngr.com/2022/12/buhari-nass-hailed-over-assent-to-national-council-for-social-work-bill/

Bakare, M. O. (2015). Demography and medical education among Nigerian final year medical students: Implication for regional and human resource development. *Health Education Research and Development, 3*(3), 1–5. 10.4172/2380-5439.1000150

Barise, A. (2005). Social work with Muslims: Insights from the teachings of Islam. *Critical Social Work Online, 6*(2). 10.22329/csw.v6i2.5660

Barner, J. R., Okech, D., & Camp, M. A. (2018). 'One size does not fit all': A proposed ecological model for human trafficking intervention. *Journal of Evidence-Informed Social Work, 15*(2), 137–150. 10.1080/23761407.2017.1420514

Bashir, A. H., Hassan, A. B., & Ibrahim,Y. G. (2020). Community-Based Rehabilitation in Nigeria: A scoping study of literature. *Disability, CBR & Inclusive Development, 31*(3), 151–163. 10.47985/dcidj.389

Berghs, M. (2017). Practices and discourses of ubuntu: Implications for an African model of disability? *African Journal of Disability, 6*, 1–8. 10.4102/ajod.v6.292

Biklen, D. P. (1983). *Community organizing: Theory and practice.* Englewood Cliffs, N.J.: Prentice-Hall.

Birchall, J. (2019). *Overview of social exclusion in Nigeria.* K4 Helpdesk.

Boahen, A. A. (1987). *African perspectives on colonialism.* Baltimore, ML: Johns Hopkins University Press.

Botha, R., & Warria, A. (2020). Social service provision with adult victims of trafficking at shelters in South Africa. *Practice, 32*(1), 3–20. 10.1080/09503153.2019.1567702.

Bromfield, N. F., & Capous-Desyllas, M. (2012). Underlying motives, moral agendas and unlikely partnerships: The formulation of the U.S. Trafficking in Victims Protection Act through the data and voices of key policy players. *Advances in Social Work, 13*(2), 243–261.

Burchardt, T., LeGrand, J., & Piachaud, D. (2002a). Degrees of exclusion: Developing a dynamic, multidimensional measure. In J. Hills, J. LeGrand, & D. Piachaud (Eds.), *Understanding social exclusion* (pp 30–43). Oxford: Oxford University Press.

Burchardt, T., LeGrand, J., & Piachaud, D. (2002b). Introduction. In J. Hills, J. LeGrand, & D. Piachaud (Eds.), *Understanding social exclusion* (pp. 1–12). Oxford: Oxford University Press.

Burton, A. (2006). Raw youth, school leavers and the emergence of structural unemployment in late-colonial urban Tanganyika. *Journal of African History, 47*(3), 363–387.

Busari, K. (2019, May 16). Senate reconsiders, passes social work bill. *Premium Times.* Retrieved from https://www.premiumtimesng.com/news/more-news/330165-senate-reconsiders-passes-social-work-bill.html

Cadmus, E. O., Adebusoye, L. A., & Owoaje, E. T. (2022). Rural-urban differences in quality of life and associated factors among community-dwelling older persons in Oyo state, South-Western Nigeria. *Quality & Quantity, 56*, 1327–1344. 10.1007/s11135-021-01178-8

Canavera, M., Akesson, B., Landis, D., Armstrong, M., & Meyer, E. (2020). Mapping social work education in the West Africa region: Movements toward indigenization in 12 countries' training programs. *International Journal of Social Welfare, 29*, 83–95. 10.1111/ijsw.12372

Chapdelaine, R. P. (2020). Margaret Belcher and the Calabar remand home: 'Saving' trafficked children in colonial Nigeria 1950s. *Bulletin of Ecumenical Theology, 32*, 6–37.

Change.org. (n.d.). *End the Almajiri education system in Northern Nigeria*. Retrieved from https://www.change.org/p/president-of-the-federal-republic-of-nigeria-end-the-almajiri-education-system-in-northern-nigeria

Chikadzi, V., & Warria, A. (2022). Social work as an unwitting enabler of oppression and disenfranchisement of the masses: A Freirean analysis of social workers' perspectives on the government of Zimbabwe's COVID-19 response. In M. C. S. Gonçalves, R. Gutwald, T. Kleibl, R. Lutz, N. Noyoo, & J. Twikirize (Eds.), *The coronavirus crisis and challenges to social development* (pp. 307–321). New York: Springer.

Child Rights International Network (CRIN). (2013). *Inhuman sentencing of children in Nigeria*. Briefing for the 17th session of the Human Rights Council Universal Periodic Review in October 2013. Retrieved from https://archive.crin.org/en/library/publications/nigeria-inhuman-sentencing-children.html

Chitereka, C. (2009). The challenges of social work training. *International Social Work 52*(6), 823–830.

Chukwu, N. E., & Idemili-Aronu, N. (2019). Cross sectional survey of access to social services by families of persons with intellectual disability (PIDs) in Imo State, Nigeria. *Journal of Social Work in Developing Societies, 1*(2), 3–14.

Chukwu, N., Chukwu, N. N., & Nwadike, N. (2017). Methods of social practice. In U. Okoye, N. Chukwu, & P. Agwu (Eds.), *Social work in Nigeria: Book of readings* (pp. 44–59). Nsukka, Nigeria: University of Nigeria Press Ltd.

Chukwu, N. E., Levy, S., & Agbawodikeizu, P. U. (2022). Social work education in Nigeria and the search for enhanced local relevance: Perspectives from social work academics. *Social Work Education*. 10.1080/02615479.2022.2103528

Chukwu, N. E., Okoye, U. O., Onyeneho, N. G., & Okeibunor, J. C. (2019). Coping strategies of families of persons with learning disability in Imo state of Nigeria. *Journal of Health, Population and Nutrition, 38*(9), 1–9. 10.1186/s41043-019-0168-2

Clark, C. I. D., & Yesufu, S. (2016). Child street trading as an aspect of child abuse and neglect Oredo Municipality of Edo State, Nigeria as case study. *European Scientific Journal, 8*(5), 148–158. https://eujournal.org/index.php/esj/article/view/89/94

Clawson, H. J., & Dutch, N. (2007). *Addressing the needs of victims of human trafficking: Challenges, barriers, and promising practices*. Issue Brief. Washington, DC: US Department of Health and Human Services, Office of the Assistant Secretary for Planning and Evaluation. Retrieved from https://aspe.hhs.gov/reports/addressing-needs-victims-human-trafficking-challenges-barriers-promising-practices-0

Clawson, H. J., Salomon, A., & Grace, L. G. (2008). *Treating the hidden wounds: Trauma treatment and mental health recovery for victims of human trafficking*. Washington, DC: Office of the Assistant Secretary for Planning and Evaluation, US Department of Health and Human Services. Retrieved from https://aspe.hhs.gov/sites/default/files/migrated_legacy_files//42706/ib.pdf

Coates, J., Gray, M., & Hetherington, T. (2006). An 'ecospiritual' perspective: Finally, a place for indigenous approaches. *British Journal of Social Work, 36*(3), 381–399. 10.1093/bjsw/bcl005

Colaridge, A., & Hartley, S. (2010). *CBR stories from Africa: What can they teach us?* East Anglia: University of East Anglia.

Collings, S., & Spencer, M. (2020). Mums with an intellectual disability already risk family violence and losing their kids. Coronavirus could make things worse. *The Conversation*. Retrieved from Mums with an intellectual disability already risk family violence and losing their kids. Coronavirus could make things worse (theconversation.com)

Connelly, G., & Ikpaahindi, S. (2016). *Alternative child care and deinstitutionalisation: A case study of Nigeria*. Retrieved from https://www.sos-childrensvillages.org/getmedia/dd26f0b6-fe9f-4769-8c29-03551237a883/Nigeria-Alternative-Child-Care-and-Deinstitutionalisation-Report.pdf

Constance-Huggins, M., Moore, S., & Slay, Z. M. (2022). Sex trafficking of Black girls: A Critical Race Theory approach to practice. *Journal of Progressive Human Services*, 33(1), 62–74. 10.1080/10428232.2021.1987755.

Crampton, A. (2015). Decolonizing social work: 'Best practices' through a philosophy of impermanence. *Journal of Indigenous Social Development*, 4(1), 1–11. https://epublications.marquette.edu/socs_fac/159/

Dahal, P., Kumar, S., & Swahnberg, K. (2015) 'We are looked down upon and rejected socially': A qualitative study on the experiences of trafficking survivors in Nepal. *Global Health Action*, 8(1), 1–9. 10.3402/gha.v8.29267

Dauda, R. S. (2019). The paradox of persistent poverty amidst high growth: The case of Nigeria. In P. Shaffer, R. Kanbur, & R. Sandbrook (Eds.), *Immiserating growth: When growth fails the poor*. Oxford Scholarship Online. 10.1093/oso/9780198832317.003.0011

Dave-Odigie, C. P. (2008). Human trafficking trends in Nigeria and strategies for combating the crime. *Peace Studies Journal*, 1, 63–75.

DeAngelis, D., & Monahan, M. J. (2012). Professional credentials and professional regulations: Social work professional development In C. Dulmus, & K. Sowers (Eds.), *The profession of social work: Guided by history, led by evidence* (pp. 91–103). Hobeken, NJ: Wiley.

Dhemba, J. (2012). Fieldwork in social work education and training: Issues and challenges in the case of Eastern and Southern Africa. *Social Work & Society*, 10(1), 1–16.

Diptee, A. A., & Klein, M. A. (2010). African childhoods and the colonial project. *Journal of Family History*, 35(1), 3–6. 10.1177/0363199009350880

Du Bois, B., & Miley, K. K. (1992). *Social work: An empowering profession*. Boston, MA: Allyn and Bacon.

Dziro, C. (2013). Trends in social work education and training: The case of Zimbabwe. *International Journal of Development and Sustainability*, 2(2), 1423–1435.

Eaton, J., & Agomoh, A. O. (2008). Developing mental health services in Nigeria: The impact of a community-based mental health awareness programme. *Social Psychiatry & Psychiatric Epidemiology*, 20, 1–8. 10.1007/s00127-008-0321-5

Ebere, S. C. (2016). *Factors that hinder effective use of information communication technology (ICT) in social work practice and teaching in Enugu state*. Nsukka: Department of Social Work, University of Nigeria.

Ebimgbo, S. O., Obi-Keguna, C. N., Chukwu, N. E., Onalu, C. E., Abonyi, S. E., & Okoye, U. O. (2019). Culture-based social support to older adults in Nnewi, South-East Nigeria. *African Population Studies*, 33(2), 4891–4900. 10.11564/33-2-1402

Ebimgbo, S. O., Agwu, P., Chukwu, N., & Okoye, U. (2020). *Appraising sufficiency of financial support for older adults in Anambra State, Nigeria*. Ageing International. 10.1007/s12126-020-09379-6.

Ebimgbo, S. O., Atama, C. S., Onalu, C. E., Obasi-Igwe, I. A., & Aghedo, G. U. (2021). Predictors of loneliness among older adults in South-Eastern Nigeria: Implications for social workers. *European Journal of Mental Health*, *16*, 3–19. 10.5708/EJMH.16. 2021.1.1

Eboiyehi, F. A. (2017). Convicted without evidence: Elderly women and witchcraft accusations in contemporary Nigeria. *Journal of International Women's Studies*, *18*(4), 247–265.

Ebue, M., Uche, O., & Agha, A. (2017). Levels of intervention in social work. In U. Okoye, N. Chukwu, & P. Agwu (Eds.), *Social work in Nigeria: Book of readings* (pp. 84–92). Nsukka: University of Nigeria Press Ltd.

Effiong, U. U., Mboho, K., & Wordu, S. (2018). Post-civil war experience and women with disabilities in Nigeria. *Journal of Research in Education and Society*, *9*(2), 104–126.

Ehigie, E. K., & Omorogiuwa, T. B. E. (2022). The scourge of child defilement and the implication for social work practice. *Benin Journal of Social Work and Community Development*, *4*, 41–54.

Eide, A. H., & Ingstad, B. (2013). Disability and poverty: Reflections on research experiences in Africa and beyond. *African Journal of Disability*, *2*(1), 1–7. 10.4102/ajod.v2i1.31

Ejikeme, G. G. (2010). The state of social work education and practice in Nigeria. In F. A. D. Oyekanmi, F. A. Badru, & F. Bammeke (Eds.), *Rethinking the state of social welfare in Nigeria*. Lagos: Department of Sociology, University of Lagos.

Eke, S. C., & Onwuatuegwu, I. N. (2021). The significance and the role of ubuntu philosophy in the Nigerian society. *South Asian Research Journal of Humanities and Social Sciences*, *3*(5), 344–349. 10.36346/sarjhss.2021.v03i05.015.

Ekoh, P. C., Agbawodikeizu, P. U., Ejimkararonye, C., George, E. O., Ezulike, C. D., & Nnebe, I. (2020a). COVID-19 in rural Nigeria: Diminishing social support for older people in Nigeria. *Gerontology and Geriatric Medicine*, *6*, 1–7. 10.1177/233372142 0986301

Ekoh, P. C., George, E. O., Ejimakaraonye, C., & Okoye, U. O. (2020b) An appraisal of public understanding of dementia across cultures. *Journal of Social Work in Developing Societies*, *2*(1), 54–67.

Ekpe, C. P. (1983). Social welfare and family support: The Nigerian experience. *Journal of Sociology and Social Welfare*, *10*(3), 488–496. https://scholarworks.wmich.edu/jssw/vol10/iss3/11

Ekpe, C. P., & Mamah, S. C. (1997). *Social work in Nigeria: A colonial heritage*. Enugu, Nigeria: UNIK-Oriental Print.

Eleweke, J., & Soje, G. (2016). Challenges of empowering people with disabilities in Nigeria for national development. *Journal of Special Education and Rehabilitation*, *17*(3/4), 122–138. 10.19057/jser.2016.14

Emelonye, U. (2020). Normative evolution of child rights in Nigeria. *Journal of Advanced Research in Social Science and Humanities*, *6*(9), 1–8. 10.53555/nnssh.v6i9.870

Etieyibo, E., & Omiegbe, O. (2016). Religion, culture and discrimination against persons with disabilities in Nigeria. *African Journal of Disability*, *5*(1), 1–6. 10.4102/ajod.v5 i1.192

European Asylum Support Office (EASO). (2018). *Country Intelligence Report Nigeria*. Retrieved from: https://www.easo.europa.eu/information-analysis/country-origin-information/country-reports

Enwereji, E. E. (2008). Assessing interventions available to Internally Displaced Persons in Abia State, Nigeria. *Libyan Journal of Medicine*, *AOP: 080725*, 17–22.

Falola, T., & Heaton, M. H. (2008). *A history of Nigeria.* Cambridge, UK: Cambridge University Press.

Fatile, J. O. (2012). Corruption and the challenges of good governance in the Nigerian public sector. *Africa's Public Service Delivery and Performance Review, 1*(3), 46–65. 10.4102/apsdpr.v1i3.35

Faulkner, D. (1941). *Social welfare and juvenile delinquency in Lagos.* London: The Hereford Times Limited, 1950, 2.

Fawcett, B., Goodwin, S., Meagher, G., & Phillips, R. (2009). *Social policy for social change.* Australia: Palgrave Macmillan.

Federal Ministry of Education (2006). *National Gender Policy on Education.* Lagos: Federal Government Press. Retrieved from https://planipolis.iiep.unesco.org/sites/default/files/ressources/nigeria_policy_gender_basic_education.pdf

Federal Ministry of National Planning. (1981). *Guidelines for the Fourth National Development Plan 1981-85.* Lagos: Federal Government Press. Retrieved from https://invenio.unidep.org/invenio//record/23810/files/NGA_S5020_3.pdf

Federal Ministry of Social Development. (1977). *Introduction to the Social Development Division.* Lagos: Federal Government Press.

Federal Ministry of Women Affairs and Social Development. (2006). *National Gender Policy.* Abuja: Federal Ministry of Women Affairs and Social Development.

Federal Ministry of Women Affairs and Social Development. (2007). *National guidelines and standards of practice on orphans and vulnerable children.* Retrieved from https://bettercarenetwork.org/sites/default/files/attachments/National%20Guidelines%20and%20Standards%20of%20Practice%20on%20Orphans%20and%20Vulnerable%20Children.pdf

Federal Ministry of Women Affairs and Social Development (FMWASD). (2013). *National priority agenda for vulnerable children in Nigeria 2013-2020.* Abuja. Nigeria: Federal Ministry of Women Affairs and Social Development.

Federal Ministry of Women Affairs and Social Development (FMWASD). (2014). *National standards for improving the quality of life of vulnerable children in Nigeria.* Abuja, Nigeria: Federal Ministry of Women Affairs and Social Development.

Federal Ministry of Women Affairs and Social Development. (2017). *National Action Plan for the implementation of UNSCR 1325 and related resolutions on women, peace and security in Nigeria 2017-2020.* Federal Ministry of Women Affairs and Social Development. Retrieved from https://www.peacewomen.org/sites/default/files/NAPNigeria.pdf

Federal Republic of Nigeria (FRN). (1970). *Second National Development Plan 1970-74.* Federal Ministry of Information. Lagos, Nigeria: Government Printer.

Federal Republic of Nigeria (FRN). (1974). *Social Development Act (No. 12 of 1974).* Retrieved from https://www.ilo.org/dyn/natlex/natlex4.detail?p_isn=58982&p_lang=en

Federal Republic of Nigeria (FRN). (1975). *Third National Development Plan 1975-80.* Federal Ministry of National Planning. Lagos, Nigeria: Government Printer.

Federal Republic of Nigeria (FRN). (1981). *Fourth National Development Plan 1981-85.* Federal Ministry of National Planning. Lagos, Nigeria: Government Printer.

Federal Republic of Nigeria (FRN). (1991). *National Mental Health Policy for Nigeria.* Lagos: Federal Ministry of Health (FMOH).

Federal Republic of Nigeria (FRN). (1995). *National Human Rights Commission Act 1995.* Retrieved from https://www.nigeriarights.gov.ng/files/nhrcact.pdf

Federal Republic of Nigeria (FRN). (1999a). *Constitution of the Federal Republic of Nigeria 1999.* Retrieved from https://www.nigeriarights.gov.ng/files/constitution.pdf

Federal Republic of Nigeria (FRN). (1999b). *National Policy on Women in Constitution of the Federal Republic of Nigeria 1999*. Retrieved from https://www.nigeriarights.gov.ng/files/constitution.pdf

Federal Republic of Nigeria (FRN). (2002). *National Disaster Response Plan (NDRP)*. Retrieved from https://www.preventionweb.net/publication/nigeria-national-disaster-response-plan

Federal Republic of Nigeria (FRN). (2004). *Compulsory, Free Universal Basic Education Act, 2004*. Retrieved from http://nigeria-education.org/literature/compulsory-free-universal-basic-education-act-2004

Federal Republic of Nigeria (FRN). (2005). *Infrastructure Concession Regulatory Commission (Establishment etc) Act, 2005*. National Assembly of the Federal Republic of Nigeria. Retrieved from https://www.icrc.gov.ng/assets/uploads/2018/12/ICRC-Act-2018.pdf

Federal Republic of Nigeria (FRN). (2006). *National Gender Policy: Situation Analysis/Framework*. Federal Ministry of Women Affairs and Social Development, Abuja. Retrieved from https://nigerianwomentrustfund.org/wp-content/uploads/National-Gender-PolicySituation-Analysis.pdf

Federal Republic of Nigeria (FRN). (2010). *Employee's Compensation Act, 2010*. Retrieved from https://www.ilo.org/dyn/natlex/natlex4.detail?p_isn=87608&p_lang=

Federal Republic of Nigeria (FRN). (2012). *National Policy on Internally Displaced Persons (IDPs) in Nigeria*. Retrieved from https://www.refworld.org/pdfid/5a7ae2324.pdf

Federal Republic of Nigeria (FRN). (2013a). *Nation Action Plan for the Elimination of Child Labour (2013-2017)*. Federal Ministry of Labour and Productivity. Retrieved from https://www.ilo.org/wcmsp5/groups/public/—africa/—ro-abidjan/—ilo-abuja/documents/publication/wcms_303410.pdf

Federal Republic of Nigeria (FRN). (2013b). *National Policy on Education*. Nigerian Educational Research and Development Council. Retrieved from https://education.gov.ng/wp-content/uploads/2020/06/NATIONAL-POLICY-ON-EDUCATION.pdf

Federal Republic of Nigeria (FRN). (2013c). *National Policy for Mental Health Services Delivery*. Abuja, Nigeria: Federal Ministry of Health. Retrieved from https://www.healthnews.ng/wp-content/uploads/2018/07/national_policy_for_mental_health_service_delivery.pdf

Federal Republic of Nigeria (FRN). (2013d). *National Mental, Neurological and Substance Use Programme and Action Plan*. Abuja, Nigeria: Federal Ministry of Health.

Federal Republic of Nigeria (FRN). (2013e). *Same Sex Marriage (Prohibition) Act, 2013*. Retrieved from https://www.refworld.org/pdfid/52f4d9cc4.pdf

Federal Republic of Nigeria (FRN). (2014). *HIV and AIDS (Anti-Discrimination) Act, 2014*. Retrieved from https://www.ilo.org/wcmsp5/groups/public/—ed_protect/—protrav/—ilo_aids/documents/legaldocument/wcms_398045.pdf

Federal Republic of Nigeria (FRN). (2015a). *Trafficking in Persons (Prohibition), Enforcement and Administration Act, 2015*. Lagos: Federal Government Printer. https://www.ilo.org/dyn/natlex/docs/ELECTRONIC/101267/121929/F958851509/NGA101267%20Part%201.pdf

Federal Republic of Nigeria (FRN). (2015b). *National Migration Policy 2015*. Retrieved from https://publications.iom.int/system/files/pdf/national_migration_policy_2015.pdf

Federal Republic of Nigeria (FRN). (2015c). *Violence Against Persons (Prohibition) Act, 2015*. Retrieved from https://www.nigeriarights.gov.ng/files/vapp.pdf

Federal Republic of Nigeria (FRN). (2015d). *Administration of Criminal Justice Act, 2015.* Retrieved from https://policehumanrightsresources.org/content/uploads/2017/09/Administration-of-Criminal-Justice-Act-2015-2.compressed.pdf?x96812

Federal Republic of Nigeria (FRN). (2016). *Draft National Social Protection Policy.* Ministry of Budget and National Planning. Retrieved from https://socialprotection.org/discover/legal_policy_frameworks/nigeria-national-social-protection-policy

Federal Republic of Nigeria (FRN). (2017). *Anti-torture Act, 2017.* Retrieved from https://www.ilo.org/dyn/natlex/docs/ELECTRONIC/108562/134257/F-1021277030/NGA108562.pdf

Federal Republic of Nigeria (FRN). (2018). *Discrimination Against Person with Disabilities (Prohibition) Act 2018.* Retrieved from https://www.nigeriarights.gov.ng/files/disability.pdf

Federal Republic of Nigeria (FRN). (2019). *Mental Health and Substance Abuse Bill.* Retrieved from https://placbillstrack.org/upload/SB66.pdf

Federal Republic of Nigeria (FRN). (2021a). *National Policy for Internally Displaced Persons (IDPs) in Nigeria.* Federal Ministry of Humanitarian Affairs, Disaster Management and Social Development.

Federal Republic of Nigeria (FRN). (2021b). *National Development Plan (NDP) 2021-2025, Volume I.* Federal Ministry of Finance, Budget and National Planning.

Federal Republic of Nigeria (FRN). (2021c). *The National Poverty Reduction with Growth Strategy: A strategy for accelerated reduction in poverty through economic growth, redistributive programs and shared prosperity.* Presidential Economic Advisory Council. Retrieved from https://nationalplanning.gov.ng/wp-content/uploads/2021/08/NPRGS-Final_23April-2021.pdf

Federal Republic of Nigeria (FRN). (2021d). *National Policy on Ageing for Older Persons in Nigeria.*

Federal Republic of Nigeria (FRN). (2022a). *National Action Plan on Human Trafficking in Nigeria 2022-2026.* National Agency for the Prohibition of Trafficking in Persons (NAPTIP) and Federal Ministry of Humanitarian Affairs Disaster Management and Social Development. Retrieved from https://www.unodc.org/documents/nigeria/National_Action_Plan_on_Human_Trafficking_in_Nigeria.pdf

Federal Republic of Nigeria (FRN). (2022b). *Chartered Institute of Social Work Practitioners (Establishment) Act, 2022.* Lagos, Nigeria: Federal Government Printer.

Federation of Nigeria. (1962). *National Development Plan 1962-68.* Federal Ministry of Economic Development. Lagos, Nigeria: Government Printer.

Felbab-Brown, V. (2018, March 30). *Nigeria's troubling counterinsurgency strategy against Boko Haram: How the military and militias are fueling insecurity.* Foreign Affairs. Retrieved from https://www.foreignaffairs.com/articles/nigeria/2018-03-30/nigerias-troubling-counterinsurgency-strategy-against-boko-haram

Flexner, A. (1915). Is social work a profession? *Proceedings of the National Conference of Charities and Corrections, 1915* (pp. 576–590). Chicago, IL: Hildmann.

Folaranmi, O. O., & Omotayo, O. T. (2013). Appraisal of traditional social welfare practices: A Review of Things Fall Apart. *Journal of English Studies, 9,* 323–340.

Folayan, M. O., Odetoyinbo, M., Harrison, A., & Brown, B. (2014). Rape in Nigeria: A silent epidemic among adolescents with implications for HIV infection. *Global Health Action, 7,* 1–2. 10.3402/gha.v7.25583

Folgheraiter, F. (2004). *Relational social work: Toward networking societal practices.* London: Jessica Kingsley Publishers.

Fourchard, L. (2006). Lagos and the invention of juvenile delinquency in Nigeria. *Journal of African History, 47*(1), 115–137.

Fourchard, L. (2010). The making of the juvenile delinquent in Nigeria and South Africa, 1930–1970. *History Compass, 8*(2), 129–142.

Funk, M. K., & Drew, N. J. (2015). Mental health legislation. *Eastern Mediterranean Health Journal, 21*(7), 527–530.

Garcia-Zamor J-C (2015) Quality of governance and ethical public service delivery (PSD) in developing countries. *Journal of Management and Strategy 6*(3): 28–37.

Garland, D. (2002). *The culture of control: Crime and social order in contemporary society.* Oxford: Oxford University Press.

GBV Sub-Sector Nigeria. (2019). *National Guidelines and Referral Standards Policy on Gender-Based Violence Prevention and Response: Nigeria.* Developed by the GBV Sub Sector in Collaboration with United Nations Population Fund (UNFPA), International Medical Corps (IMC) and Plan International: Validated & Endorsed by the GBV SS partners on 10th October 2019.

George, A. (2011). Within salvation: Girl hawkers and the colonial state in development era Lagos. *Journal of Social History, 44*(3), 837–859. 10.1353/jsh.2011.0034

George, A. A. (2014). *Making modern girls: A history of girlhood, labor, and social development in colonial Lagos.* Athens, GA: Ohio University Press.

George, E. O., & Ekoh, P. C. (2020). Social workers' perception of practice with lesbians, gays and bisexuals (LGBs) in Nigeria. *Journal of Comparative Social Work, 2*, 56–78. 10.31265/jcsw.v15.i2.306

George, T. O., Onwumah, A. C., Ozoya, M. I., & Olonade, O. Y. (2021). Good governance, social order, and development in Nigeria: The critical role of gender inclusion. *African Journal of Reproductive Health, 25*, 201–208. 10.29063/ajrh2021/v25i5s.18

Gerassi, L. B., & Nichols, A. J. (2021). Social work education that addresses trafficking for sexual exploitation: An intersectional, anti-oppressive practice framework. *Anti-Trafficking Review, 17*, 20–37. Retrieved from antitraffickingreview.org

Gesinde, A. M., & Elegbeleye, A. (2011). An investigation into push factors sustaining human trafficking in Nigeria. *Journal of Functional Management, 41*(1), 147–157.

Gibbelman M. (1999). The search for identity: Defining social work – past, present, future. *Social Work, 44*(4), 298–310.

Gimba, B. (2016). Internal displacement in Nigeria and the case for human rights protection of displaced persons. *Journal of Law, Policy and Globalization, 51*, 26–33.

Global Terrorism Index. (2016). *Measuring and understanding the impact of terrorism.* New York: Institute for Economics and Peace. Retrieved from https://www.economicsandpeace.org/wp-content/uploads/2016/11/Global-Terrorism-Index-2016.2.pdf

Goodwin, S. (2003). Gender and social exclusion in Australia. In Weiss (Eds.), *Social Exclusion: An Approach to the Australian Case* (pp. 375–390). Germany: Peter Lang Publishing.

Graham, M. J. (1999). The African-centred worldview: Developing a paradigm for social work. *British Journal of Social Work, 29*(2), 251–267.

Gray, M. (2000). Social work and the 'social service professions'. *Social Work/ Maatskaplike Werk, 36*(1), 99–109.

Gray, M. (2010). Social development and the status quo: Professionalisation and Third Way cooptation. *International Journal of Social Welfare, 19*(4), 463–470. 10.1111/j.1468-2397.2009.00714.x.

Gray, M. (2016). 'Think globally and locally, act globally and locally': A new agenda for international social work education. In I. Taylor, M. Bogo, M. Lefevre, & B. Teater (Eds.), *The Routledge International Handbook of Social Work Education* (pp. 3–13). London: Routledge.

Gray, M. (Ed.). (2017). *The Routledge handbook of social work and social development in Africa.* London: Routledge.

Gray, M., & Allegritti, I. (2002). Cross-cultural practice and the indigenisation of African social work. *Social Work/Maatskaplike Werk,* 38(4), 324–336.

Gray, M., & Allegritti, I. (2003). Towards culturally sensitive social work practice: Re-examining cross-cultural social work. *Social Work/Maatskaplike Werk,* 39(4), 312–325.

Gray, M., & Amadasun, S. (2022). Strategic processes to further the professional status of social work in Nigeria. *International Social Work,* 0(0). 10.1177/00208728221123193.

Gray, M., & Ariong, S. B. (2017). Discourses shaping development, foreign aid, and poverty reduction policies in Africa: Implications for social work. In M. Gray (Ed.), *The Routledge handbook of social work and social development in Africa* (pp. 15–32). London: Routledge.

Gray, M., & Hetherington, T. (2013). Indigenization, Indigenous social work, and decolonization: Mapping the theoretical terrain. In M. Gray, J. Coates, M. Yellow Bird, & T. Hetherington (Eds.), *Decolonizing social work* (pp. 25–41). Aldershot, Hants: Ashgate.

Gray, M., & Lombard, A. (2022). Progress of the social service professions in South Africa's developmental social welfare system: Social work and child and youth care work. *International Journal of Social Welfare.*

Gray, M., & Simpson, B. (1998). Developmental social work education: A field example. *International Social Work,* 41(2), 227–237.

Gray, M., & Webb, S. A. (2014). The making of a civil society politics in social work: Myth and misrepresentation in the global agenda. *International Social Work,* 57(4), 346–359. 10.1177/0020872814524965 (Special Issue on the Global Agenda).

Gray, M., Agllias, K., Boddy, J., & Schubert, L. (2015). Doctoral research from a feminist perspective: Appreciating feminist research: Acknowledging, advancing and aligning women's experience. *Qualitative Social Work,* 14(6), 758–775. 10.1177/14733250145 65148.

Gray, M., Agllias, K., Mupedziswa, R., & Mugumbate, J. (2018). The expansion of developmental social work in Southern and Eastern Africa: Opportunities and challenges for social work field programs. *International Social Work,* 61(6), 974–987.

Gray, M., Coates, J., & Yellow Bird, M. (Eds.). (2008). *Indigenous social work around the world: Towards culturally relevant education and practice.* Aldershot, Hants: Ashgate.

Gray, M., Coates, J., Yellow Bird, M., & Hetherington, T. (Eds.). (2013). *Decolonizing social work.* Aldershot, Hants: Ashgate.

Gray, M., Kreitzer, L., & Mupedziswa, R. (2014). The enduring relevance of in-digenisation in African social work: A critical reflection on ASWEA's legacy. *Ethics and Social Welfare,* 8(2), 101–116. 10.1080/17496535.2014.895397.

Gray, M., Mazibuko, F., & O'Brien, F. (1996). Social work education for social development. *Journal of Social Development in Africa,* 11(1), 33–42.

Guardian (The). (2021). *Social workers appeal to NASS on passage of Social Work Bill.* Retrieved from https://guardian.ng/news/social-workers-appeal-to-nass-on-passage-of-social-work-bill/

Gureje, O., Ogunniyi, A., Kola, L., & Afolabi, E. (2006). Functional disability in elderly Nigerians: Results from the Ibadan study of aging. *Journal of the American Geriatrics Society, 54*(11), 1784–1789.

Gureje, O., Oladeji, B. B., Abiona, T., & Chatterji, S. (2014). Profile and determinants of successful ageing in the Ibadan study of aging. *Journal of the American Geriatrics Society, 62*(5), 836–842. 10.1111/jgs.12802

Gureje, O., Abdulmalik, J., Kola, L., Musa, E., Yasamy, M. T., & Adebayo K. (2015). Integrating mental health into primary care in Nigeria: Report of a demonstration project using the mental health gap action programme intervention guide. BMC *Health Services Research 15*, 242–250. 10.1186/s12913-015-0911-3

Gwadabe, N. M., Salleh, M. A., Ahmad, A. A., & Jamil, S. Forced displacement and the plight of Internally Displaced Persons in Northeast Nigeria. *Humanities and Social Science Research, 1*(1), 46–52. 10.30560/hssr.v1n1p46

Hamilton, R. (1976). Social work: An aspiring profession and its difficulties. *British Journal of Social Work, 4*(3), 333–341.

Harms-Smith, L. (2017). 'Blaming-the-poor': Strengths and development discourses which obfuscate neo-liberal and individualist ideologies. *International Social Work, 60*(2). 336–350. 10.1177/0020872815594218.

Harms-Smith, L., & Nathane, M. (2018). #Not domestication #Not indigenisation: Decoloniality in social work education. *Southern African Journal of Social Work and Social Development, 30*(1), 1–18.

Harré, T. (2022). Human traffickers' fair trial rights and transnational criminal law. *Anti-Trafficking Review, 18*, 159–173. 10.14197/atr.2012221810

Haruna, M. A. (2017). The problems of living with disability in Nigeria. *Journal of Law, Policy & Globalization, 65*, 103–113.

HassanWuyo, I. (2020, September 18). Nigeria sliding into Hobbesian state, NGOs defrauding int'l organisations—Anglican Bishop [Rt. Rev. Timothy Yahaya]. *Vanguard News Nigeria*. Retrieved from https://www.vanguardngr.com/2020/09/nigeria-sliding-into-hobbesian-state-ngos-defrauding-intl-organisations-%e2%80%95-anglican-bishop/

Healy, K. (2013). Professional registration and title protection for social workers in Australia: Past, present and future. Address to *Social Work Registration Board Conference*, Wellington, New Zealand, November 11. Retrieved from https://www.aasw.asn.au/document/item/5717

Heap, S. (1997). 'Jaguda boys': Pickpocketing in Ibadan, 1930-60. *Urban History, 24*(3), 324–343.

Heap, S. (2010). 'Their days are spent in gambling and loafing, pimping for prostitutes, and picking pockets': Male juvenile delinquents on Lagos Island, Nigeria, 1920s–60s. *Journal of Family History, 35*(1), 48–70.

Heap, S. (2015). Processing juvenile delinquents at the Salvation Army's Boys' Industrial Home in Lagos, 1925-1944. In S. Aderinto (Ed.), *Children and Childhood in Colonial Nigerian Histories* (pp. 49–76). New York: Palgrave Macmillan. 10.1057/9781137492937_3

Heldring, L., & Robinson, J. A. (2012). *Colonialism and economic development in Africa.* Working Paper 18566. Cambridge, MA: National Bureau of Economic Research. Retrieved from http://www.nber.org/papers/w18566.

Hochfeld, T., Selipsky, L., Mupedziswa, R., & Chitereka, C. (2009). *Developmental social work education in southern and east Africa.* University of Johannesburg, Johannesburg: Centre for Social Development in Africa.

Holmes, R., Akinrimisi, B., Morgan, J., & Buck, R. (2012). Social protection in Nigeria. In *Mapping Programs and Their Effectiveness*. London, UK: Overseas Development Institute. Retrieved from https://cdn.odi.org/media/documents/7582.pdf

Hopp, J. G., & Pinderhughes, E. B. (1987). Profession of social work: Contemporary characteristics. *Encyclopedia of Social Work* (18th ed.). (pp. 351–366). Silver Spring, MD: National Association of Social Workers.

Hopper, E. K. (2017). Trauma-informed psychological assessment of human trafficking survivors. *Women & Therapy, 40*(1-2), 12–30. 10.1080/02703149.2016.1205905

Hu, R. (2019). Examining social service providers' representation of trafficking victims: A feminist postcolonial lens. *Journal of Women and Social Work, 34*(4), 421–438.

Hume, D. L., & Sidun, N. M. (2017). Human trafficking of women and girls: Characteristics, commonalities, and complexities. *Women & Therapy, 40*(1-2), 7–11. 10.1080/02703149.2016.1205904

Human Development Report. (2020). *The next frontier: Human development and the Anthropocene*. Briefing note for countries on the 2020 Human Development Report. Nigeria: UNDP. Retrieved from https://hdr.undp.org/sites/default/files/hdr2020.pdf

Human Rights Watch. (2019). *Nigeria Passes Disability Rights Law*. Retrieved from https://www.hrw.org/news/2019/01/25/nigeria-passes-disability-rights-law

Husted, T. F., & Blanchard, L. P. (2020). *Nigeria: Current issues and U.S. policy*. Washington, DC: Congressional Research Service. Retrieved from https://www.fas.org/sgp/crs/row/RL33964.pdf

Hutton, M., & Mwansa, L-K. (Eds.). (1996). *Social work practice in Africa: Social development in a community context*. Gaborone: PrintConsult.

Ibekwe, C. S., & Uduma, O. C. (2019). The evolution of disability rights in Nigeria: Pitfalls and prospects. *African Journal of Law and Human Rights, 3*(2), 137–147.

Ibiezugbe, M. I. (2018). Social analysis of the living conditions of the elderly in selected communities in Edo Central Senatorial District. *International Journal of Humanities and Social Science, 8*(3), 35–42. 10.30845/ijhss.v9n3p6

Ibrahima, A., & Mattaini, M. (2019). Social work in Africa: Decolonizing methodologies and approaches. *International Social Work, 62*(2), 799–813. 10.1177/0020872817742702.

Idyorough, A. E. (2013). Social work administration in Nigeria: Challenges and prospects. *Keynote address Professionalization of Social Work in Nigeria*. Nigerian Association of Social Workers (NASoW), Abuja, Nigeria, March 26-27.

Iguh, N. A., & Nosike, O. (2011). An examination of the child rights protection and corporal punishment in Nigeria. *Nnamdi Azikiwe University Journal of International Law and Jurisprudence, 2*, 97–111. Retrieved from https://www.ajol.info/index.php/naujilj/article/view/82391

Iguh, N. A., & Oti-Onyema, L. A. (2020). Statutory rape under the Child's Right Act of Nigeria: Analysis of the criminal responsibility of a child offender. *International Journal of Comparative Law and Legal Philosophy, 2*(3), 184–191.

Iheanacho, E. N. (2014). National development planning in Nigeria: An endless search for appropriate development strategy. *International Journal of Economic Development Research and Investment, 5*(2), 49–60.

Iliffe, J. (1987). *The African poor: A history*. New York: Cambridge University Press.

Iloh, J. O., & Bahir, M. (2013). Public private partnership (PPP) and social service reform in Nigeria: 1999-2007. In A. N. Nosike, P. U. Akanwa, K. A. Anele, & D. Iornem (Eds.), *Proceedings of the Abuja International Conference on Human and Social Sciences*, (pp. 323–330). Granada, Spain: International Association for Teaching and Learning.

Imam, I., & Abdulraheem-Mustapha, M. M. (2016). Rights of people with disability in Nigeria: Attitude and commitment. *African Journal of International and Comparative Law, 24*(3), 439–459.

International Association of Schools of Social Work (IASSW) and International Federation of Social Workers (IFSW). (2012). *Global Agenda for Social Work and Social Development*. Retrieved from https://www.iassw-aiets.org/global-agenda/global-agenda-2010-2020/

International Federation of Social Workers (IFSW) and International Association of Schools of Social Work (IASSW). (2020). *Global standards for social work education and training*. Retrieved from https://www.ifsw.org/global-standards-for-social-work-education-and-training/?hub=main

International Association of Schools of Social Work (IASSW), International Federation of Social Workers (IFSW), and International Council on Social Welfare (ICSW). (2020). *2020 to 2030 Global Agenda for Social Work and Social Development Framework: Co-Building Inclusive Social Transformation*. Retrieved from https://www.iassw-aiets.org/global-agenda/

International Labour Organisation (ILO). (1930). *Convention concerning Forced or Compulsory Labour*. Retrieved from https://documentation.lastradainternational.org/doc-center/1065/convention-concerning-forced-or-compulsory-labour

International Labour Organisation (ILO). (1951). *Equal Remuneration Convention*. Retrieved from https://www.ilo.org/dyn/normlex/en/f?p=NORMLEXPUB:12100:0::NO::P12100_Ilo_Code:C100

International Labour Organisation (ILO). (1957). *Abolition of Forced Labour Convention*. Retrieved from https://www.ilo.org/dyn/normlex/en/f?p=1000:12100:0::NO::P12100_ILO_CODE:C105

International Labour Organisation (ILO). (1958). *Discrimination (Employment and Occupation) Convention*. Retrieved from https://www.ilo.org/dyn/normlex/en/f?p=NORMLEXPUB:12100:0::NO::P12100_ILO_CODE:C111

International Labour Organisation (ILO). (1999). *Convention Concerning the Prohibition and Immediate Action for the Elimination of the Worst Forms of Child Labor*. Retrieved from https://www.ilo.org/dyn/normlex/en/f?p=NORMLEXPUB:12100:0::NO::P12100_ILO_CODE:C182

International Organisation for Migration (IOM). (2019). *'Voodoo curses' keep victims of trafficking under bondage*. Retrieved from https://www.iom.int/news/voodoo-curses-keep-victims-trafficking-under-bondage

International Program on the Elimination of Child Labor (IPEC). (2002). *Unbearable to the heart: Child trafficking and action to eliminate it*. Retrieved from http://www.unicf.org/violencestudy/pdf/2002-traff-unbearable.en.pdf

Isaac, O. A., & Tanga, P. T. (2014). Income and occupation as correlates of well-being of caregivers of children with disabilities in South-Western Nigeria. *Mediterranean Journal of Social Sciences, 5*(2), 111–119.

Isangha, S. O., Olaitan, T. M., Ogar, L. E., Obasi-Igwe, I. A., Aghedo, G. U., & Iweagwu, A. O. (2020). Child witchcraft confession: Parental reaction and implication for social work practice. *Advances in Social Sciences Research Journal, 7*(12), 691–704.

Isichei, E. (1978). *Igbo worlds: An anthology of oral histories and historical descriptions*. Philadelphia, PA: Institute for the Study of Human Issues.

Iweriebor, E. E. G. (1982). State systems in pre-colonial, colonial and post-colonial Nigeria: An overview. *Rivista trimestrale di studi e documentazione dell'Istituto italiano per l'Africa e l'Oriente, 37*(4), 507–513. Retrieved from https://www.jstor.org/stable/40759619

Iwobi, U. (2008). No cause for merriment: The position of widows under Nigerian law. *Canadian Journal of Women and the Law, 20*(1), 37–86.

Iyayi, R. I. (2017). *Nigeria, arise and embrace Ubuntu.* Retrieved from http://saharareporters. com/2017/08/30/nigeria-arise-and-embrace-ubuntu-rukayya-ibrahim-iyayi

Izzett, A. (1955). *The Yoruba young delinquent in Lagos, Nigeria.* B. Litt thesis, University of Oxford.

Izzett, A. (1973). The fears and anxieties of young Yoruba children. *ODU: Journal of Yoruba and Related Studies, 1*, 211–217.

Jack-Ide, I. O., & Uys, L. R. (2013). Barriers to mental health services utilization in the Niger Delta region of Nigeria: Service users' perspectives. *Pan African Medical Journal, 14*, 159–166. 10.11604/pamj.2013.14.159.1970

Jack-Ide, I. O., Uys, L. R., & Middleton L. E. (2012). A comparative study of mental health services in two African countries: South Africa and Nigeria. *International Journal of Nursing and Midwifery, 4*(4), 50–57. 10.5897/IJNM12.002

Jayasooria, D. (2016). Sustainable Development Goals and social work: Opportunities and challenges for social work practice in Malaysia. *Journal of Human Rights and Social Work, 1*(1), 19–29. 10.1007/s41134-016-0007-y

Jegede, A. S. (2002). The Yoruba cultural construction of health and illness. *Nordic Journal of African Studies, 11*(3), 322–335.

Jegede, A. S. (2005). The notion of 'were' in Yoruba conception of mental illness. *Nordic Journal of African Studies, 14*(1), 117–126.

Jidong, D. E., Bailey, D., Sodi, T., Gibson, L., Sawadogo, N., Ikhile, D., Musoke, D., Madhombiro, M., & Mbah, M. (2021). Nigerian cultural beliefs about mental health conditions and traditional healing: A qualitative study. *Journal of Mental Health Training, Education and Practice, 16*(4), 285–299. 10.1108/JMHTEP-08-2020-0057

Jidong, D. E., Ike, T. J., Tribe, R., Tunariu, A. D., Rohleder, P., & Mackenzie, A. (2022) Berom cultural beliefs and attitudes towards mental health problems in Nigeria: A mixed-methods study. *Mental Health, Religion & Culture, 25*(5), 504–518. 10.1080/ 13674676.2021.2019205

Jinadu, G. M. (1985). Social development in Nigeria: A case analysis. *Journal of Sociology & Social Welfare, 12*(4), 850–877. Retrieved from https://scholarworks.wmich.edu/cgi/ viewcontent.cgi?article=1730&context=jssw, Article 10.

John, M. E., Nsemo, A. D., John, E. E., Opiah, M., Robinson-Bassey, G. C., & Yagba, J. (2015). Indigenous child care beliefs and practices in the Niger Delta Region of Nigeria: Implications for health care. *International Journal of Health Sciences & Research, 5*(11), 235–247.

Johnson, A. (2019). *The voiceless woman: Countering dominant narratives concerning disabled women in Nigeria.* PhD thesis. Pretoria, SA: University of Pretoria.

Johnson, A. (2020). Hush woman! The complex 'disabled' woman in Nigeria's legal and human-rights framework: A deconstruction. *African Disability Rights Yearbook, 8*, 3–30. Retrieved from https://www.adry.up.ac.za/articles-2020/johnson-a-2020

Jones, D. N., & Truell, R. (2012). The global agenda for social work and social development: A place to link together and be effective in a globalized world. *International Social Work, 55*(4), 454–472. 10.1177/0020872812440587

Kazeem, K. (2011). An integrated approach to social work practice in Nigeria. *College Student Journal, 45*(1), 122–133.

Lamai, S. (2021, February 11). *FG Approves National Policy on Ageing for Older Persons in Nigeria.* Federal Ministry of Information and Culture. Retrieved from https://fmic.gov. ng/fg-approves-national-policy-on-ageing-for-older-persons-in-nigeria/

Lawal, T., & Oluwatoyin, A. (2011). National development in Nigeria: Issues, challenges and prospects. *Journal of Public Administration and Policy Research, 3*(9), 237–241. 10.5897/JPAPR11.012

Levy, S., Okoye, U. O., & Ingram, R. (2022). Making the 'local' visible in social work education: Insights from Nigeria and Scotland on (re)balancing and contextualising indigenous and international knowledge. *British Journal of Social Work*. 10.1093/bjsw/bcac028

Lombard, A. (2015). Global agenda for social work and social development: A path toward sustainable social work. *Social Work/Maatskaplike Werk, 50*(4), 482–499. http://dx.doi.org/51-3-462

Lombard, A., Grobbelaar, M., & Pruis, S. (2003). Standards for social work qualifications in South Africa. *Social Work/Maatskaplike Werk, 39*(1), 1–17. 10.15270/39-1-375

Louw, L. R. (1998). Changing social welfare policy in South Africa. *Social Work/Maatskaplike Werk, 34*(1), 134–143.

Lovat, T. (2010). Islam and ethics. In M. Gray, & S. A. Webb (Eds.), *Ethics and value perspectives in social work* (pp. 185–195). London: Palgrave.

Ma, D., Qin, K., Shi, T., & Gai, K. (2015). Qingshaonian shehui gongzuo xietong fazhan moshi tanxi (The cooperative development model of adolescent social work). *Youth & Adolescence Studies, 23*(3), 51–54.

Mabvurira, V. (2020). Hunhu/ubuntu philosophy as a guide for ethical decision making in social work. *African Journal of Social Work, 10*(1), 73–77.

MacDonald, D., Dew, A., & Boydell, K. (2020). Structuring photovoice for community impact: A protocol for research with women with physical disability. *Forum: Qualitative Social Research, 21*(2), 1–17. 10.17169/fqs-21.2.3420

Makinde, O. A. (2016). Infant trafficking and baby factories: A new tale of child abuse in Nigeria. *Child Abuse Review, 25*, 433–443. 10.1002/car.2420

Makinde, O. A., Makinde, O. O., Olaleye, O., Brown, B., & Odimegwu, C. O. (2016). Baby factories taint surrogacy in Nigeria. *Reproductive BioMedicine Online, 32*(1), 6–8. 10.1016/j.rbmo.2015.10.001

Makinde, O. A., Odimegwu, C. O., & Babalola, S. O. (2017a). Reasons for infertile couples not to patronize baby factories. *Health & Social Work, 42*(1), 57–59. 10.1093/hsw/hlw054

Makinde, O. A., Olaleye, O., Makinde, O. O., Huntley, S. S., & Brown, B. (2017b). Baby factories in Nigeria: Starting the discussion toward a national prevention policy. *Trauma, Violence & Abuse, 18*(1), 98–105. 10.1177/1524838015591588

Mamman-Daura, F. (2022). *Forced migration in Nigeria is a development issue*. OECD Development Matters. Retrieved from https://oecd-development-matters.org/2022/02/02/forced-migration-in-nigeria-is-a-development-issue/

Marris, P. (1966). *Family and social change in an African city*. London: Routledge and Kegan Paul.

Mayah, E., et al. (2017). *Inequality in Nigeria: Exploring the drivers*. Even it up series. Oxfam International. Retrieved from https://www.oxfam.org

Mazibuko, F. N. M., & Gray, M. (2004). Social work professional associations in South Africa. *International Social Work, 47*(1), 129–142.

Mbah, P., & Nwangwu, C. (2013). Sub-ethnic identity and conflict in Nigeria: The policy option for the resolution of the conflict between Ezza and Ezillo in Ebonyi state. In A. N. Nosike, P. U. Akanwa, K. A. Anele, & D. Iornem (Eds.), *Proceedings of the Abuja International Conference on Human and Social Sciences* (pp. 415–424). Granada, Spain: International Association for Teaching and Learning.

Mbah, F., Ebue, M., & Ugwu, C. (2017). History of social work in Nigeria. In U. Okoye, N. Chukwu, & P. Agwu (Eds.), *Social work in Nigeria: Book of readings* (pp. 1–14). Nsukka, Nigeria: University of Nigeria Press Ltd.

Mboto, W. A., Akah, P. E., & Bukie, F. B. (2021). Family values, human rights and challenges of modernization in Nigeria. *British International Journal of Education and Social Sciences*, 8(12), 18–23.

McCurdy, S., Sreekumar, S., & Mendes, P. (2020). Is there a case for the registration of social workers in Australia? *International Social Work*, 63(1), 18–29.

Meng, Q., Gray, M., Bradt, L., & Roets, G. (2018). Emergence of social work practice in rural China: A way forward? *International Social Work*, 62(2), 933–943. 10.1177/002 0872818755859.

Mere, A. A. (1981). Field work instruction in Nigerian schools of social work. *International Social Work*, 24, 41–45. 10.1177/002087288102400307.

Meyer, S. R., Stöckl, H., Vorfeld, C., Kamenov, K., & Garcia-Moreno, C. (2022). A scoping review of measurement of violence against women and disability. *PLoS ONE*, 17(1), e0263020. 10.1371/journal.pone.0263020

Midgley, J. (1981). *Professional imperialism: Social work in the Third World*. London: Heinemann Educational Books.

Midgley, J. (1995). *Social development: The developmental perspective in social welfare*. London: Sage.

Mohamed, K., & Shefer, T. (2015). Gendering disability and disabling gender: Critical reflections on intersections of gender and disability. *Agenda*, 29(2), 2–13. 10.1080/1013 0950.2015.1055878

Monye, S., Ansah, E., & Orakwue, E. (2010). Easy to declare, difficult to implement: The disconnect between the aspirations of the Paris Declaration and donor practice in Nigeria. *Development Policy Review*, 28(6), 749–770.

Moore, M., Wilson, E., Campaign, R., Hagiliassis, N., McGillivray, J., Graffam, J., & Bink, M. (2010). *Measuring the social inclusion of people with a disability in Australia: The first national 1 in 4 poll*. Deakin and SCOPE. Retrieved from http://dro.deakin.edu.au/eserv/DU:30041561/moore-measuringthe-2010-1.pdf

Moshood, Y. (2020, July 20). Nigeria's growing problem of child abandonment. *Punch Healthwise*. Retrieved from https://healthwise.punchng.com/nigerias-growing-problem-of-child-abandonment/

Milner, A. (1972). *The Nigerian Penal System*. London: Sweet & Maxwell.

Mimiko, O. (1998). The State and the growth/Development Agenda: Africa and East/Asia in context. In D. Kolawole (Ed.), *Issues in Nigerian government and politics* (pp. 163–166). Ibadan, Nigeria: Dekaal Publishers.

Ministry of Civil Affairs (MOCA) [China]. (2019). *The Third Quarter of 2019 Routine Press Conference*. Retrieved from http://lyzx.mca.gov.cn:8280/asop/login.asop

Minnesota University Library, Human Rights Library. (n.d.). *Ratification of International Human Rights Treaties: Nigeria*. Retrieved from http://hrlibrary.umn.edu/research/ratification-nigeria.html

Mojoyinola, J. K. (2006). Social work interventions in the prevention and management of domestic violence. *Journal of Social Sciences*, 13(2), 97–99. 10.1080/09718923.2006. 11892537

Mojoyinola, J. K., & Ayangunna, J. A. (2012). Social work and welfare of the aged in Nigeria. In H. O. Osinowo, O. A. Moronkola, & D. O. Egunyomi (Eds.), *The adults and aged in Nigeria: Issues and researches* (pp. 17–29). Ibadan, Nigeria: Royal People (Nigeria) Ltd.

Mugumbate, J., & Chereni, A. (2019). Using African Ubuntu theory in social work with children in Zimbabwe. *African Journal of Social Work, 9,* 27–34.

Mugumbate, J., & Nyanguru, A. (2013). Exploring African philosophy: The value of Ubuntu in social work. *African Journal of Social Work, 3,* 82–100.

Mupedziswa, R. (1992). Africa at a crossroads: Major challenges for social work education and practice towards the year 2000. *Journal of Social Development in Africa, 7*(2), 19–38.

Mupedziswa, R. (1993). *Social work in Äfrica: Critical essays on the struggle for relevance.* Draft Manuscript. Harare: School of Social Work.

Mupedziswa, R., Rankopo, M., & Mwansa, L-K. (2019). Ubuntu as a pan-African philosophical framework for social work in Africa. In J. M. Twikirize, & H. Spitzer (Eds.), *Social work practice in Africa: Indigenous and innovative approaches* (pp. 21–38). Kampala, Uganda: Fountain Publishers.

Muzaale, P. (1987). Social development, rural poverty and implications for fieldwork practice. *Journal of Social Development in Africa, 2*(1), 75–87.

Naab, F., Lawali, Y., & Donkor, E. S. (2019). 'My mother in-law forced my husband to divorce me': Experiences of women with infertility in Zamfara State of Nigeria. *PLoS One, 14*(12), e0225149. 10.1371/journal.pone.0225149

National Assembly of the Federal Republic of Nigeria. (2019). *A Bill for an Act to establish the Nigerian Council for Social Work to Regulate the Practice of Professional Social Work in Nigeria, and for Related Matters, 2019.* Retrieved from https://placng.org/i/wp-content/uploads/2019/12/A-Bill-for-an-Act-to-Establish-the-Nigerian-Council-for-Social-Work-2019.pdf

National Emergency Management Agency (NEMA). (2010). *National Disaster Framework.* Retrieved from https://www.preventionweb.net/files/21708_nigherianationaldisastermanagementf.pdf

National Bureau of Statistics (NBS). (2019). *Poverty and inequality in Nigeria.* Abuja, Nigeria: NBS. Retrieved from https://nigerianstat.gov.ng

National Human Rights Commission (NHRC). (2003). *Child Rights Act 2003.* Retrieved from https://www.nigeriarights.gov.ng/files/childrightact.pdf

National Human Rights Commission (NHRC). (2010). *National Human Rights Commission (Amendment) Act, 2010.* Retrieved from

National Human Rights Commission (NHRC). (2021). *National Action Plan for the Promotion and Protection of Human Rights 2022-2026.* Retrieved from https://www.nigeriarights.gov.ng/activities/nap.html

National Planning Commission (NPC). (2004). *National Economic Empowerment and Development Strategy (NEEDS).* Abuja: NPC. Retrieved from https://www.nigeriarights.gov.ng/about/nhrc-mandate.html#:~:text=The%20NHRC%20(Amendment)%20Act%2C,rights%20and%20enforcement%20of%20decisions. https://www.cbn.gov.ng/out/publications/communique/guidelines/rd/2004/needs.pdf

National Planning Commission (NPC). (2009). *Nigeria Vision 20:2020 Document.* Abuja: National Planning Commission.

National Planning Commission (NPC). (2020). *Nigeria Vision 20:2030 Document.* Abuja: National Planning Commission.

National Population Commission (NPC). (2018). *Nigeria Demographic and Health Survey, 2018.* Abuja, Nigeria: National Population Commission. Retrieved from https://drive.google.com/file/d/1Y9dm9Mhr1KjLj9asOYuXkutGIxW8wY06/view

National Population Commission (NPC) [Nigeria] and International Classification of Functioning, Disability and Health (ICF). (2019). *Nigeria Demographic and Health Survey 2018*. Abuja, Nigeria, and Rockville, Maryland, USA: NPC and ICF. Retrieved from https://dhsprogram.com/pubs/pdf/FR359/FR359.pdf

National Universities Commission (NUC). (2017). Benchmark Minimum Academic Standards (BMAS) guidelines for undergraduate bachelors and masters courses in social work. *NUC Bulletin, 12*(30), 8–9. Retrieved from https://nuc.edu.ng/wp-content/uploads/2017/07/MB-24th-July-2017-ilovepdf-compressed.pdf

National Universities Commission (NUC). (2017). *Benchmark Minimum Academic Standards for Undergraduate Programme in Nigerian Universities: Social Work*. Abuja: NUC.

Nigeria Association of Social Workers (NASoW), Lagos State Chapter. (2022). *About*. Retrieved from https://nasowlagos.org/

Nigeria CEDAW NGO Coalition. (2008). *Nigeria CEDAW NGO Coalition Shadow Report*. Submitted to the 41st Session of the United Nations Committee on the Elimination of all Forms of Discrimination Against Women. Retrieved from https://www.fidh.org/IMG/pdf/Nigeria-report.pdf

Niu, D., & Østbø Haugen, H. (2019). Social workers in China: Professional identity in the making. *British Journal of Social Work, 49*(7), 1932–1949.

Nnama-Okechukwu, C. U., & McLaughlin, H. (2022). Indigenous knowledge and social work education in Nigeria: Made in Nigeria or made in the West? *Social Work Education*, 1–18. 10.1080/02615479.2022.2038557

Nnama-Okechukwu, C., Agwu, P., & Okoye, U. (2020). Informal foster care practice in Anambra State, Nigeria and safety concerns. *Children and Youth Services Review, 112*, 1–7. 10.1016/j.childyouth.2020.104889

Nnama-Okechukwu, C., McLaughlin, H., Okoye, U., Hendricks, E., Imaan, L., Malinga, T., Wizi-Kambala, A., Ebimgbo, S., Veta, O., & Imo, N. (2022). Indigenous knowledge and social work education in Nigeria: Challenges and need for sustainable development. *International Social Work, 0*(0), 1–15. 10.1177/00208728221098511

Nnamani, D. O., & Obinna, A. S. (2013). Local government administration and opposition parties in Nigeria: 1999-2011. In A. N. Nosike, P. U. Akanwa, K. A. Anele, & D. Iornem (Eds.), *Proceedings of the Abuja International Conference on Human and Social Sciences* (pp. 284–294). Granada, Spain: International Association for Teaching and Learning.

Nonomura, R. (2020). *Trafficking at the intersections: Racism, colonialism, sexism, and exploitation in Canada*. Brief 36. London, ON: Learning Network. Retrieved from https://www.vawlearningnetwork.ca/our-work/briefs/briefpdfs/Brief-361.pdf

Ntusi, T. M. (1998). Professional challenges for South African social workers: Response to recent political changes. *Social Work/Maatskaplike Werk, 34*(4), 380–388.

Nwakasi, C. C., Hayes, C., Fulton, J., & Roberts, A. R. (2019). A pilot qualitative study of dementia perceptions and experiences of Nigerian migrant caregivers. *International Journal of Africa Nursing Sciences, 10*, 167–174. 10.1016/j.ijans.2019.03.003

Nwalieji, R. I., & Oyebanjo, A. (2019). Nigeria's Internally Displaced Persons: A humanitarian priority. *AU ECHO, 10*. Retrieved from https://www.researchgate.net/profile/Raymond_Inkabi/publication/334466238_Nigeria's_Internally_Displaced_Persons_A_Humanitarian_Priority/links/5d2c8e5f299bf1547cb88c2b/NigeriasInternally-Displaced-Persons-A-Humanitarian-Priority.pdf

Nwanna, C. R., & Ogunniran, I. (2019). Challenges of Lagos State child's rights law: Social welfare officers' perspective. *African Journal of Criminology and Justice Studies: AJCJS*, *12*(1), 1–20. Retrieved from https://www.umes.edu/uploadedFiles/_WEBSITES/AJCJS/Content/VOL12.1.%20NWANNA%20FINAL.pdf

Nwanna, C. R., & Oparaoha, N. U. (2018). The role of social workers in ameliorating the plight of internally displaced persons (IDPs) in Nigeria. *Nigerian Journal of Social Psychology*, *1*(1), 61–73.

Nwatu, U. L., Ebue, M. O., Iwuagwu, A. O., Ene, J. C., & Odo, C. O. (2020). Perception of witchcraft practice in Oredo Local Government Area of Edo State, Nigeria. *Advances in Social Sciences Research Journal*, *7*(12), 514–527.

Nwogu, P. (2021). *A report on poverty rates in Lagos State*. Retrieved from https://twentytendaily.com/a-report-on-poverty-rates-in-lagos-state/

Nwokolu-Nte, M. S., & Onyige, C. D. (2020). Family welfare: Implications for child development in Nigeria. *American Scientific Research Journal for Engineering, Technology, and Sciences (ASRJETS)*, *67*(1), 144–154.

Nyeche, F. M. (n.d.). *Critical analysis of Abacha's Vision 2010*. Retrieved from https://www.academia.edu/4020714/Critical_Analysis_of_Abachas_Vision_2010

Obaji, P. Jnr. (2020, May 3). Human trafficking: Survivors of Nigeria's 'baby factories' share their stories. *Aljazeera*. Retrieved from https://www.aljazeera.com/indepth/features/survivors-nigeria-baby-factories-share-stories-200420091556574.html

Obidi, S. S. (2005). *Culture and education in Nigeria: A historical analysis*. Ibadan: University Press.

Obidimma, A. E., & Obidimma, E. O. C. (2012). Challenges and prospects of the juvenile justice administration in South East Nigeria. *Nnamdi Azikiwe University Journal of International Law and Jurisprudence*, *3*, 83–96.

Obikeze, D. S. (1979). Evacuation as a child welfare intervention measure: The case of the Nigerian Civil-War. *International Social Work*, *22*(2), 2–8.

Odiah, C. A. (1991). *Identification of gaps in social work education on Nigeria*. PhD dissertation, Canada: University of Toronto.

Oduor, R. M. J. (2014). A critical review of Leonhard Praeg's 'A Report on Ubuntu'. *Thought and Practice: A Journal of the Philosophical Association of Kenya (PAK) New Series*, *6*(2), 75–90.

Office of the National Security Advisor. (2016). *National Counter Terrorism Strategy (NACTEST), 2016*. Federal Ministry of Interior. Retrieved from http://ctc.gov.ng/onsa-reviews-national-counter-terrorism-strategy-nactest/

Office of the National Security Advisor. (2017). *Policy Framework and National Action Plan for Preventing and Countering Violent Extremism (PCVE)*. Retrieved from http://ctc.gov.ng/pcve-nsa-book/

Offiong, E. E., & Uduigwomen, G. A. (2021). Socio-cultural values and children's rights in Calabar. *Society Register*, *5*(2), 13–30. 10.14746/sr.2021.5.2.02

Ogbonna, A. (2018, February 6). Buhari declines assent to three bills passed by NASS. *The Vanguard*. Retrieved from http://www.vangauardngr.com/2018/02/buhari-declines-assent-three-bills-passed-nass/

Ogbonna, B. O. (2017). Social welfare scheme; a neglected component of public health care services in Nigeria. *MOJ Public Health*, *5*(3), 101–104. 10.15406/mojph.2017.05.00132

Ogundipe, A., & Edewor, P. A. (2012). Sociology and social work in Nigeria: Characteristics, collaborations and differences. *African Sociological Review*, *16*(2), 40–55.

Ogundola, O. J. (2013). *Framing disability: A content analysis of newspapers in Nigeria.* Media Studies - Theses. 15. New York: Syracuse University. https://surface.syr.edu/ms_thesis/15

Ogundola, O. (2019). Disability narratives in the news media: A spotlight on Africa. In K. Ellis, G. Goggin, B. Haller, & R. Curtis (Eds.), *The Routledge Companion to Disability and Media (Chpt 15).* London: Routledge.

Ogunniran, I. (2015). A centurial legal history of child justice reforms in Nigeria 1914-2014. *Law, Crime and History, 5*(2), 44–68. Retrieved from https://pearl.plymouth.ac.uk/handle/10026.1/8924

Ogunniyi, A., Hall, K. S., Baiyewu, O., Gureje, O., Unverzagt, F. W., Gao, S., & Hendrie, H. C. (2005). Caring for individuals with dementia: The Nigerian experience. *West African Journal of Medicine, 24*(3), 259–262. 10.4314/wajm.v24i3.28211. PMID: 16276708.

Ogwumike, F. (1995). The effects of macrolevel government policies on rural development and poverty alleviation in Nigeria. *Ibadan Journal of Social Sciences, 1*(1), 85–101.

Ohachenu, E. I. (2020). African ideologies, human security and peace building: The case of child adoption in Igbo communities. *IGWEBUIKE: An African Journal of Arts and Humanities, 6*(5), 229–248.

Ojagbemi, A., & Gureje, O. (2019). Social relationships and the association of loneliness with major depressive disorder in the Ibadan Study of Aging. *World Social Psychiatry, 1*, 82–88. https://www.worldsocpsychiatry.org/temp/WorldSocPsychiatry1182-2008556_053445.pdf

Ojanuga, D. N. (1985). The Mujedawa Dispensary Project: An experiment in social work education in Nigeria. *Journal of Social Work Education, 21*(3), 125–130.

Ojelabi, O. A., Osamor, P. E., & Owumi, B. E. (2015). Policies and practices of child adoption in Nigeria: A review paper. *Mediterranean Journal of Social Sciences, 6*(1) S1, 75–81. https://www.mcser.org/journal/index.php/mjss/article/view/5511

Ojembe, B. U., & Kalu, M. E. (2018). Describing reasons for loneliness among older people in Nigeria. *Journal of Gerontological Social Work, 61*(6), 640–658. 10.1080/01634372.2018.1487495.

Ojembe, B. U., & Kalu, M. E. (2019). Television, radio, and telephone: Tools for reducing loneliness among older adults in Nigeria. *Gerontechnology, 18*(1), 36–46. 10.4017/gt.2019.18.1.004.00.

Ojewale, O. (2021a). *Community resilience to violent conflict in north central Nigeria.* PhD Thesis. Nigeria: Obafemi Awolowo University, Ile-Ife.

Ojewale, O. (2021b, June 23). Violence is endemic in north central Nigeria: what communities are doing to cope. *The Conversation.* Retrieved from https://theconversation.com/violence-is-endemic-in-north-central-nigeria-what-communities-are-doing-to-cope-157349#:~:text=North%20central%20Nigeria%2C%20known%20as,militia%20attacks%20and%20sectarian%20crises

Ojua, T. A., Ishor, D. G., & Ndom, P. J. (2013). African cultural practices and health implications for Nigeria rural development. *International Review of Management and Business Research, 2*(1), 176–183. https://irmbrjournal.com/papers/1367572437.pdf

Okali, D., Okpara, E., & Olawoye, J. (2001). *The case of Aba and its region, southeastern Nigeria.* International Institute for Environment and Development Report. Retrieved from https://www.jstor.org/stable/resrep01762

Okech, D., Morreau, W., & Benson, K. (2012). Human trafficking: Improving victim identification and service provision. *International Social Work, 55*, 488–503. 10.1177/0020872811425805

Okech, D., Choi, Y., Elkins, J., & Burns, A. (2018). Seventeen years of human trafficking research in social work: A review of the literature. *Journal of Evidence-Informed Social Work*, 15(2), 103–122. 10.1080/23761407.2017.1415177.

Okeshola, F. B., & Adenugba, A. A. (2018). Human trafficking: Modern-day slavery in Nigeria. *American International Journal of Contemporary Research*, 8, 40–44.

Okigbo, P. (1989). *National Development Planning in Nigeria 1900-1992*. Enugu, Nigeria: Fourth Dimension Publishers Ltd.

Okoli, R. C. B., & Udechukwu, N. S. (2019). Child adoption, child trafficking and illegal surrogate parenting practices in Nigeria: The need for social work intervention. *Journal of Social Work in Developing Societies*, 1(1), 46–60. https://journals.aphriapub.com/index.php/JSWDS/article/download/664/647

Okongwu, O. C. (2021). Are laws the appropriate solution: The need to adopt non-policy measures in aid of the implementation of sex discrimination laws in Nigeria. *International Journal of Discrimination and the Law*, 21(1), 26–46. 10.1177/1358229912 0978915

Okowa, W. (1991). *Political economy of development planning in Nigeria*. Port Harcourt, Nigeria: Pam Unique Publishers.

Okoye, E. I., & Yugu, Y. G. (2009). Evaluating the critical factor for the realisation of Vision 20-2020 and the 7-point agenda of the Yar'Adua's administration in Nigeria. *The University Advanced Research Journal*, 1, 87–103.

Okoye, U. O. (2013). Community-based care for home bound elderly persons in Nigeria: A policy option. *International Journal of Innovative Research in Science, Engineering and Technology*, 2(12), 7089–7091.

Okoye, U. O. (2014). Trends and challenges of social work practice in Nigeria. In V. E. Cree (Eds.), *Becoming a social worker* (pp. 166–174). London: Routledge.

Okoye, U. O. (2019). Health care social work in Nigeria. In R. Winnett, R. Furman, D. Epps, & G. Lamphear (Eds.), *Health Care Social Work: A Global Perspective* (pp. 149–161). New York: Oxford University Press.

Okoye, U. O., & Eromosele, I. E. (2013). The Nigerian social worker and the challenge of practicing in a multi-cultural society. Paper presented at the Second National Conference of the Nigerian Association of Social Work Educators (NASWE) *Social Work Practice in a Diverse Society: Meeting the Challenges of Contemporary Nigeria*, 13-16 March, University of Benin, Benin-city. Retrieved from https://www.researchgate.net/publication/281935788_The_Nigerian_Social_Worker_and_the_challenge_of_practicing_in_a_multi-cultural_society

Olaitan, M. F. (2021). *Victimisation experiences and coping strategies of women with disabilities in Lagos state*. PhD Thesis. Department of Sociology, University of Ibadan.

Olaleye, Y. L. (2013). Community social work programme interventions on Nigerian families living in poverty. *Journal of Environment and Culture*, 10(1-2), 62–74.

Olaore, A. Y., & Drolet, J. (2017). Indigenous knowledge, beliefs, and cultural practices for children and families in Nigeria. *Journal of Ethnic & Cultural Diversity in Social Work*, 26(3), 254–270. 10.1080/15313204.2016.1241973

Olatunji, O. A. (2012). Penetration, corroboration and non-consent: Examining the Nigerian law of Rape and addressing its shortcomings. *University of Ilorin Law Journal*, 8, 79–105.

Olusola, A. I., & Ogunlusi, C. (2020). Recurring cases of child rape in Nigeria: An issue for church intervention. *INSANCITA: Journal of Islamic Studies in Indonesia and Southeast Asia*, 5(1), 55–72. https://journals.mindamas.com/index.php/insancita/article/view/1331/1158

Omigbodun, O. O., & Olatawura, M. U. (2008). Child rearing practices in Nigeria: Implications for mental health. *Nigerian Journal of Psychiatry*, 6(1), 10–15. 10.4314/njpsyc.v6i1.39904

Omobowale, A. O., Omobowale, M. O., & Falase, O. S. (2019). The context of children in Yoruba popular culture. *Global Studies of Childhood*, 9(1), 18–28. 10.1177/2043610618815381

Omoniyi, M. B. I. (2014). Parental attitude towards disability and gender in the Nigerian context: Implications for counseling. *Mediterranean Journal of Social Sciences*, 5(20), 2255–2260. 10.5901/mjss.2014.v5n20p2255

Omorogiuwa, T. B. E. (2017). The impacts of mental disability: Implications for social work practice. *African Journal of Social Work*, 17(1), 1–8.

Omorogiuwa, T. B. E. (2020). Troubling childhood: the physical and health issues experienced by child labourers. *Social Work in Public Health*, 35(8), 679–688. 10.1080/19371918.2020.1823928

Onalu, C. E., & Okoye, U. O. (2021). Social justice and social work curriculum at the University of Nigeria, Nsukka, Nigeria. *Research on Social Work Practice*, 31(6), 576–583. 10.1177/10497315211001532

Onalu, C. E., Chukwu, N. E., & Okoye, U. O. (2020). COVID-19 response and social work education in Nigeria: Matters arising. *Social Work Education*, 39(8), 1037–1047. 10.1080/02615479.2020.1825663

Onayemi, O. M., & Aderinto, A. A. (2019). Child adoption investigation in Nigeria: Challenges and options. *Nigerian Journal of Sociology and Anthropology*, 15(2), 87–100. 10.36108/NJSA/7102/51(0260)

Onyeiwu, S. (2021). Nigeria's poverty profile is grim: It's time to move beyond handouts. *The Conversation*, June 27, 2021. Retrieved from https://theconversation.com/nigerias-poverty-profile-is-grim-its-time-to-move-beyond-handouts-163302#:~:text=The%20Nigerian%20National%20Bureau%20of,million%20Nigerians%20live%20in%20poverty.&text=If%20the%20World%20Bank's%20income,Nigeria's%20poverty%20rate%20is%2071%25

Onyejekwe, C. J. (2005). Influences of global human trafficking issues on Nigeria: A gender perspective. *Journal of International Women's Studies*, 7(2), 141–151. https://vc.bridgew.edu/jiws/vol7/iss2/9

Onyemelukwe, C. (2016). Stigma and mental health in Nigeria: Some suggestions for law reform. *Journal of Law, Policy and Globalization*, 55, 63–68.

Osiakwan, E. M. K. (2017). The KINGS of Africa's digital economy. In B. Ndemo, & T. Weiss (Eds.), *Digital Kenya: An entrepreneurial revolution in the making* (pp. 56–83). London: Palgrave Macmillan.

Organisation of African Unity (OAU). (1969). *Convention Governing the Specific Aspects of Refugee Problems in Africa*. Adopted by the Assembly of Heads of State and Government at its Sixth Ordinary Session, Addis-Ababa, 10 September 1969. Retrieved from https://www.unhcr.org/en-au/about-us/background/45dc1a682/oau-convention-governing-specific-aspects-refugee-problems-africa-adopted.html

Orikpe, E. A. (2013). Education and national security: Challenges and the way forward. In A. N. Nosike, P. U. Akanwa, K. A. Anele, & D. Iornem (Eds.), *Proceedings of the Abuja International Conference on Human and Social Sciences* (pp. 44–51). Granada, Spain: International Association for Teaching and Learning.

Osawe, T. O. (2018) Mapping international social work education: A research proposal toward rethinking social work education and professional practice in Nigeria. *Transnational Social Review*, 8(3), 331–336. 10.1080/21931674.2018.1504159

Osayi, K. K. (2015). *A theoretical assessment of the reformation and rehabilitation programmes of the federal prisons in Nigeria: Implications for social work profession.* Retrieved from https://www.researchgate.net/publication/280298911_A_THEORETICAL_ASSESSMENT_OF_THE_REFORMATION_AND_REHABILITATION_PROGRAMMES_OF_THE_FEDERAL_PRISONS_IN_NIGERIA_IMPLICATIONS_FOR_SOCIAL_WORK_PROFESSION?channel=doi&linkId=55b01bb808aeb0ab466985eb&showFulltext=true

Osei-Hwedie, K. (1990). Social work and the question of social development in Africa. *Journal of Social Development in Africa,* 5(2), 87–99.

Osei-Hwedie, K. (1993). The challenge of social work in Africa: Starting the indigenisation process. *Journal of Social development in Africa,* 8(1), 19–30.

Osei-Hwedie, K. (1995). *A search for legitimate social development education and practice models for Africa.* Lewiston, New York: Edwin Mullen.

Osei-Hwedie, K. (1996). The indigenisation of social work education and practice in South Africa: The dilemma of theory and method. *Social Work/Maatskaplike Werk,* 32(3), 215–225.

Osei-Hwedie, K. (2002a). Indigenous practice – Some informed guesses: Self evident and possible. *Social Work/Maatkaplike Werk,* 38(4), 311–329.

Osei-Hwedie, K. (2002b). Indigenous practice – Some informed guesses. Part II: Self-evident and possible. *Social Work/Maatskaplike Werk,* 38(4), 311–336.

Osei-Hwedie, K. (2007). Afro-centrism: The challenge of social development. *Social Work/Maatskaplike Werk,* 43(1), 106–116.

Osei-Hwedie, K., & Rankopo, M. J. (2008). Developing culturally relevant social work education in Africa: The case of Botswana. In M. Gray, J. Coates, & M. Yellow Bird (Eds.), *Indigenous social work around the world: Towards culturally relevant education and practice* (pp. 203–218). Aldershot, Hants: Ashgate.

Otabor, B., & Shodeinde, J. (2018). *Social integration of Internally Displaced Person into the community in Nigeria: The role of non-governmental organization.* Helsinki: Diaconia University of Applied Sciences Degree program in Social Service Focus on Community Development, Bachelor of Social Service.

Paddock, A. (2015). A world of good to our boys: Boys scouts in Southern Nigeria, 1934-1951. In S. Aderinto (Ed.), *Children and childhood in colonial Nigeria histories* (pp. 123–146). New York: Palgrave MacMillan.

Patel, L. (2005). *Social welfare and social development in South Africa.* Cape Town: Oxford University Southern Africa.

Pathfinders Justice Initiative (PJI). (2022). *Nigeria: Human Trafficking Factsheet.* Retrieved from http://pathfindersji.org/nigeria-human-trafficking-factsheet/.

Pawar. M. (2019). Social work and social policy practice: Imperatives for political engagement. *International Journal of Community and Social Development,* 1(1), 15–27. 10.1177/2516602619833219

Pearce, D. (1978). The feminization of poverty: Women, work, and welfare. *Urban and Social Change Review,* 11: 28–36.

Phillips, R. (2006). Women and poverty: The application of feminism in overcoming women's poverty in the global context. In K. Serr (Eds.), *Thinking about poverty* (pp. 24–34). Sydney: The Federation Press.

Praeg, L. (2014). *A report on Ubuntu.* Pietermaritzburg: University of KwaZulu-Natal Press.

Public Health Nigeria. (2020). *Complete list of skills offering social work education in Nigeria.* Retrieved from https://www.publichealth.com.ng/complete-list-of-schools-offering-social-work-courses-in-nigeria/

Rabbort, P., & Wallace, C. (1990). *An introduction to sociology: Feminist perspectives.* New York: Brooks/Cole Publishing.

Ragab, I. (1982). *Authentization of social work in developing countries.* Tanta, Egypt: The Integrated Social Services Project (Arabic/English).

Ragab, I. (1990). How social work can take root in developing countries. *Social Development Issues, 12*(3), 38–51.

Ragab, I. A. (2016). The Islamic perspective on social work: A conceptual framework. *International Social Work, 59*(3), 325–342. 10.1177/0020872815627120

Ragab, I. A. (2017). Has social work come of age? Revisiting the authentisation debate 25 years on. In M. Gray (Ed.), *The Routledge Handbook of Social Work and Social Development in Africa* (pp. 33–45). London: Routledge.

Rankin, P. (1997). Developmental social welfare: Challenges facing South Africa. *Social Work/Maatskaplike Werk, 33*(3), 184–192.

Rasheed, M. N., & Rasheed, J. M. (2011). Reflection on King's 'Beloved Community' and Tutu's Ubuntu theology, and implications for multicultural social work practice. Paper presented at the *Convention of the North American Association of Christians in Social Work,* Pittsburgh, PA.

Riddick, J. F. (1966). *Sir Frederick Lugard, World War I and the Amalgamation of Nigeria 1914-1919.* Master's Theses. 3848. Retrieved from https://scholarworks.wmich.edu/masters_theses/3848

Rohwerder, B. (2018). *Disability stigma in developing countries.* K4D Helpdesk Report. Brighton, UK: Institute of Development Studies.

Ross-Sheriff, F., & Orme, J. (2015). Human trafficking: Overview. *Encyclopedia of Social Work.* National Association of Social Work Press and Oxford University Press. 10.1093/acrefore/9780199975839.013.945

Ryan, G. K., Nwefoh, E., Aguocha, C., Ode, P. O., Okpoju, S. O., Ocheche, P., Woyengikuro, A., Abdulmalik J., & Eaton, J. (2020). Partnership for the implementation of mental health policy in Nigeria: A case study of the Comprehensive Community Mental Health Programme in Benue State. *International Journal of Mental Health Systems, 14*(10), 1–13. 10.1186/s13033-020-00344-z

Sa'ad, A-M. (2008). Juvenile justice in Nigeria. *Nigerian Journal of Sociology and Anthropology, 6*(1), 71–83. 10.36108/NJSA/8002/60(0140)

Sadruddin, H., Walter, N., & Hidalgo, J. (2005). Human trafficking in the United States: Expanding victim protection beyond prosecution witnesses. *Stanford Law & Policy Review, 16*(2), 379–416.

Salami, K. K. (2016). Housing facilities and realities of health of the elderly in Nigerian cities. Nigerian. *Journal of Economics and Social Studies, 58*(1), 53–75.

Salawu, B., & Hassan A. O. (2011). Ethnic politics and its implications for the survival of democracy in Nigeria. *Journal of Public Administration and Policy Research, 3*(2), 28–33. http://www.academicjournals.org/jpapr

Saliu, H. A. (2007). Facing the challenges of reforms. In H. Saliu, E. Amali, & R. Olawepo (Eds.), *Nigeria's reform programme: Issues and challenges* (pp. 608–622). Ilorin, Nigeria: Faculty of Business and Social Sciences, University of Ilorin.

Samphina Academy. (2022). *List of universities in Nigeria that offers social work.* Retrieved from https://samphina.com.ng/universities-offering-social-work-nigeria/

Schmid, H., & Sheikhzadegan, A. (Eds.). (2022). *Exploring Islamic social work: Between community and the common good.* Open access, Springer. https://link.springer.com/book/10.1007/978-3-030-95880-0

Schön, D. (1983). *The reflective practitioner: How professionals think in action.* New York: Basic Books.

Secker, E. (2012). Witchcraft stigmatisation in Nigeria: Challenges and successes in the implementation of child rights. *International Social Work, 56*(1), 22–36.

Sekudu, J. (2019). Ubuntu. In A. van Breda, & J. Sekudu (Eds.), *Theories for decolonial social work practice in South Africa* (pp. 105–119). Cape Town: Oxford University Press.

Sewpaul, V., & Lombard, A. (2004). Social work education, training and standards in Africa. *Social Work Education, 25*(5), 537–554.

Shawky, A. (1972). Social work education in Africa. *International Social Work, 15*(1), 3–16.

Silavwe, G. W. (1995). The need for a new social work perspective in an African setting: The case of Zambia. *British Journal of Social Work, 25*(1), 71–84.

Siollun, M. (2021). *What Britain did to Nigeria.* London: C. Hurst & Co. (Publishers) Ltd.

Smith, N. (2011). The face of disability in Nigeria: A disability survey in Kogi and Niger States. *Disability, CBR and Inclusive Development, 22*(1), 35–47. 10.5463/DCID.v22i1.11

Sossou, M-A., & Yogtiba, J. A. (2009). Abuse of children in West Africa: Implications for social work education and practice. *British Journal of Social Work, 39*(7), 1218–1234. 10.1093/bjsw/bcn033

Specht, H., & Courtney, M. (1994). *Unfaithful angels: How social work has abandoned its mission.* New York: Free Press.

SPRING. (2016). *Review of programming for orphans and vulnerable children in Nigeria: Exploring opportunities for future investments in nutrition social and behavior change communication.* Arlington, VA: Strengthening Partnerships, Results, and Innovations in Nutrition Globally (SPRING) project. Retrieved from https://www.spring-nutrition. org/sites/default/files/publications/reports/spring_ovc_in_nigeria.pdf

State Council. (2016). *China needs 1m more social workers by 2020.* Retrieved from http:// english.www.gov.cn/state_council/ministries/2016/03/15/content_281475308144616.htm

Statista. (2022, Feb 1). *Age distribution of population in Nigeria in 2021, by gender.* Published by Doris Dokua Sasu. Retrieved from https://www.statista.com/statistics/ 1121317/age-distribution-of-population-in-nigeria-by-gender/

Sule, I. D. (2022, August 29). President Muhammadu Buhari has assented to 8 Bills recently passed by the National Assembly. *Daily Trust.* Retrieved from https:// dailytrust.com/buhari-assents-civil-aviation-advertising-council-6-other-bills

Tajudeen, O. A., & Adebayo, O. F. (2013). Issues of refugees and displaced persons in Nigeria. *Journal of Sociological Research, 4*(1), 1–18. 10.5296/jsr.v4i1.3156

Tanyi, P. L., André, P., & Mbah, P. (2018). Care of the elderly in Nigeria: Implications for policy. *Cogent Social Sciences, 4*(1), 1555201. 10.1080/23311886.2018.1555201

Teoh, A. H., & Shaffie, Fuziah. (2017). Professionalization of social work in Malaysia through legislation: A literature discussion on concepts, issues and challenges. *Journal Pembangunan Sosial Jilid, 20*, 117–134. Retrieved from https://e-journal.uum.edu.my/ index.php/jps/article/view/jps.20.2017.11541/2541

Temilola, O. M. (2020). *Social workers' approach in combating domestic violence in Alimosho community, Lagos State.* Retrieved from https://ir.unilag.edu.ng/handle/123456789/9845

Todowede, B. J. (2013). Managing university finances for sustainable administration and institution-building. In A. N. Nosike, P. U. Akanwa, K. A. Anele, & D. Iornem (Eds.), *Proceedings of the Abuja International Conference on Human and Social Sciences* (pp. 342–347). Granada, Spain: International Association for Teaching and Learning.

Togonu-Bickersteth, F., & Akinyemi, A. I. (2014). Ageing and national development in Nigeria: Costly assumptions and challenges for the future. *African Population Studies*, 27(2 Supp), 361–371. http://aps.journals.ac.za

Transparency International. (2021). *Global Corruption Perception Index: Nigeria*. Retrieved from https://www.transparency.org/en/countries/nigeria

Travis, R.(Jnr), McFarlin, N., van Rooyen, C. A. J., & Gray, M. (1999). Community development in South Africa: Its use as an intervention strategy. *International Social Work*, 42(2), 177–188.

Tubor, M. (2019). *A critical analysis of the 'Trokosi' practice in parts of West Africa as a harmful tradition against women and girls: states obligations under international human rights law*. Master's Thesis in International Law and Human Rights. Helsinki, Finland: Åbo Akademi University. Retrieved from https://www.doria.fi/handle/10024/169438

Tutu, D. (1999). *No future without forgiveness*. New York: Doubleday.

Uchendu, E. (2007). Recollection of childhood experiences during the Nigerian Civil War. *Periodical: Africa: Journal of the International African Institute* 77(3), 393–418.

Uchendu, U., Roets, G., & Vandenbroeck, M. (2019). Mapping constructs of gender in research on Igbo women in Nigeria: Embracing a southern feminist theoretical perspective. *Gender and Education*, 31(4), 508–524.

Udeani, C. C. (2019). Social work in contemporary Nigerian society: Challenges and prospects. *Journal of Social Work in Developing Societies*, 1(1), 1–16.

Udechukwu, N. S. (2019). Social work intervention against illegal child adoption. *SciMedicine Journal*, 1(1), 1–11. 10.28991/SciMedJ-2019-0101-1

Udoudo, M. P., & Ubi-Abai, I. P. (2016). Vision 20:2020 and economic development in Nigeria: Gleaning from past national development plans. *International Journal of Development Strategies in Humanities, Management and Social Sciences*, 6(2), 201–215.

Ugbe, R. O., Agi, J. U., & Ugbe, A. B. (2019). A critique of the Nigerian Administration of Criminal Justice Act 2015 and challenges in the implementation of the Act. *African Journal of Criminal Law and Jurisprudence*, 4, 69–81. Retrieved from https://journals.ezenwaohaetorc.org/index.php/AFJCLJ/article/view/738

Ugiagbe, E. O. (2015). Social work is context-bound: The need for indigenization of social work practice in Nigeria. *International Social Work*, 58(6), 790–801.

Ugiagbe, E. O. (2017). Decolonising social work practice in Nigeria: Moving beyond indigenisation to development. In M. Gray (Ed.), *The Routledge Handbook of Social Work and Social Development in Africa* (pp. 271–280). London: Routledge.

Ugiagbe, E. O., & Eweka, H. E. (2014). Systemic oppression and rights of the minorities: Discourse of the reflections on Nigerian society. *Mediterranean Journal of Social Sciences*, 5(4), 16–526.

Ugiagbe, E. O., & Okaka, E. (2014). Social capital and mental health issues in the Nigerian environment. *Journal of Nursing, Social Studies, Public Health and Rehabilitation*, 3(4), 143–153.

Ugiagbe E. O., & Ugiagbe, I. (2015). Transcending the Eurocentric development paradigms in Nigeria: The traditional age grade in discourse. *Humanities and Social Sciences Journal of Siberian Federal University*, 8(3), 366–376.

Ugiagbe, E. O., & Vincent-Osaghae, G. (2014). An assessment of the barriers to women access to health facilities in Isi communities of Edo State, South-South Nigeria: Implication for policy development and social work. *Journal of Nursing, Social Studies, Public Health and Rehabilitation*, 1(2), 7–15.

Ugochukwu, O., Mbaezu, N., Lawal, S. A., Azubogu, C., Sheikh, T. L., & Vallières, F. (2020). The time is now: Reforming Nigeria's outdated mental health laws. *The Lancet: Global Health*, 8(8), E989–E990. 10.1016/S2214-109X(20)30302-8

Ugwoegbu, E. U. (2016). *Revitalization of Nigeria - equal access: A case study on people with disabilities in Nigeria*. Boston College Electronic Thesis or Dissertation, 2016. http://hdl.handle.net/2345/bc-ir:106930

Ugwu, M. O. (2021). Gender-based violence in situations of internal displacement: Realities faced by women within the IDP camps in Nigeria. *International Review of Law and Jurisprudence*, 3(1), 132–138.

Ugwuanyi, B. I., & Chukwuemeka, E. E. O. (2013). The obstacles to effective policy implementation by the public bureaucracy in developing nations: The case of Nigeria. *Kuwait Chapter of Arabian Journal of Business and Management Review*, 2(7), 59–68.

Ukelina, B. U. (2021). Making a nation modern: CIS and Nigeria's First National Development Plan. *Journal of West African History*, 7(2), 25–48. https://muse.jhu.edu/article/845931

United Nations (UN). (1965). *International Convention on the Elimination of All Forms of Racial Discrimination*. OHCHR. Retrieved from https://www.ohchr.org/en/instruments-mechanisms/instruments/international-convention-elimination-all-forms-racial

United Nations (UN). (1966a). *International Covenant on Civil and Political Rights*. OHCHR. Retrieved from https://www.ohchr.org/en/instruments-mechanisms/instruments/international-covenant-civil-and-political-rights

United Nations (UN). (1966b). *International Covenant on Economic, Social and Cultural Rights*. OHCHR. Retrieved from https://www.ohchr.org/en/instruments-mechanisms/instruments/international-covenant-economic-social-and-cultural-rights

United Nations (UN). (1979). *Convention on the Elimination of all forms of Discrimination against Women CEDAW)*. OHCHR. Retrieved from https://www.ohchr.org/en/instruments-mechanisms/instruments/convention-elimination-all-forms-discrimination-against-women#:~:text=On%2018%20December%201979%2C%20the,twentieth%20country%20had%20ratified%20it

United Nations (UN). (1984). *Convention against Torture and Other Cruel, Inhuman or Degrading Treatment or Punishment*. Retrieved from https://www.ohchr.org/en/instruments-mechanisms/instruments/convention-against-torture-and-other-cruel-inhuman-or-degrading

United Nations (UN). (1989). *Convention on the Rights of the Child*. Retrieved from https://www.ohchr.org/en/instruments-mechanisms/instruments/convention-rights-child

United Nations (UN). (1990). *International Convention on the Protection of the Rights of All Migrant Workers and Members of their Families*. OHCHR. Retrieved from https://www.ohchr.org/en/instruments-mechanisms/instruments/international-convention-protection-rights-all-migrant-workers

United Nations (UN). (1997). *Guidelines for Action on Children in the Criminal Justice System*. Retrieved from https://www.ohchr.org/en/instruments-mechanisms/instruments/guidelines-action-children-criminal-justice-system

United Nations (UN). (1999). *Optional Protocol to the Convention on the Elimination of All Forms of Discrimination against Women*. OHCHR. Retrieved from https://www.ohchr.org/en/instruments-mechanisms/instruments/optional-protocol-convention-elimination-all-forms

United Nations (UN). (2000a). *Optional Protocol to the Convention on the Rights of the Child on the sale of children child prostitution and child pornography.* OHCHR. Retrieved from https://www.ohchr.org/en/instruments-mechanisms/instruments/optional-protocol-convention-rights-child-sale-children-child

United Nations (UN). (2000b). *Optional Protocol to the Convention on the Rights of the Child on the involvement of children in armed conflicts.* OHCHR. Retrieved from https://www.ohchr.org/en/instruments-mechanisms/instruments/optional-protocol-convention-rights-child-involvement-children

United Nations (UN). (2000c). *Protocol to Prevent, Suppress and Punish Trafficking in Persons Especially Women and Children, supplementing the United Nations Convention against Transnational Organized Crime (Palermo Protocol).* UN General Assembly resolution 55/25. Office of the High Commissioner for Human Rights (OHCHR). Retrieved from https://www.ohchr.org/sites/default/files/ProtocolonTrafficking.pdf

United Nations (UN). (2002). *Optional Protocol to the Convention against Torture and other Cruel, Inhuman or Degrading Treatment or Punishment.* OHCHR. Retrieved from https://www.ohchr.org/en/instruments-mechanisms/instruments/optional-protocol-convention-against-torture-and-other-cruel

United Nations (UN). (2006a). *Convention on the Rights of People with Disabilities.* OHCHR. Retrieved from https://www.ohchr.org/en/instruments-mechanisms/instruments/convention-rights-persons-disabilities

United Nations (UN). (2006b). *Optional Protocol to the Convention on the Rights of Persons with Disabilities.* OHCHR. Retrieved from https://www.ohchr.org/en/instruments-mechanisms/instruments/optional-protocol-convention-rights-persons-disabilities

United Nations (UN). (2010). *International Convention for the Protection of All Persons from Enforced Disappearance.* OHCHR. Retrieved from https://www.ohchr.org/en/instruments-mechanisms/instruments/international-convention-protection-all-persons-enforced

United Nations (UN). (2018). *Convention against Transnational Organized Crime and the Protocols Thereto.* Office of Drugs and Crime. Retrieved from https://www.unodc.org/unodc/en/organized-crime/intro/UNTOC.html#:~:text=The%20United%20Nations%20Convention%20against,fight%20against%20transnational%20organized%20crime

United Nations (UN). (2019). *World Population Prospects 2019.* United Nations Economic and Social Affairs. Retrieved from https://population.un.org/wpp/Publications/Files/WPP2019_Highlights.pdf

United Nations Development Programme (UNDP). (2020). *Human Development Reports.* Retrieved from https://hdr.undp.org/en/content/latest-human-development-index-ranking

United Nations Education, Scientific and Cultural Organisation (UNESCO). (2006). *Human trafficking in Nigeria: Root causes and recommendations.* Policy Paper Poverty Series 14.2 (E). Retrieved from https://unesdoc.unesco.org/ark:/48223/pf0000147844

United Nations High Commissioner for Refugees (UNHCR). (2018). *Nigeria situation: UNHCR Situational Update 01-31 January 2018.* Retrieved from https://reliefweb.int/report/nigeria/nigeria-situation-unhcr-situational-update-01-31-january-2018

United Nations Children's Fund (UNICEF). (2016). *UNICEF Annual Report: Nigeria.* Retrieved from https://www.unicef.org/about/annualreport/files/Nigeria_2016_COAR.pdf

United Nations International Children's Emergency Fund (UNICEF). (2020, September 17). *Children adjust to life outside Nigeria's Almajiri system.* Retrieved from https://www.unicef.org/nigeria/stories/children-adjust-life-outside-nigerias-almajiri-system#:~:text=Under%20the%20Almajiri%20system%2C%20parents,schooling%20have%20made%20this%20choice.

United Nations Office on Drugs and Crime (UNODC). (2020). *Global Report on Trafficking in Persons 2020.* Vienna: UNODC. Retrieved from https://www.unodc.org/documents/data-and-analysis/tip/2021/GLOTiP_2020_15jan_web.pdf

United Nations Office on Drugs and Crime (UNODC). (2022). *Nigeria launches National Action Plan against human trafficking. UNODC Nigeria.* Retrieved from https://www.unodc.org/nigeria/en/nigeria-launches-national-action-plan-against-human-trafficking.html

United Nations Treaty Body Database. (n.d.). *Nigeria.* Retrieved from https://tbinternet.ohchr.org/_layouts/15/TreatyBodyExternal/Treaty.aspx?CountryID=127&Lang=EN

United States Code (USC). (2022). *22 USC 7106: Minimum standards for the elimination of trafficking.* Title 22-Foreign relations and intercourse. Chapter 78-Trafficking victims protection. Retrieved from https://uscode.house.gov/view.xhtml?req=(title:22%20section:7106%20edition:prelim)

United States Department of State (USDS). (2000). *Victims of Trafficking and Violence Protection Act of 2000.* Retrieved from https://www.govinfo.gov/content/pkg/PLAW-106publ386/pdf/PLAW-106publ386.pdf

United States Department of State (USDS). (2016). *Trafficking in Persons Report: Nigeria.* Retrieved from https://www.refworld.org/docid/577f95c46.html

United States Department of State (USDS). (2018). *2018 Trafficking in Persons Report.* Washington, DC: US Government Publishing Office.

United States Department of State (USDS). (2019). *2019 Trafficking in Persons Report: Nigeria.* Retrieved from https://www.state.gov/reports/2019-trafficking-in-persons-report-2/nigeria/

United States Department of State (USDS). (2021). *2021-Trafficking in Persons Report: Nigeria.* Office to Monitor and Combat Trafficking in Persons. Retrieved from https://www.state.gov/reports/2021-trafficking-in-persons-report/nigeria/

Upkong, D., & Orji, E. (2006). Mental health of infertile women in Nigeria. *Turkish Journal of Psychiatry, 17*(4), 259–265. https://pubmed.ncbi.nlm.nih.gov/17183442/

USAID ASSIST Project. (2014). *Community Booklet: National Standards for Improving the Quality of Life of Vulnerable Children in Nigeria.* USAID Applying Science to Strengthen and Improve Systems Project. Bethesda, MD: University Research Co., LLC (URC). Retrieved from https://pdf.usaid.gov/pdf_docs/PA00M578.pdf

Uwakwe, R., Ibeh, C. C., Modebe, A. I., Bo, E., Ezeama, N., Njelita, I., Ferri, C. P., & Prince, M. J. (2009). The epidemiology of dependence in older people in Nigeria: Prevalence, determinants, informal care, and health service utilization. *Journal of the American Geriatrics Society, 57,* 1620–1627. 10.1111/j.1532-5415.2009.02397.x

Uzuegbu, C. N. (2010). Culture and child abuse in Nigeria. *International Journal of Research in Arts and Social Sciences, 2,* 201–206.

Van Breda, A. (2018). Developmental social case work: A process model. *International Social Work, 61*(1), 66–78. 10.1177/0020872815603786.

Wada, Y. H., Rajwani, L., Anyam, E., Karikari, E., Njikizana, M., Srour, L., & Khalid, G. M. (2021). Mental health in Nigeria: A neglected issue in public health. *Public Health in Practice, 2,* 1–3. 10.1016/j.puhip.2021.100166.

Wahab, E. O., & Ikebudu, C. J. (2014). Quality of life of patients with early onset dementia in Nigeria. *International Letters of Social and Humanistic Sciences, 12,* 28–42. https://www.scipress.com/ILSHS.12.28

Walk Free Foundation (WWF). (2018). *Global Slavery Index. Country Data: Nigeria.* Retrieved from https://www.globalslaveryindex.org/2018/data/country-data/nigeria/

Walton, R. G., & Abo El Nasr, M. M. (1988). Indigenisation and authentization in terms of social work in Egypt. *International Social Work, 31*(1), 135–144.

Wang, S. B. (2013a). Different interpretations of social work in China: A comparative analysis. *Chinese Education & Society, 46*(6), 7–15.

Wang, S. B. (2013b). Social work experience and development in China. *Chinese Education & Society, 46*(6): 79–91.

Ward, Y., & Fouladvand, S. (2018). Human trafficking, victims' rights and fair trials. *Journal of Criminal Law, 82*(2), 138–155. 10.1177/0022018318761680

Warria, A. (2019). Child marriages, child protection and sustainable development in Kenya: Is legislation enough? *African Journal of Reproductive Health, 23*(2), 121–133. bioline.org.br

Warria, A. (2020). 'The child goes back to the trafficking situation': Consequences of inappropriate assistance procedures during reintegration of child victims of trafficking. *Child Abuse Research: A South African Journal, 21*(1), 47–57.

Warria, A. (2022). Decolonizing trafficking responses: Reflections on social work practice and training. *Social Dialogue online*. Retrieved from https://socialdialogue.online

Warria, A., Dixon, H., Roper, M., Marx, S., Leteane, M., & Chadambuka, C. (2021). The voices of human trafficking victims and survivors must be heard above all others to elicit change. Daily Maverick, July 29. Retrieved from dailymaverick.co.za

Webb, D. (1984). Review of 'The Flexner myth and the history of social work' by Austin, D. M. *British Journal of Social Work, 14*(2), 187–188.

Weitzer, R. (2014). New directions in research on human trafficking. *The ANNALS of the American Academy of Political and Social Science, 653*(1), 6–24. 10.1177/000271 6214521562

Williamson, E., Dutch, N. M., & Clawson, H. J. (2008). *Evidence-based mental health treatment for victims of human trafficking*. Washington, DC: Office of the Assistant Secretary for Planning and Evaluation, US Department of Health and Human Services. https://aspe.hhs.gov/reports/evidence-based-mental-health-treatment-victims-human-trafficking-0

Woermann, M., & Sanni, J. S. (2020). Ethnic and racial valorisations in Nigeria and South Africa: How ubuntu may harm or help. *South African Journal of Philosophy, 39*(3), 296–307. 10.1080/02580136.2020.1809123

Woodroofe, K. (1962). *From charity to social work*. London: Routledge and Kegan Paul.

World Bank. (2012). *World development report: Gender equality and education*. Washington, DC: World Bank.

World Bank. (2019a). *Nigeria Biannual Economic Update, April 2019: Water supply, sanitation and hygiene - a wake-up call*. Washington, DC: World Bank. Retrieved from https://openknowledge.worldbank.org/handle/10986/31514

World Bank. (2019b). *Jumpstarting inclusive growth: Unlocking the productive potential of Nigeria's people and resource endowments*. Nigeria Economic Update, Fall 2019. Washington, DC: World Bank. Retrieved from https://openknowledge.worldbank.org/handle/10986/32795

World Bank. (2020). *GDP (current US$) – Nigeria*. Retrieved from https://data.worldbank.org/indicator/NY.GDP.MKTP.CD?locations=NG

World Bank. (2021). *Poverty & equity brief, Africa Western & Central, Nigeria, April 2021*. Washington, DC: World Bank. Retrieved from https://databank.worldbank.org/data/download/poverty/987B9C90-CB9F-4D93-AE8C-750588BF00QA/AM2020/Global_POVEQ_NGA.pdf (accessed 31 January 2022)

World Bank. (2020). *Disability inclusion in Nigeria: A rapid assessment*. Washington, DC: World Bank. Retrieved from https://openknowledge.worldbank.org/handle/10986/34073

World Data Lab. (2022). *Nigeria*. World Poverty Clock. Retrieved from https://worldpoverty.io/map

World Factbook (The). (2022). *Nigeria*. Retrieved from https://www.cia.gov/the-world-factbook/countries/nigeria/#people-and-society

World Health Organisation (WHO). (2001). *International Classification of Functioning, Disability and Health (ICF)*. Retrieved from http://www.who.int/classifications/icf/en/

World Health Organisation (WHO). (2010). *Community Based Rehabilitation: CBR Guidelines*. Geneva, Switzerland: WHO.

World Health Organisation (WHO). (2011). *World Report on Disability*. Geneva, Switzerland: WHO. Retrieved from https://www.who.int/publications/i/item/9789241564182

World Health Organisation (WHO). (2013a). *Mental Health Action Plan 2013-2020*. Retrieved from https://www.who.int/mental_health/publications/action_plan/en/

World Health Organisation (WHO). (2013b). *WHO Checklist on Mental Health Legislation*. Retrieved from http://healthrights.mk/pdf/Zdravstveni%20Rabotnici/Publikacii/Mentalno%20zdravje/Dopolneti/%D0%9B%D0%B8%D1%81%D1%82%D0%B0%20%D0%B7D0%B0%20%D0%BF%D1%80%D0%BE%D0%B2%D0%B5%D1%80%D0%BA%D0%B0%20%D0%BD%D0%B0%20%D0%A1%D0%97%D0%9E%20%D0%B7%D0%B0%20%D0%BB%D0%B5%D0%B3%D0%B8%D1%81%D0%BB%D0%B0%D1%82%D0%B8%D0%B2%D0%B0%D1%82%D0%B0%20%D0%B7%D0%B0%20%D0%BC%D0%B5%D0%BD%D1%82%D0%B0%D0%BB%D0%BD%D0%BE%20%D0%B7%D0%B4%D1%80%D0%B0%D0%B2%D1%98%D0%B5.pdf

Yekini, A. O., & Salisu, M. (2013). Probation as a non-custodial measure in Nigeria: Making a case for adult probation service. *African Journal of Criminology and Justice Studies*, 7(1 &2), 101–117.

Yunusa, A. (2020). Constraints and challenges of development planning in Nigeria. *Journal of Humanities and Social Sciences Studies*, 2(1), 69–76.

Index

Page numbers in bold refer to tables.

Abari, C. A. 62
Abasilim, U. D. 46
AbdulQadir, I. A. 95
Abdulraheem-Mustapha, M. A. 56
Abo El Nasr, M. M. 5
Adah, A. A. 46
Adebiyi, A. O. 89
Adegbami, A. 44
Adegbite, O. S. 86
Adeoye, J. O. 44
Adepitan, O. 94, 98, 99, 102
Aderinto, A. A. 59
Aderinto, S. 17
Adeyemi, O. S. 62
adoption 58
adult probation 32, 120
Afolayan, G. E. 69
African Charter on Human and Peoples'
    Rights 33
African Protocols on Ageing and
    Disabilities 35
African Traditional Religion (ATR) 83
African Union (AU) 2, 29
Afrocentrism 7, 12
Agba (young elderly) 87
Agbalagba (old elderly) 87
Agbalagbakejekeje (older elderly) 87
Agbawodikeizu, P. U. 89, 125, 133, 136
Agbo, M. C. 63
age grades 16
ageing 8, 85; policies and services 86–88;
    social work role 89–91; sociocultural
    practices 88–89; stages of 87; and
    witchcraft 120
agency 70
Agugua, A. 2
Agwu, P. 138

AIDS and HIV 28, 51, 115, 120
Akinrimisi, B. 25
Akintayo, T. 25–26, 54, 56
Akinyemi, A. I. 88
Alapiki, H. 42
Almajiri (Koranic) schools 52, 95–96
Aluko, O. A. 69
Amadasun, S. 9, 74, 102, 116, 121, 136
amalgamation (1914) 2, 17
AMSWON see Association of Medical
    Social Workers of Nigeria (AMSWON)
Anah, C. 49
ancestors 10, 12, 73
Animasahun, V. J. 89
annulment, of presidential election
    (1993) 2
Anti-Torture Act 35
Anucha, A. 28
Araromi, M. A. 86
Archibong, E. P. 120
Arimoro, A. E. 76
armed banditry 45
armed groups 61
Arugbo (oldest elderly) 87
Aruna, J. O. 52, 63
Association for Social Work Education in
    Africa (ASWEA) 125
Association of Medical Social Workers of
    Nigeria (AMSWON) 116
Association of Social Work Educators in
    Nigeria (ASWEN) 116, 134
ASWEN see Association of Social Work
    Educators in Nigeria (ASWEN)
Atilola, O. 64
ATR see African Traditional
    Religion (ATR)
AU see African Union (AU)

AU Draft Policy Framework and Action Plan on Ageing 35
Audu, D. T. 62
AU Social Agenda 2063 35
authentisation, of social work 5
Avidime, S. 58
awareness: about cause of disabilities 72; decolonisation 7; of human trafficking 95; mental illness 82
Ayangunna, J. A. 87, 90
Ayegboyin, M. 87
Ayobade, A. 2
Ayodele, O. S. 74
Azi, S. A. 62
Azorondu, A. A. 102

baby factories 60–61, 101
Badru, A. 134
Barner, J. R. 103
Bashir, A. H. 68
Belcher, M. 21, 23
Benchmark Minimum Academic Standards (BMAS) 28, 34, 35, 111, **130–132**
Benin kingdom 15
Berghs, M. 67
Berom people 83
Biklen, D. P. 110
Birchall, J. 69
birth rates 38
Blanchard, L. P. 3
BMAS *see* Benchmark Minimum Academic Standards (BMAS)
Boko Haram 38, 44, 45, 93
Boy Scouts 17, 21
bride price 11
Britain, abolition movement in 15
British ships, in Bight of Benin 15
British unification (1914) 1
Bromfield, N. F. 94
Buhari, Muhammadu 93
Burchardt, T. 70
burial plans 89
Burton, A. 24

Calabar (remand home) 21
Canavera, M. 126, 133, 135
Capous-Desyllas, M. 94
CBR *see* community-based rehabilitation (CBR)
Center for International Studies (CIS) 39–40
Change.org 96

Chapdelaine, R. P. 20, 21, 23
Chapman, H. J. 89
Charity Organisation Society (COS) 127
Chartered Institute of Social Work Practitioners of Nigeria (C-ISOWN) 35, 112–113, 116
child abuse 11, 52–53
child labour 17, 20, 61–62
childlessness 59–60, 83
child marriage 43, 53
childrearing practices 53, 75, 83
children 11; abandonment of 59; adoption 58–59; in conflict 61; fostering 83, 99; illegal adoption 60–61; international laws 55; protection of 26, 57–58; rape of 62–63; rights 30; sexual abuse in 52–53; socialisation of 10; witchcraft confession 11
Children and Young Persons Act 21, 32, 56, 58
Child Rights Act in 2003 31, 34, 54, 58
child trafficking 53
child welfare 8, 51; child abandonment 59; child labour 61–62; childlessness 59–60; child protection 57–58; child rape 62–63; children in conflict 61; cultural acceptability of child adoption 58–59; illegal child adoption and baby factories 60–61; indigenous childcare practices 52–54; juvenile justice in crisis 63–64; policies 54–57
China 111, 115
Christianity 16–18, 23, 83
Chukwu, N. 74–75, 135
Chukwuemeka, E. E. O. 31
C-ISOWN *see* Chartered Institute of Social Work Practitioners of Nigeria (C-ISOWN)
civil war (1967–1970) 2, 24
climate, inhospitability of 3, 18
Coates, J. 5
"Co-building a new Eco-Social World: Leaving no one behind" 49
Colonial Development and Welfare Act 21, 32
communitarianism 13
community-based rehabilitation (CBR) 68, 78
community support 27
Constitution of the Republic of Nigeria 34
contemporary social work 8
contributory benefits 4
Convention against Torture and Other

Cruel, Inhuman or Degrading Treatment or Punishment 34
Convention for the Protection and Assistance of Internally Displaced Persons in Africa 34
Convention for the Protection of All Persons from Enforced Disappearance 34
Convention on the Elimination of all forms of Discrimination against Women (CEDAW) 66
Convention on the Rights of People with Disabilities 34, 66
Convention on the Rights of the Child (UN, 1989) 26, 33
Corporate Affairs Commission (CAC) 33
corruption 37, 46, 63
COVID pandemic 138–139
criteria approach, of professionalisation 108–109
cultural diversity 6

dan Fodio, Usman 3
decolonisation xx, 4, 7, 14, 19
deindustrialisation 2
dementia 89
digital technology 138–139
disabilities 8, 11, 66; African understandings 67–68; legislation and policies 76; religious-medical conception of 68, 73; rights 30; social inclusion barriers 71–74; social models 69–71; social response 74–78
"disability-is-poverty" 70
disabled peoples' organisations (DPO) 68
discrimination: and disability 72–73; against women 43–44, 66
Discrimination Against Persons with Disability (Prohibition) Act 35, 66, 73
Discrimination (Employment and Occupation) Convention 34
displaced people 30, 92
divination 12
divorce 11
domestication *see* localisation
DPO *see* disabled peoples' organisations (DPO)
Draft Social Protection Policy 35
Drew, N. J. 81
dynamics 70

early marriages 54
Ebere, S. C. 138

Eboiyehi, F. A. 120
Economic Community of West African States (ECOWAS) 2
Economic Recovery and Growth Plan (ERGP) 35, 43
economic stress 90
ECOWAS *see* Economic Community of West African States (ECOWAS)
Edo people 16, 98–99
Ehigie, E. K. 52
Eide, A. H. 70, 74
Ejikeme, G. G. 134
Ekoh, P. C. 125, 133, 136
Ekpe, C. P. 10–11, 24, 52
Eleweke, J. 76
Employee's Compensation Act 34, 73
employment 26, 29
end-of-life planning 89
Equal Remuneration Convention 33
ethnoreligious diversities/differences 45
Eweka, H. E. 118
exorcism 59
extended families 10, 52, 57
extremist groups 45

Falola, T. 1
family 10–11, 27
farmers-herders' conflicts 45
farming 11
Fatile, J. O. 46
Faulkner, Donald 21, 32
FCPTSWN *see* Forum of Concerned Professional and Trained Social Workers in Nigeria (FCPTSWN)
Federal Ministry of Culture and Social Welfare 24 25
Federal Ministry of Social Development, Youth, and Sports 33
Federal Ministry of Women Affairs and Social Development (FMWASD) 51, 76, 127
Federal Republic of Nigeria (FRN) 3
Felbab-Brown, V. 98
"feminisation of poverty" 71
Flexner, Abraham 108–109
Folaranmi, O. O. 10
Folgheraiter, F. 118
forced labour 29
forced marriage 61
Forum of Concerned Professional and Trained Social Workers in Nigeria (FCPTSWN) 116–117
foster care 57–58

Fouladvand, S. 94
Fourchard, L. 20, 22–23
Freeman, Thomas 32
FRN *see* Federal Republic of
  Nigeria (FRN)
Fulani herdsmen 45
functional independence 90
Funk, M. K. 81

GDP *see* gross domestic product (GDP)
gender: disparities based on 66;
  inequality 95
Gender-Based Violence Prevention and
  Response 35
Geneva Declaration of the Rights of the
  Child (1924) 20
George, A. 22, 27
George, E. O. 47
Gerassi, L. B. 105
Gibbelman, M. 109
Girl Guides 17, 21
Global Agenda xx, 13, 141
Global Agenda on Social Work and Social
  Development (2010–2020) 49
Global Corruption Perception Index 46
Global Slavery Index 98, 100
Global Terrorism Index 45
Graham, M. J. 133
Gray, M. 5, 7, 125
Green Triangle Club 20
Green Triangle Group 32
gross domestic product (GDP) 2
Guardianship of Infants Act 32
Guardianship of Infants Act of 1886 18
Guidelines for Action on Children in the
  Criminal Justice System 26
Gureje, O. 70, 81

Hamilton, R. 109
Harms-Smith, L. 7
Harré, T. 94
Haruna, M. A. 76
HassanWuyo, I. 102
Hausa 16, 19
hawking 17
healing rituals 12
health and education 26
healthcare services 90
Heap, S. 21, 22
Heaton, M. H. 1
Heidegger, Martin 13
HIV and AIDS (Anti-Discrimination) Act 35
Holmes, R. 25, 57

Hopper, E. K. 104
human trafficking 8, 29, 92–93; 5-year
  National Action Plan on 97; policies
  94–97; political problem 97–99;
  postcolonial construction 99–100;
  prostitution 100–101; provision for
  survivors 101–106
Hume, D. L. 105
Husted, T. F. 3

Ibekwe, C. S. 69, 76
Ibiezugbe, M. I. 89, 90
Idemili-Aronu, N. 75
IDS *see* Institute for Development
  Studies (IDS)
Idyorough, A. E. 126, 138
Igbo people 16, 19, 20, 58, 60, 74–75, 84
Iguh, N. A. 62
Iliffe, J. 23
illegal child adoption 60–61
illiteracy 38
impunity culture 45
income inequality 37
indigenisation xx, 4–6, 7, 108,
  124–125, 136
indigenous childcare practices 52–54
indirect rule 16, 19
industrial production 2
inequality 37–38, 45
infertility 11
Ingstad, B. 70, 74
Institute for Development Studies (IDS)
  70, 72
institutional failures 37, 49
insurgency 45, 93
intellectual disability 73–75
internally displaced persons (IDPs) 27, 35,
  92–93, 98, 103
International Classification of
  Functioning, Disability, and Health 68
International Convention on the
  Elimination of All Forms of Racial
  Discrimination (1967) 33
International Council on Social Welfare
  (ICSW) 49
International Labour Organisation (ILO)
  55, 62
international laws 55
International Program on the Elimination
  of Child Labour (IPEC) 62, 101
Isaac, O. A. 76
Islam: education 95–96; Sharia law 2, 38,
  54, 58; Zakat system 52

Iweriebor, E. E. G. 2–3, 16
Iwobi, U. 88

jaguda (pickpockets) 21
Jayasooria, D. 49
Jegede, A. S. 84–85
Jidong, D. E. 80, 83
Jinadu, G. M. 9, 24–25
John, M. E. 53
Johnson, A. 68, 73
Joint National Association of Persons with
  Disabilities (JONAPWD) 72
JONAPWD *see* Joint National
  Association of Persons with Disabilities
  (JONAPWD)
Jones, D. N. 49
*Journal of Nigerian Social Work
  Educators* 34
juvenile delinquency 4, 17, 20, 23
juvenile justice 56, 63–64

Kainji hydroelectric dam project 40
kidnapping, of children 56
kinship 10, 52
Koranic education 56, 95–96

Lagos 2, 20, 27; , 1st juvenile court in 1942
  21; poverty rate 38
Lagos Women's League (LWL) 22, 32
land 11
Lawal, T. 14, 46, 47
leadership, poor 37, 42, 49–50
legislation and regulation 27
LGA *see* local government area (LGA)
livelihood support 26, 82
Lizzett, A. 22
local government area (LGA) 3, 47, 71
localisation 6
Lunacy Ordinance (1916) 79

Makinde, O. A. 60
Malaysia 111
malnutrition 39
Mamah, S. C. 24
marriage 11
mass education 47, 75–76, 83
Mayah, E. 38, 46
Mbada, K. 69
Mbah, P. 9, 69
Mboto, W. A. 10
mental health 8; cultural perceptions of
  mental illness 83–85; legislation and
  policies 79–82, **80**; trafficked people 104

Mental Health and Substance Abuse
  Bill 82
mental illness: cultural perceptions of
  83–85; ignorance of 81–82
Midgley, J. 5
migrants 30, 92
military: coups 1; rule 3
Milner, A. 22
Mimiko, O. 19
Ministry of Humanitarian Affairs, Disaster
  Management and Social Development
  25, 27, 92
Ministry of Social Development 24, 39,
  41, 115
Ministry of Women Affairs and Social
  Development 25, 27
missionary education 16–17
Mojoyinola, J. K. 87, 90
Monye, S. 42–43
Moore, M. 69
mortality rates 43
Muslims 4, 19, 58, 93

NASoW *see* Nigerian Association of
  Social Workers (NASoW)
Nathane, M. 7
Nation Action Plan for the Elimination of
  Child Labour (2013–2017) 35
National Action Plan for the Promotion
  and Protection of Human Rights 35, 36
National Action Plan on Human
  Trafficking in Nigeria 35
National Agency for the Prohibition of
  Trafficking in Persons (NAPTIP)
  96–97, 102
National Board for Technical Education
  (NBTE) 126
National Bureau of Statistics (NBS) 37–38
National Council of Social Work
  (NCSW) 112, 116
National Development Plans (NDPs):
  1st (1962–68) 33, 39–40; 2nd
  (1970–74) 33, 40; 3rd (1975–80) 33,
  40–41; 4th (1981–85) 33, 41–42;
  5th (2021–2025) 35, 43–44, 56;
  cessation 33, 42–43; National Economic
  Empowerment and Development
  Strategy (NEEDS) 34, 42; rolling plan
  era (1990–1998) 42; structural
  adjustment (1986–1990) 42
National Economic Empowerment and
  Development Strategy (NEEDS) 34, 42
National Gender Policy 34, 67

National Guidelines and Standards of Practice on Orphans and Vulnerable Children 34

National Human Rights Commission Act 33–34

National Mental Health Policy for Nigeria 79

National Mental, Neurological and Substance Use Programme and Action Plan 35

National Migration Policy 96

National Policy for Mental Health Services Delivery in Nigeria 35, 80

National Policy on Ageing for Older Persons in Nigeria 35

National Policy on Education 35

National Population Commission (NPC) 72

National Poverty Reduction with Growth Strategy 35

National Priority Agenda 55

National Universities Commission (NUC) 28, 34–35, 111, 124, 126, **130–132**

Native Children (Custody and Reformation) Ordinance 21, 32

natural resources 37

NBS *see* National Bureau of Statistics (NBS)

NDPs *see* National Development Plans (NDPs)

NGO *see* non-government organisation (NGO)

Nichols, A. J. 105

Nigeria: anti-discriminatory policies 67, 73; Civil War 33; colonisation in 3; first republic (1963–1966) 3; independence from Britain (1960) 1; ineffectiveness of foreign aid 42–43; Jihad of Usman dan Fodio in 19th century 3; lacking service-delivery system 25; legal system 29; natural resources 37; policies and laws 31; population 2; social welfare and social work **32–35**; *see also* precolonial Nigeria (1472–1850)

Nigerian Association of Social Workers (NASoW) 28, 33–34, 112–113, 116

Nigerian Council of Social Work (Establishment) Bill 2017 *see* Social Work Bill

Nnamani, D. O. 47

Nnama-Okechukwu, C. 53

non-government organisation (NGO) 25, 75, 77, 102, 115

NUC *see* National Universities Commission (NUC)

Nwalieji, R. I. 93

Nwangwu, C. 69

Nwanna, C. R. 103

Nwatu, U. L. 73, 120

Nwokolu-Nte, M. S. 57

Obasa, C. 22

Obasanjo, O. 3

Obidimma, A. E. 63

Obidimma, E. O. C. 63

Obikeze, D. S. 61

Obinna, A. S. 47

Odiah, C. A. 136

Office of the National Security Adviser 44

Offiong, E. E. 53

Ogbonna, B. O. 25, 121

Ogundola, O. J. 68

Ogunniran, I. 54

Ohachenu, E. I. 58

Ojanuga, D. N. 27

Ojelabi, O. A. 58

Ojewale, O. 93

Ojua, T. A. 83

Okoye, U. O. 121, 126, 134, 137, 138

Olatawura, M. U. 83

Olatunji, O. A. 62

older people *see* ageing

Oluwaseun, O. 62

Oluwatoyin, A. 14, 46, 47

Omigbodun, O. O. 83

Omobowale, A. O. 59–60

Omorogiuwa, T. B. E. 52, 62, 75

Onalu, C. E. 134, 137, 138

Onayemi, O. M. 59

online learning 139

ontological hermeneutics 13

Onyemelukwe, C. 84

Onyige, C. D. 57

Oparaoha, N. U. 103

oral traditions 15

Orikpe, E. A. 9

Orji, E. 83

orphans 21–22, 51, 115, 126, 137

Osawe, T. O. 133

Osei-Hwedie, K. 6, 7

Osiakwan, E. M. K. 138

Oti-Onyema, L. A. 62

out-of-home care 57–58

out-of-school children 55–56

Oyebanjo, A. 93

Paddock, A. 23
Palermo Protocol 96
Pathfinders Justice Initiative (PJI) 97, 99
Patterson, A. 32
Phillips, R. 71
pickpockets (*jaguda*) 21
political problem, human trafficking as
    97–99
poor leadership/governance 37, 42, 49–50
Portugal 15
postcolonial construction, of human
    trafficking 99–100
postcolonial scholarship 4–8
poverty 37, 42, 45, 69, 74, 136–137
Praeg, L. 12–13
precolonial Nigeria (1472–1850) 14–18;
    and British (precolonial period) 14–16;
    economic interests, political fluidity
    14–16; governance systems 16;
    missionary education 16–17; Portugal
    15; Spain 15; troubled children 17–18
prevention, human trafficking 95–96
primacy healthcare 41
Professional Imperialism in the Third World
    (Midgley) 5
professionalisation 108, 109–110;
    recognition 114–117, 122; registration
    and regulation 112–113, 122; relational
    connection 118, 122; relevance
    113–114, 122; representation 117–118,
    122; research and theory 119, 122;
    rights 118–119, 122
prosecution, human trafficking 94–95
prostitution 23, 100–101
protection, human trafficking 96–97
*Provisions for the Welfare of the Young and
    the Treatment of Offenders* 22
psychosocial support 82
public ignorance 72–73
Punch Editorial Board 42, 48

Ragab, I. 4–5
Rankopo, M. 6
rape 62–63
recognition, and professionalisation
    114–117, 122
reconceptualisation, of social work 5
reform schools 22–23
refugees 30, 92
registration, and professionalisation
    112–113, 122
regulation 112–113, 122
relational connection 118, 122

relativity 70
relevance 113–114, 122
religious extremism 45
remand homes 21, 22–23
rent seeking 46
representation 117–118, 122
research, and professionalisation 119, 122
responsibilisation 95
rights, and professionalisation
    118–119, 122
River Niger 15
Rohwerder, B. 72–73, 75
rolling plan era, of NDP (1990–1998) 42

Sa'ad, A.-M. 63
sacrificial rituals 60
Salami, K. K. 87
Salisu, M. 63
Salvation Army 20, 32
Sanni, J. S. 6
Secker, E. 54
Sekudu, J. 14
self-help movement 110
sex: education 53; trafficking 100
sexual abuse, in children 52–53
sexual violence 61
Sharia law 2, 38, 54, 58
Shawky, A. H. 24, 33, 124–125
Sidun, N. M. 105
Siollun, M. 1, 14, 18
slave trade 15, 16
Smith, N. 74
social assistance 26
social class xx, 18
social contract failure 45
social development 4, 5, 8, 37–38; factors
    impacting 44–47; government's lack of
    commitment 46–47; National
    Development Plans (NDPs) 39–44;
    portfolio 39; and postcolonial welfare
    24–27; and social work 47–49; violent
    conflict 44–46
Social Development Act (1974) 24
Social Development Decree (1974) 41
Social Development Institute, Iperu, Ogun
    State 33
Social Development Policy for Nigeria
    (SDPN) 24, 33
social exclusion 69–70; absence of
    statistical information 71–72; core
    features of 70; lack of measures 73–74;
    public ignorance, stigma, and persistent
    discrimination 72–73

social housing 26
social insurance 26
social integration 109–112
social models, of disability: disability-is-poverty discourse 70; feminist discourse 71; social exclusion discourse 69–70
social protection policy 25–26
social response, for disability 74–78; research and advocacy 77–78; social interventions and mass education 75–76; state obligations 76; strong representation 76–77
Social Security Act (1961) 24, 33
social solidarity xx, 10–11, 14, 141
social welfare 8, 9–36; authoritarian administrative state 18–19; and child protection 26; chronology **32–35**; colonial Nigeria (1850s-1960) 18–24; constructions of social problems 20–24; economic interests and political fluidity 14–16; indigenous support systems 10–11; indirect rule 16, 19; missionary education 16–17; national guidelines 41–42; policies and laws 31; postcolonial welfare and social development 24–27; post-independence Nigeria (1960s onwards) 24–36; precolonial Nigeria (1472–1850) 14–18; ratifying human rights charters and enacting social policies 29–36; reclamation-of-culture discourse 11–14; revisiting history 10–14; social work education 27–28; troubled children 17–18
social work 107, 122–123; contemporary practice 119–121; criteria approach 108–109; definition of 114–115; postcolonial scholarship 4–8; professionalisation 112–119; reconceptualisation 5; reiteration of 8; social integration 109–112
Social Work Bill 28, 36, 117
social work education 8, 27–28, 105–106, 124; BMAS curriculum guidelines **130–132**; curriculum content 136; developmental perspective 136–137; development of 24; digital connectivity 138–139; educational standards 134; educators' standards 134–135; fieldwork practice 137–138; in Nigeria 125–132; programs **128–129**; remit agreement 115–116, 133–134; systematic curriculum revision 135–136

Social Work Proficiency Certificate Examination (SWPCE) 112–113
social work response: for disabilities 74–78; human trafficking 102–105
Sossou, M.-A. 53
Spain 15
spirit mediums 12
SSA *see* sub-Saharan Africa (SSA)
statutory rape 62–63
stigmatisation 52–53, 60, 72–73, 120
Stolper, Wolfgang 40
street: children 62; hawking 56; labour 55; trading 17
structural adjustment, of NDP (1986–1990) 42
sub-Saharan Africa (SSA) 2
supernatural causes 12
surrogacy 61
SWIN-P Project 34

Tanga, P. T. 76
Tanyi, P. L. 87
Temilola, O. M. 121
terrorism 44
therapeutic counseling 104
Tiv 16, 93
torture, Charter for 30
traditional healing/medicine 83–85, 90
Trafficking in Persons (Prohibition), Enforcement, and Administration Act (2015) 35, 96, 102, 105
Trafficking in Persons (TIP) Act 96–97
Trafficking Victims Protection Act (TVPA) framework: prevention 95–96; prosecution 94–95; protection 96–97
transnational criminal law (TCL) 94
trauma-informed therapy 104
Tribalism 19
Trokosi (voodoosi/vudusi) 53
troubled children 17–18
Truell, R. 49

ubuntu 6–7, 12–14, 141
"Ubuntu: Strengthening Social Solidarity and Global Connectedness" 49
Udechukwu, N. S. 60
Uduigwomen, G. A. 53
Uduma, O. C. 69, 76
Ugiagbe, E. O. 27–28, 118, 125
Ugochukwu, O. 81, 82
Ugwuanyi, B. I. 31
Ugwu, M. O. 44
Ukelina, B. U. 39–40

UN *see* United Nations (UN)
UNDP *see* United Nations Development Program (UNDP)
unemployment 42, 45
Unemployment Inquiry Commission (1935) 32
UNIBEN *see* University of Benin (UNIBEN)
UNICEF *see* United Nations Children's Fund (UNICEF)
United Nations (UN) 27, 29
United Nations Children's Fund (UNICEF) 54, 95
United Nations Development Program (UNDP) 37
United Nations High Commissioner for Refugees (UNHCR) 93
United Nations Office on Drugs and Crime (UNODC) 97, 100
United States Code (USC) 97
United States Department of State (USDS) 97–98
University of Benin (UNIBEN) 28, 33, 125
University of Nigeria, Nsukka (UNN) 28, 33, 125
UN Monitoring Report 70
UNN *see* University of Nigeria, Nsukka (UNN)
unsettled returnees 92
unwanted pregnancy 61
Upkong, D. 83
Uzuegbu, C. N. 53

Van Breda, A. 14
violence, against women 44
Violence Against Persons (Prohibition) Act 59, 96
violent conflict 37

Vision 20:2020 43
Vision 20:2030 35

Walk Free Foundation 98
Walton, R. G. 5
Ward, Y. 94
Weitzer, R. 101
Western colonisation 7
WHO *see* World Health Organisation (WHO)
widows/widowhood 11, 88–89
Williamson, E. 104
witchcraft 12, 53–54, 59, 120
Woermann, M. 6
women: and childlessness 59–60, 83; with disabilities 66, 73; discrimination against 43–44, 66; "feminisation of poverty" 71; measures to improve security for 44; rights 30; violence 44
Women Trafficking and Child Labor Eradication Foundation (WOTCLEF) 102
World Bank 38, 47, 72
World Factbook 3
World Health Organisation (WHO): International Classification of Functioning, Disability, and Health 68, 72; Mental Health Action Plan 82; World Report on Disability 71–72
World Poverty Clock 37
World Report on Disability 71–72

Yekini, A. O. 63
Yogtiba, J. A. 53
Yoruba 16, 19, 20, 58, 60, 84–85
youth crime 23

Zakat Islamic system 52